ANIMATED LANDS

**Cultural Geographies
+ Rewriting the Earth**

Series Editors
Paul Kingsbury, Simon Fraser University
Arun Saldanha, University of Minnesota

ANIMATED LANDS

Studies in Territoriology

Andrea Mubi Brighenti and Mattias Kärrholm

University of Nebraska Press | Lincoln

Acknowledgments for the use of previously
published material appear on page xi, which
constitutes an extension of the copyright page.

Library of Congress Cataloging-in-Publication Data
Names: Mubi Brighenti, Andrea, author. |
Kärrholm, Mattias, author.
Title: Animated lands: studies in territoriology /
Andrea Mubi Brighenti and Mattias Kärrholm.
Description: Lincoln: University of Nebraska
Press, [2020] | Series: Cultural geographies +
rewriting the earth | Includes bibliographical
references and index.
Identifiers: LCCN 2019052219
ISBN 9781496213396 (hardback)
ISBN 9781496221773 (paperback)
ISBN 9781496222367 (epub)
ISBN 9781496222374 (mobi)
ISBN 9781496222381 (pdf)
Subjects: LCSH: Human territoriality.
Classification: LCC GN491.7 .M83 2020 |
DDC 304.2/3—dc23
LC record available at
https://lccn.loc.gov/2019052219

Designed and set in Minion Pro by L. Auten.

For Mari and Rebecka

Contents

List of Illustrations   ix

Acknowledgments   xi

Introduction   1

1. For a Science of Territories   9

2. Environments, Atmospheres,
   and Networks   37

3. The Multitemporality of
   Territorial Production   55

4. Morphogenesis and
   Animistic Moments   82

5. Domesticity and Animation   114

6. Territorializing Rhythms   136

7. Affording Play   166

Conclusion   187

Notes   195

References   203

Index   225

Illustrations

1. Caper bush 13

2. Colosseum archway 13

3. Diagram of the three presents 69

4. Main entrance to Sir John
   Soane's museum 71

5. Dome in the Sepulchral Chamber 72

6. Sarcophagus of King Seti I 75

7. Breakfast Room at 13 Lincoln's
   Inn Fields 79

8. Brick making in Ahmedabad 96

9. Experimental Arch 107

10. Indian Institute of Management,
    Ahmedabad 107

11. Wooden sculpture of a tomte 126

12. Wander lines of Janmari in Le Serret 161

13. Sand play in the Frederik
    Henrikplantsoen playground 172

14. Swinging at the Jonas Daniël
    Meyerplein playground 174

Acknowledgments

Chapters 3, 4, 5, and 6 are revised and extended versions of articles originally published as A. M. Brighenti and M. Kärrholm, "Three Presents: On the Multi-Temporality of Territorial Production and the Gift from John Soane," *Time and Society* 28, no. 1 (2019): 375–98; Brighenti and Kärrholm, "Morphogenesis and Animistic Moments: On Social Formation and Territorial Production," *Social Science Information* 57, no. 2 (2018): 249–72; Brighenti and Kärrholm, "Domestic Territories and the Little Humans: Understanding the Animation of Domesticity," *Space and Culture* 21, no. 4 (2018): 395–407; and Brighenti and Kärrholm, "Beyond Rhythmanalysis: Towards a Territoriology of Rhythms and Melodies in Everyday Spatial Activities," *City, Territory and Architecture* 5, no. 4 (2018): 1–12.

Small parts of the following texts are revised and used in, respectively, chapters 2 and 6: A. M. Brighenti and M. Kärrholm, "Atmospheres of Retail and the Asceticism of Civilized Consumption," *Geographica Helvetica* 73, no. 3 (2018): 203–13; and Brighenti and Kärrholm, "Introduction: The Life of Walls in Urban, Spatial and Political Theory," in *Urban Walls: Political and Cultural Meanings of Vertical Structures and Surfaces*, ed. A. M. Brighenti and M. Kärrholm (London: Routledge, 2018), 13–28.

The authors would like to thank Takahiko Ueno for his help with translations from Japanese sources in chapter 5. We would also like to thank Jesper Magnusson and Amit Srivastava for generously providing us with photographs.

ANIMATED LANDS

Introduction

Our aim in this book is to revive and enrich the project of territoriology (or territorology).[1] In short, territoriology could be defined as a theoretical as well as empirical science of territories and territorial formations. We seek to show how the two sides of this science may cooperate so that each studied phenomenon reveals new facets of territorial life, transforming theory itself as the exploration progresses. While the domain and outreach of territoriology may not be of universal applicability—insofar as there certainly exist nonterritorial phenomena and formations—we believe that this science contains a number of insights that can be extremely fruitful to deepen our understanding of social life as it unfolds in space and time or, as we detail later, in time-spaces. But our effort here is not simply to recapitulate the tenets of territoriology. Rather, we seek to propose an original development that avoids a number of pitfalls that have traditionally afflicted this type of analysis. Indeed, it is important to remind ourselves that territoriology has recurrently been regarded as a somewhat "suspect" science, allegedly compromised with a primordialist and reactionary political worldview. It is certainly not a chance that twentieth-century ethnonationalist political theories have long cherished the notion of territory and that in the twenty-first century the resurgence of populist and nativist politics in Europe, for instance, has once again pushed the notion of "territories of belonging" to the fore.

If territory has been recurrently mobilized by political rhetoric, the science of territory itself has long been soaked in a reductionist and polarized worldview we must be aware of too. To overcome what we believe are the distortions and limitations inherent in classical territoriology, we refine our understanding of how we might think about territorial existence and experience in a more pluralist and open-ended way. To study how territories function in practice, we thus suggest to initiate a rich dialogue between territorial analysis and a number of other spatial concepts and approaches currently more fashionable in the academia, such as networks, atmospheres, and rhythms. By engaging such dialogue, we propose to rework classical territorial studies advancing toward the piecemeal construction of a new territoriology, whose outline we submit to the reader. In our view such an attempt is warranted by the potential insight enveloped by the very word *territory*—a term rich in history and vision, which always comprises aspects of materiality and meaning, of sociality and space, of imagination and practice. To territorialize is to turn stone, clay, or even dust into a vehicle of transformative power; it is a way of animating the land by envisioning and deploying the potentials of materials. If we speak of a piecemeal construction of such a new territoriology, this is because of the organization of the book itself, which has grown out of a number of parallel explorations, already partly published in separate papers. These explorations were, however, already from the beginning part of the larger project of trying to consolidate and define a single field of inquiry. Although to some extent the chapters of this book can be seen as tackling distinct phenomena, they are also interconnected in a number of ways at a deeper level.

Some of the case studies tackled in the book include, for instance, the house museum of John Soane, the urban playgrounds of Amsterdam, the history of European urban walls, the brick architecture of Louis Kahn in Ahmedabad, and peculiar house spirits such as the *munaciello*, the *tomte*, and the *domovoj*. The choice of less obvious and not so expected examples is a deliberate one. First of all, each case enables us to explore a territorial theme, a facet of what we are interested in highlighting as relevant in the general life of territories. For example, in chapter 3 we chose John Soane's museum in London to discuss territorial temporalities. John Soane's troublesome transformation of his house into a house-museum is richly riddled with examples of how different temporal borders or moments of change play into a specific process of territorialization. Second, we have also been interested in widening the discussion of territoriality beyond the classical examples—the latter typically include, on the one hand, nations and different kinds of legal jurisdictions and local governance and, on the other, the behavior of animals, persons, and groups claiming space for themselves. But in our view the making of territories presents us with much richer phenomena than it is generally credited for. If we want to broaden our sensitivity to territorial issues, we might prefer to skip the good old textbook examples of territoriality and try something novel instead. Bringing our disparate cases together is thus meant to facilitate the fleshing out of the ways in which theory and empirical research might work jointly toward a rich and possibly nondogmatic understanding of territories at the interplay of ecology and phenomenology. In fact, whereas the ecology of territories illuminates how territories work together and affect one another, the phenomenology of territories explains how imagination and experience come to be constituent parts of their existence. Territories are constantly changing, and this change must be studied in relation to, and together with, the environments in which they exist and with which they coevolve.

Which readership do we address in this book? If it exists, territoriology is necessarily a transdisciplinary science, one that spans across several disciplines. As such, it necessarily entails a specifically *risky* type of knowledge that draws insights from a disparate body of sciences, each endowed with its own episteme, methods, and communities—necessarily without pretending to master the whole of current science. The disciplines involved in the territoriological attempt certainly include the social and human sciences (such as geography, anthropology, sociology, urban studies, and political science) but also encompass the natural sciences (such as ethology and ecology). It is a rich mixture—the sort of rich mixture scientists are usually quite wary of. Indeed, the risk of confusion, misunderstanding, self-deception, and error is great. This consideration invites caution. At the same time our argument is that the theoretical stake entailed by territorial life could not be fully excavated and appreciated without recourse to the interplay of diverse disciplinary perspectives. Our strategy in this book thus consists in keeping alive a multiplicity of references, playing wherever necessary each of them against what we perceive as the reductionism (the weak side and the blind spot, we may also say) of the other. The type of attitude that informs this book is neither relativist nor postmodernist. On the contrary, we believe that science must operate in a positivist way—that is, drawing from actual data and facing evidence, but this does not at all mean to renounce intuition, speculation, and counterintuitiveness. All cross-disciplinary, transdisciplinary, and even nondisciplinary movements must not be understood as antipositivist; rather, we suggest, they should be seen as contributing a second reading of positive science results as well as, possibly, a third eye to the common binocular vision of the scientist. Rereading what we have and adding new dimensions of existence are what territories themselves constantly do as they unfold.

Animated Lands is divided into seven chapters, presenting different (melodic) themes in territoriology and, correlatively, different takes on territorial life. In the first chapter we give an introduction to the field of territoriology. Starting with a short introduction to the sources of territoriality research, we go on to outline some of the key insights that may serve as referent points for discussion and establish some first basic assumptions for a more general theory of territories. We rationalize these as "operations" performed by territories so that a general territoriology can be configured as a theory of operations (or, following Gilbert Simondon, "allagmatics"). Finally, we introduce the neovitalist sensitivity that informs our inquiry and some of the insights and intentions associated with it. While we do not venture into metaphysical vitalism (i.e., the claim that life contains some sort of immaterial driving principle), we frame vitalism especially as an attitude that, resisting easy reductionism, invites us to attend the unexpected "animations" of territories. We thus seek to highlight how, contrary to the general tendency to take territories as passive backgrounds for action, territorial operations always give rise to new and unexpected phenomena, with the typical suddenness that characterizes all life—in a way, one could say that territories are always and inherently exercises in *emergence*.

The theoretical framework for the book is refined in the second chapter, where we situate our proposal for territoriology within the wider field of existing sociospatial inquiry. We thus set territories in relation to the key concepts of *environment*, *atmosphere*, and *network*. We have singled out these notions because of the interest that they have sparked in recent literature, but above all in connection with our belief that these notions genuinely mirror important facets of territorial phenomena. Broadly speaking, we could say that environments, atmospheres, and networks correspond to certain fundamental motifs in territories: *living*, *feeling*, and *making*. Whereas the exploration of environments guides us through literature and theories that have emerged in mostly biology and ecology (sciences of life and environments), a discussion of atmospheres brings us into aesthetic philosophy and human geography (sciences of perception and spatial experience). And finally, taking networks into account implies venturing into social theory, notably through an engagement with actor-network theory and its socioanthropological import (theory of connections, action chains, and morphologies of action distribution and transfer). Our hope is that an albeit summary discussion of these concepts may help the reader to get a more rounded idea of how we suggest to proceed in laying out a theoretical background and a suitable lexicon for the following discussion of the life of territories. Indeed, taken jointly, ways of living, ways of feeling, and ways of acting contribute to shaping the topology of inhabited, imagined, and projected territories.

By and large, territoriality has been seen mostly as a spatial rather than temporal phenomenon. In the third chapter we want to investigate how time functions in territorializing processes. In particular, we are attracted by the multitemporality that is co-present in each process of territorialization (i.e., processes in which time and space are used as means of measure, control, and expression). The chapter is divided into two main parts. In the first part we draw inspiration from Gilles Deleuze's *Logic of Sense*, as well as from authors such as Georg Simmel, Alfred Whitehead, Walter Benjamin, and Furio Jesi, to articulate three different types of the present—which we call, respectively, Aion, Kronos, and Chronos. In the second part of the chapter, we move to a case study of the architect and collector Sir John Soane, and the establishment of his house-museum in London. The case is used to exemplify how these three presents can be used to discuss temporal aspects of territorialization in general and the production of a specific sort of territory—the house-museum as a new building type—in particular.

One of our aims with this chapter is to point out how every territory is contradistinguished by multiple borders, in time no less than in space. A territory does not start its existence (and become present) at any single given moment; rather, it makes—and marks—its progressive appearance and its actualization through a series of articulated temporal thresholds.

The actualization of forms in time and in a material substrate space thus becomes key in the description of territorialization. Such actualization is what can also be called *morphogenesis*. Chapter 4 articulates issues of morphogenesis and metamorphosis in territorial formations, with an eye to what we propose to call the *animistic moment* in form-taking processes. We believe that a conceptualization of animistic moments might help us to better focus on not simply the coming about of new forms but also the elusive yet distinct power forms are endowed with. The general social-theoretical horizon is an approach to social collectives as forms of territorialization and territorial stabilization. We suggest that an inquiry into the genesis and the transformation of forms through animistic moments might also be employed in the study of an array of processes of social territorialization. Introducing the theme of the wall as morphogenetic artifact, we look at two examples of the materialization and animation of social-territorial boundaries: the first one relates to the architectural construction of brick arches and walls, while the second leads to urban warfare and the piercing of walls during swarming and guerrilla warfare operations. The question of animation comes into full play at this point and contributes to elucidate how, for better or worse, territorializations impact people. Animation, we argue, is not just a possible result of a well-crafted territory (cf. Latour 1999b, 2010); rather, it is an important part of its very formation since the outset.

The fact that animistic moments are important revelatory moments in the probing of territorial constitutions can also be seen in our discussion of domesticity in chapter 5. Our approach to domesticity and domestication may appear idiosyncratic, yet we are surprised by how curiously the phenomena of domesticity fit well with the framework of territoriology. Home is a territory in a more complex and more multifaceted way than is usually assumed. Rather than looking at the classical analysis of the more or less symbolic topography of home space, as has been classically done in anthropology, we are interested in tackling the expressive dimensions of domesticity by revealing how both ecological and spiritual factors are intermingled. We emphasize that the expressiveness of home inherently includes the register of the familiar as well as that of the unfamiliar (Freud's *unheimlich*). The constant negotiations between these two registers can be appreciated as carried out *at the limits of control*. To highlight this fact, we focus on the case of the "little humans," miniature humanoid creatures well attested in traditional mythologies and folktales across different civilizations. Drawing from anthropological and ethnological literature, yet with a leading interest in spatial theorizing, we seek to untangle the relations between humans and the little humans—these "elusive others" living with us—to clarify some of the deep meanings ingrained in domestic territories. Like all territories, home is not so much defined by its perimeters or by a codified mapping of its symbolic parts but rather by the constant rewriting of multiple borders as correlative to the possibilities and the limits in taming the energies and the forces that cross the domestic domain.

An analysis of domestic territories as animated also opens up consideration of the role of rhythms. The latter forms the pivot of the sixth chapter. The chapter starts with a quick recapitulation of urban walls in European history to illustrate how territories and rhythms have always intersected in different ways. Territoriology thus intersects rhythmanalysis. The recent, rich scholarship on rhythms, following in the wake of Henri Lefebvre's book *Éléments de rythmanalyse* (1992), proves that rhythmanalysis is an important sensitizing notion and research technique. Despite its increasing recognition, however, rhythmanalysis has not become a proper science as its proponents had initially hoped. For how much essential rhythmanalysis is to territoriology, we also believe that the former could benefit from being further developed and integrated into a wider science of territories. What research must attain is, we suggest, not simply a recording, description, or analysis of rhythms; instead, the goal is to capture the life of rhythms as they enter territorial formations. Once again a neovitalist perspective could enrich the standard social-scientific understanding of the relation between rhythms and territories. More specifically, we submit that the notion of rhythm could be explored not only in terms of the recurrent patterns of association it defines but also with essential reference to the intensive situations and moments it generates and, in the end, territorializes. In short, this chapter suggests not only that rhythms are a vital part of territoriology but also that territorialization is an ever-present part of rhythms and rhythmic life.

Out of enclosed spaces another humble and yet interesting urban territory is the playground. The seventh chapter investigates urban playgrounds from the point of view of territorial production and affordance analysis. As we know, the playground was primarily an invention of the nineteenth century, linked to the accelerated territorialization of society in the aftermath of the Industrial Revolution. As such, it clearly retains an association with various processes of disciplination coessential to the turn toward modern society. But while the playground certainly contains a disciplinary dimension, we suggest that it also allows for the production of new perceptual, spatial, and social affordances in the city. The twin guiding questions of this chapter thus concern, respectively, how the playground has affected the possibility of children to take part in the everyday life of the city and how in turn the possibility of play has affected the urban landscapes outside of the playground itself. We reconstruct in particular the case of the Amsterdam playgrounds, looking at how historical, societal, cultural, and aesthetical rhythms manifest themselves through the playground and have impact far beyond it in the larger urban realm.

In sum, this book represents an invitation to undertake, practice, and develop territoriology by all suitable means. Rather than an overarching or imperialist discipline endowed with a strong, univocal paradigm ("paradigms always live above their means," as René Thom [1988, 50] once said), we portray territoriology foremost as research practice and a research attitude—certainly a science, but perhaps more in the sense of the Goethe-Ritter *Kunde* tradition. Instead of either a technical methodological recipe or a grandiloquent new theory, with this book we would, above all, like to bear testimony of how a commitment to the development of spatial and social knowledge can be carried out in everyday practice.

1   For a Science of Territories

In this first chapter we offer an introduction to territoriology, tracing its sources and methods. By doing so we also seek to situate our study in the history of scientific research on territories as institutions (agencies and structures of authority) and behavior (territoriality, i.e. territorial behavior). Thus, we gauge various ways in which territories and territorial life can be approached and review some basic assumptions that can be used for preliminary definitional purposes. Within the rich scenery of territorial studies, what contradistinguishes our approach is, in particular, an attempt to inherit and further develop what could be described as a vitalistic sensitivity toward territories, which runs like a motif through the subsequent chapters of this book. Indeed, we are specifically interested in drawing attention to a series of peculiar moments when territories reveal properties of animation and life. Besides being a form of institutionalized behavior and a type of decision space, territory—we think—also reveals something inherent in the experience and the possibilities of social life at large. This elusive quid is, in a sense, at the center of our quest. We stress, however, that territoriology is not a metaphysical enterprise but a research approach that seeks to remain faithful to the possibilities of a science. This first chapter sets a broad stage of our inquiry, starting with a visit to a famous arena of spectacles.

A Visit to the Roman Colosseum

Let us place ourselves inside the Roman Colosseum, a well-known place that may provide us with a first short illustration of how territories are made and how they *animate the land*. Changing ceaselessly through history, the Colosseum has undergone a number of territorializations that have produced meanings and effects. Many of these have been overlapping, feeding on one another or working side by side. In general, the history of the Colosseum is well known: the building project was started by Vespasianus but finished and inaugurated under his son Titus in 80 AD. In his classical study, *Animals for Show and Pleasure in Ancient Rome*, George Jennison tells us how the Colosseum hosted chariot races and gladiator fights alongside animal parades and animal fights. During the first hundred days after the Colosseum's opening, no fewer than nine thousand animals were killed (1937, 62). This sort of territorialization belongs, we could say, in our collective visual imagery, not least thanks to 1950s Hollywood movies. The games died out somewhere during the sixth century BC, but the greatness of the building lived on, as did the echoes of its large spectacles. During the eleventh century the arena was used as a fortification, first by the Frangipane family, then by the Annibaldi. Later it was successively turned into gardens, churches, hospitals, craftspeople's workshops, markets, a bullfighting arena, and so forth. Up until the seventeenth century, parts of the structure were used as a sanctuary by outlaws, and it was only when the building became a memorial for Christian martyrs in 1750 that its use as a free quarry for travertine ended (Caneva et al. 2003, 212–13; cf. Gibbon 1896–1900, 317–18).

Despite its many uses, some more joyous, others more destructive, the Colosseum was mostly seen as a bastion. Edward Gibbon, for example, recalls a saying that the English monk Bede the Venerable seems to have picked up from pilgrims coming back from Rome during the eighth century: "As long as the Coliseum stands, Rome shall stand; when the Coliseum falls, Rome will fall; when Rome falls, the world will fall" (1900, 316).[1] Outside of Rome the building thus became a symbol for the stability of the Western world and Christendom itself. The old saying is very interesting especially if we consider it in the light of scale: the Colosseum appears as an intensive point endowed with transscalar properties—an *omphalos*, if one wishes, or what in mathematics is know as a singularity. In the course of our explorations, we'll return recurrently to the notion of singularity in relation to territory. Today the Colosseum is most of all a tourist site—in fact, it has been seen as one of the earlier examples of "dark tourism" (Stone 2006). It is, however, also an archaeological site, a place of inspiration for architects and architectural students, a symbol of Rome, a postcard motif, and so on.

One particular, if sometimes overlooked, feature of the Colosseum is that over the centuries it has been—and still is, it seems—an exceptional place for botanical studies. From the many seeds brought there by animals from different parts of the world—together with its use for markets, gardens, grazing sheep, and so on—the Colosseum shows an exceptional richness in terms of plants and flowers. A first inventory of the flora was made already in 1643. Francesco Antonio Sebastiani did a major one in 1815, while in 1855 Richard Deakin reached a comprehensive inventory in his *Flora of the Colosseum*, where no fewer than 420 species are listed. Subsequently, Elisabetta Fiorini Mazzanti also published a series of texts in 1874–78. Although the twentieth century has been marked by restoration works, weed killing, and sanitation, new inventories have been made, for example, in 1951 and 2002 (Caneva et al. 2003, 211–12). So the Colosseum, apart from everything else, has also appeared as a kind of unplanned botanical garden of its own—perhaps even one of the first botanical gardens in Europe—at least, one with a clear focus on exotic imported plants. This is interesting for us, because we could suggest that plants bring historical events to life again. Deakin, for example, cannot help but summon the scene of gladiators and lions as he investigates local plants, hinting at what might be called the especially "animating power" of flowers:

> Flowers are perhaps the most graceful and most lovely objects of the creation but are not, at any time, more delightful than when associated with what recalls to the memory time and place, and especially that of generations long passed away. They form a link in the memory, and teach us hopeful and soothing lessons, amid the sadness of by-gone ages: and cold indeed must be the heart that does not respond to their silent appeal; for, though without speech, they tell of that regenerating power which reanimates the dust of mouldering greatness, and clothes their sad and fallen grandeur with graceful forms and curiously constructed leaves and flowers, resplen-

dent with their gay and various colours, and perfume the air with their exquisite odours. (1855, vi)

The impact that the Colosseum as a territory for plants had on the physician and botanist Deakin can, in fact, also be seen from the curious way in which he illustrated his book (see figs. 1 and 2): rather than directing his attention exclusively to plants—which of course is the common thing to do in flora studies—Deakin's focus is actually on architecture and how it became covered in plants and greenery.

Urban space can, in a sense, be imaged as possessing a vegetative stratum of its own (Brighenti 2018). A specific aspect of the "plant territorialization" of the city is, as Sarah Besky and Jonathan Padwe (2016, 21) also argue, its slowness. Indeed, plants play their territorial part in a peculiarly slow fashion, imperceptibly but inexorably covering buildings and cracking the asphalt. Here we have a hint for a form of temporality that we are going to explore as "aeonic" (see chapter 3). By their temporal existence, plants also remind us of the more-than-human character of all territorializations. Not only do plants claim space; they also make space available to animals: through their slowness and persistence, plants make space materializing new interspecific associations and keeping those associations stable despite material and social transformations. New ecologies appear, and there's a way in which architecture also learns from plants (Gruber 2011). Deakin's (1855) territorial association between the plants of the arena and the Roman animal fights are, in one way, produced by his imagination. We like to believe that he found these images while he roamed in the arena collecting specimens, perhaps again later as he sat in his studio writing and illustrating his book. Territorial associations also have a continuity that connects them to one another—now, and now, and yet again on these pages—and that draws its intensity from written texts, stories told through centuries, and indeed from the thread of continuous life that can be traced back from rocks, through plants, to animals themselves.

It is impossible to account for all the territorializations associated with the Colosseum. Our purpose with this example is just to show how even a

1. An illustration of the caper bush, from Richard Deakin's book *Flora of the Colosseum* (1855).

2. A Colosseum archway, from Richard Deakin's book *Flora of the Colosseum* (1855).

single and well-defined place is necessarily always entangled in an ecology of fleeting, disappearing, reappearing, ongoing, and overlapping territories. Every subsequent territorialization has a vibrant transformative intensity that in different ways evokes and enacts other territorializations and reacts to them. Reducing the Colosseum, as so many books of history and architecture have done, to be one specifically decaying architectural form related to successive changes of function offers only a poor picture of its exuberant territoriality. As soon as we start to follow the abundance of territorializations of this single building, we see that they overlap both in time and space and play into one another's rhythms and melodies. In practice most territorial forms and their associated activities or meanings could be said to be in a fluid situation (Kärrholm 2013; cf. Law and Mol 1994; Law 2002). We return to these theoretical issues later. But this story suffices to remind us that a territory can be analytically investigated through these questions: Who draws it? How is it drawn and why? Which evocations and associations follow from its drawing? These questions, we believe, must be studied over time through the effects and the ongoing *revelations* that territory itself offers. Each territory is but a site of passage. Only then can we discover that each and every territory is drawn by many different hands, with many different overlapping and crisscrossing borders, according to constrains as well as affordances that have evolved continuously, perhaps even over centuries if not millennia. It is in this sense that territory is a vibrant entity (Bennett 2010): as it changes its qualities and traits over time, with some things remaining and others going, it affords associations that might live on, disappear, and return.

Territories are not simple obedient objects; they cannot always be turned off and on at will. Even when they seem stabilized, they are indeed pulsating and full of rhythms, melodies, memories, and desires. When they seem dead, they might be just dormant. The qualities of complexity and experience have often been assigned to place rather than to territory (Casey 1997). And places certainly are complex spaces: a single place can, for example, consist of several different territorializations and several imaginations. In this regard the Colosseum is just, as any other place, an assemblage of

For a Science of Territories

multiple territories. But as we inspect these processes of territorialization closer, we also notice that they are quite impossible to pin down individually. Territories are animated objects entangled with intentions, wills, imperatives, dreams, imaginations, and multifarious life forms. In short, territories seem to have life written all over them. At least this is an assumption that we are prepared to investigate and to hopefully make use of in this book. Often it is in the moment when we think we know what a certain territory is about and how it works that it surprises us by taking another direction, disappearing, and perhaps reappearing in different guises. How then can we follow territorial trajectories, understood not simply as trajectories in the territory but veritable trajectories *of* territories themselves? This amounts to asking what the role of territorialization in social life is and how we can investigate it while keeping its ever-changing ways in mind.

Sources and Studies in Territoriology

The processes of territorialization and their ensuing territorial effects are at the heart of our study. Some sources and previous investigations we deem most fruitful can now be reviewed. The concept of territoriology was used early on by Heini Hediger in his essay "The Evolution of Territorial Behavior," where he curiously claims that territoriology is a "broad and fairly well-cultivated field of science" (1961, 34). For Hediger territoriology, firmly placed within a behavioral biological field, combines a mix of ecology, ethology, and animal psychology (1961; cf. Malmberg 1980, 16–17). Torsten Malmberg, although also coming from a behavioral perspective (starting as a zoologist and then moving on to human ecology) is a bit broader in scope in his call for a "science of territory." Malmberg interestingly suggests that "facts at the border between separate sciences run great risks of being neglected" (1980, 13) and advocates a bridging of the many gaps between natural science and the humanities or between a behavioral-biological side and a sociopolitical side of territories. Certainly, Malmberg at the time was optimistic about the gaps being bridged; however, almost fifty years later, gaps still persist. In his important book *The Birth of Territory*, for example, Stuart Elden states that it is unclear how a biological perspective studying animal association can "tell us something about 'territory'" and goes on to explain that "in part this is due to the obvious point that human social organization has changed more rapidly than biological drives" (2013, 4). Similarly, in his introductory book to territory, the legal geographer David Delaney acknowledges biological approaches but concludes that the "explicit theorization of territory and territoriality is a comparatively recent phenomenon that emerged under a specific set of (geo)political and historical conditions" (2005, 34), quickly moving the discussion to exclusively (geo)political phenomena. Barbara Brown, on the other hand, seems to suggest that behavioral analysis is advantaged over social and cultural analysis, owing a stronger paradigm: "Unlike the biological approach," she writes, "the social approach cannot claim a unified theoretical heritage" (1987, 506). More recently, scholars working in the domains of ecology and zoology simply seem to completely neglect insights from the social sciences.

In a sense it is as if a "classic," foundational season—with some bold attempts at advancing encompassing definitions of territory—has ended, and scholars have retreated in their own disciplinary turfs.[2] Although many studies conducted inside specific disciplines are rewarding and precise, they tend to rule out other ways of looking at territories as irrelevant or even straightforwardly tagging them as "non-territorial" (Halvorsen 2018, 793). This suggests that the territorialization of the concept of territory is quite a widespread theoretical practice. In this book we are not interested in taking side in any controversy between behavioral-biological or sociopolitical perspectives. Simply put, we are convinced that both biological and social aspects might have parts to play in the life of a territory, but calling some aspects biological and some social does not mean that the territory itself is somehow divided into two realms. In other words, we believe it is more promising to acknowledge that we are looking at a complex entity from different perspectives that can be simultaneous and do not rule one another out. Consequently, rather than trying to explain territories by reducing them to the myth of a single origin (whether a political strategy, a biological drive, or anything else), we want to investigate the complexity of the territorial productions and effects in social life.

For a Science of Territories

Eschewing from the debates seeking to identify the "real" foundation of territorial existence, we rather build on the insight by Walter Benjamin, who distinguished between origin or better source (*Ursprung*) and beginning or genesis (*Entstehung*).[3] Following his lead, we are interested not so much in understanding the (biological or political) beginnings of the notion of territory and its practices but in analyzing its living sources in medias res. Thus we focus our attention on certain peculiar, qualitative moments when territories become *animated*. We believe there are specific conditions for the "activation" of territories that enable territorial composition to become expressive, to convey meaning. We thus subscribe to an approach that might be loosely called *neovitalistic*. In this context the notion of animation is particularly interesting: when space is set into play, and different aspects of life are at stake, it is through animation that territories can be best studied and understood. A caveat is needed: just as we do with territoriology, our placement with the vitalist perspective also entails an elaboration on our part. In particular, as we shall detail, we are not so much interested in reproposing some variant of the Schopenhauerian notion of Will, nor of the Bergsonian élan vital. We take a phenomenologically inspired, rather than metaphysical, view on life, approaching the dynamic "livingness" of phenomena that manifest across vegetative and "animational" thresholds. The Canguilhem-Deleuze lineage seems to us more interesting to outline a space where vital phenomena can be articulated with, yet not reduced to, either organic or rational-logical ones.

A more general view on territoriology is now perhaps called forth. Although the divisions in disciplines and perspectives still exist, there are also attempts at bridging these divisions, and these attempts are the most inspiring for us. But specialized research and empirical studies are also necessary. In our view the development of a territoriology requires a mature and nontrivial combination of insights derived from at least four main threads of research:

1. biology, zooethology, and human ethology (Altum 1868; Howard 1920; Uexküll [1934] 1957; Tinbergen 1951; Ardrey 1966; Etkin 1967; Lorenz 1966; Hediger 1969; Eibl-Eibesfeldt 1970; Krebs 1977; Lorenz 1981);

2. human ecology, anthropology, environmental psychology, social psychology, and interactionism (Speck 1915; Hall 1959; Sommer 1959; Lyman and Scott 1967; Roos 1968; Sommer 1969; Goffman 1971; Edney 1974; Altman 1975; O'Neal, Caldwell, and Gallup 1977; Dyson-Hudson and Smith 1978; Ericksen 1980; Malmberg 1980; Ingold 1986; Brown 1987; Taylor 1988; Tonboe 1994; Jacobson 1997);

3. human, political and legal geography, and planning (Soja 1971; Gottman 1973; Lefebvre [1974] 1991; Ley and Cybriwsky 1974; E. Maier 1975; Raffestin 1980; Sack 1986; Soja 1989; Agnew 1994; Agnew and Corbridge 1995; Blomley 1994; Häkli 1994; Herbert 1996; Paasi 1996; Healey 1997; Blomley, Delaney, and Ford 2001; Storey 2001; Holder and Harrison 2003; Delaney 2005; Elden 2005, 2007; Sassen 2006); and

4. social and natural philosophy (in particular, Merleau-Ponty 1945; Husserl 1973; Foucault 1975, [1978] 2004; Deleuze and Guattari 1980; Steinbock 1995).[4]

In the course of this book, we retrieve and highlight the insights that these different traditions have brought to the study of territorial phenomena. In a preliminary way we could begin by stating:

1. Within biological research ethology has inaugurated the interest for the special coupling that certain animals develop with given regions of space at given times. Ethology has strictly correlated space and behavior as a function of given "releasers"—that is, signs to which the animal reacts immediately.

2. Interactionism has provided a wealth of detailed phenomenological observations of how people act and react to one another in local situations, managing space to assert property and maintain meaningful reciprocal distances.

3. Human geography has furthered the view that territories are not just natural occurrences but derive from planned strategies to master space in various ways and institute organizations to control space and movement.

4. Some major authors in (especially contemporary French) philosophy, while not clearly belonging in a single school of thought, have elaborated subtle and nuanced descriptions of how bodies can live in an environ-

ment, how the environment can be used to govern human masses, and how territories are ongoing vital dynamic creations.

Besides these four large and established fields, however, the notion of territoriality has lately also been addressed through more interdisciplinary approaches, such as market theory (Cheetham, McEachern, and Warnaby 2018; Warnaby 2018), plant geography (Besky and Padwe 2016), and urban design (Magnusson 2016; Keswani 2017; Manfredini and Ta 2017)—to mention just a few.

In our own studies the interdisciplinary ambitions have also been important. Mattias Kärrholm has, in a series of theoretical and empirical studies, focused on materiality and the territorial production of public spaces (2004, 2005, 2007, 2008, 2012, 2017; Citroni and Kärrholm 2017; Kärrholm and Wirdelöv 2019). Here the different kinds of territorializations and spatial (or spatiotemporal) claims—which traditionally have been treated within different disciplines—have been jointly investigated (as formal strategies, informal tactics and appropriations, and more vague associations). Territorial strategies and tactics are meant to capture those intentional territorial productions that are either planned from another time and space than the territorial effect (territorial strategies) or produced as part of an ongoing local life (territorial tactics). Territorial appropriations and associations, on the other hand, result from practices that do not specifically aim at producing a certain territory but nevertheless involve one or several processes of territorialization. This can be accomplished through the connection of a time-space, either to certain individuals or groups (appropriation) or to a specific practice or use (association) (Kärrholm 2007, 2012). By studying these different forms of territorialization side by side, the idea of multi-territoriality, or rather territorial complexity, and how different territories intermingle and coexist can be outlined.

In several articles this notion of territorial complexity has then been investigated and discussed as an important aspect of how public places actually and practically are produced and used (Kärrholm 2005, 2007, 2008, 2009). In the book *Retailising Space* (2012), further aspects of territorializations are discussed through the case of retail and the retailization of urban space. Different forms of territorial stabilizations are identified, such as networks, sorts, bodies, and framings, with a specific interest into how materialities and design play a part—or, in fact, multiple parts—in the territorialization of specific urban locales. Another interesting feature that has been documented concerns territorial synchronization—that is, how the synchronization of urban rhythms with retail contributes to processes of territorialization—and territorial singularization, or the strategy of making certain spaces or time-spaces unique, setting the ground for reproduction and typologization (which, for example, has been a strategy for advancing certain building types of consumption). In later articles Kärrholm has focused on some temporal aspects of territorializations, tracking how different territories of public space might last for centuries or decades or only for minutes or even seconds. These different temporal scales of territorial production often interact and depend on one another (2015, 2017). Finally, some articles have looked more closely at the different territorial negotiations of local public spaces and events in the suburban neighborhood (Citroni and Kärrholm 2017; Kärrholm and Wirdelöv 2019).

For his part Andrea Mubi Brighenti has started his research with a reflection on the relation between law and space, puzzling about the restricted notion of territoriality mirrored in modern jurisdictional theories (2006c, 2009a). Commands, in particular, can be regarded as basic yet forceful territorializing devices for the synchronization of action within a social multiplicity (2006a). Widening the notion of territory—or arguing for a sociorelational notion of territory instead of a referential one—has led into focus the interweaving of territories, power, and identity, as well as of territories and movement (2009b, 2010a). While the law has often been criticized for foregrounding stability over mobility, promoting a sedentarist territoriality, an analysis of some constitutional premises of modern law, in fact reveals how deep the notion of movement is ingrained in the legal imagination and in the foundations of social power (2014b). In Brighenti's (2007, 2008, 2010b, 2010d, 2017) subsequent analyses, of interest has been the interweaving of territory and visibility: in a way—as we also explore later on in this book—territories have to do with displaying, presenting, and becoming visible to someone for some purposes or in some respects or capacities. Exceeding the merely visual dimension, visibility thus concerns the meanings, the framings, and the keyings of social meetings and the geometries of territorialization that ensue from such meetings. Besides that, visibility is not merely extensive, logistic, or strategic but also intensive, affective, and critical.

In this sense the notion of territory can be widened to include an array of "critical moments" (critical distances, tipping points, turning events, etc.), where encounters occur capable of affecting the very topology and the constitution of entailed actors (Brighenti 2016b). This has led to the idea of territories as measure-setting environments and as attempts to set certain measures for coexistence (Brighenti 2013a). In an urban ethnography of graffiti writing (Brighenti 2010c) as well as in subsequent empirical studies of how graffiti writers, street artists, and other informal actors use city space (Brighenti and Mattiucci 2012; Brighenti 2015, 2016a), a panoply of possibilities for multiple territorializations has been described as emerging in contextual situations. Urban space in particular is perceived and experienced by graffiti writers as well as by other actors interested in intervening through the series of affordances and possibilities to act evoking different possible territorializations. Notably, emerging territorializations are never deterministic; rather, a relative indetermination is generated within social multiplicities each time surging events like crowding and swarming unsettle them (Brighenti 2014a). Public space and the public domain could thus be integrally interpreted through the notions of circulation, dispersal, and the synthesisless dialectic of appropriation and resistance (Brighenti 2010c, 2010d, 2016c). Research on specific urban artifacts such as walls (Brighenti 2009a, 2013b; Brighenti and Kärrholm 2018b) has similarly illustrated the richness and unpredictability of territorializing devices in urban space. In another parallel stream of research, Brighenti and Mattiucci (2008) and Brighenti (2012) have investigated how the use of new media technologies can be explained in terms of new territorial production and territorial multiplication. This thread of research has highlighted that territories are constitutionally open and permeable to the series of events that affect them and that new media illustrate and clarify the phenomenon of the stratification of territories.

The Operations of Territory

If territorial studies are varied and rich (and something we have been struggling with for more than fifteen years now), how can we summarize this heterogeneous field and lay out the table for an enlarged territoriological investigation? We believe that the joint contribution of the diverse and varied literature of the field has converged on a series of key insights. First, a territory is not an object and should not be confused with the space where it takes place. The once mainstream view that sees territory as the hard fact that merely provides the visible support or backup for invisible social ties has been challenged. For instance, it would not make much sense to affirm that "the state extends its power over a territory," because that "territory" is precisely the outcome and effect of a specific social relation that includes power relations. The image of the modern territorial state is a mythic-ideological self-representation that would not have been possible without a number of requirements: first, a certain configuration of political power; second, a whole technosocial and biopolitical apparatus that encompasses technologies (military, cartographic, transport technologies, etc.), disciplines, and their professional knowledge (medicine, school, police, administration, etc.; for a historical example, see Alliès 1980). If the state is an abstract construct, town halls, city districts, and neighborhood councils are no less so. While not of the same scale, nor endowed with the same degree of centripetal power, all these institutions lie at the same level of abstraction. As we shall see better later, they all require a special imagination to make sense.

Importantly, then, territory is not defined by space; rather, it defines spaces through patterns of relations. Every type of social tie can be imagined and constructed as territorial. Territories differ dramatically in scale and visibility, as well as in expression, function, organization, and technology. As a consequence, only the most visible territories are usually recognized

For a Science of Territories

as proper territories, whereas the others are relegated to the realm of metaphor. Visibility is, in this sense, an important predictor of the definitional fault lines that will be adopted by scientists and laypeople. Interestingly, the effects of visibility depend in their turn on specific expressive, functional, relational, organizational, and technological territorial arrangements. In other words, only once relations among actors, rather than space, are put at the conceptual core of territory, does it become possible to capture the ways in which spatial and nonspatial territories are superimposed one onto the other and endowed with multiple linkages. Territories are interactional: they result from encounters and from the effects developed during those encounters. Territories are the effect of material inscriptions of social relationships. In fact, actors do inscribe an ensemble of cognitive and normative plans into given material supports, such as procedures (e.g., procedures for navigating a certain space), ways of doing things conveniently (proper behavior, efficient action, etc.), expectations about mutual recognition (interaction rituals, reparations, etc.), power claims and hierarchies (both personal and impersonal), and so on. Because more or less complex plans are always territorially inscribed by the different actors who compose a territory, territories are as heterogeneous as the ensemble of actors present in them. In fact, a territory designates a convergence of actors who attempt to manage reciprocal visibilities and invisibilities and reciprocal affections (including, notably, the spread of moods, attitudes, desires, beliefs, etc.).

Second, territory is an imagined (not imaginary) entity. Benedict Anderson's (1983) famous idea of nation as an imagined community is extremely important and inspiring but should not mislead us about the fact that clans too are imagined entities. The difference is that the clan territorializes its members through myths and narratives that focus on bodies, whereas the nation territorializes its members through myths and narratives that focus on places. Outside these acts of imagination, neither the nation nor the clan can be visible, working entities. When space is carved out and circumscribed by an animal to create a territory, this implies a fundamental transformation of previous environments. Territorial practice is an imaginative mechanism whereby someone is initially recognized as an intruder or insider (or other equivalent qualification) in relation to one's territory. Spaces and places can be urbanistically and architecturally planned to support certain activities, but if the capacity to imagine relationships were lost, even the most carefully planned space would be an empty shell. It is imagination that enables classification, distinction, and recognition. For its part territory is not simply the physical setting for such recognition. Rather, recognition and separation of two basic types of conspecifics (members of the same species) is what the territory is in the first place about. *Selective* inclusion and exclusion combine into a series to form an ordering mechanism that becomes the basis for the formation of social groups. Most important, inclusion and exclusion are not totalizing acts; they correspond to partial and reversible openings and closures that enact the basic operations of the territorial machine. As such, they can be applied differently to various relational dimensions, giving birth to patterns of hegemony, control, and resistance.

Third, territory has both expressive and functional components. Expression marks the emergence of a territory, given that a territory appears when some qualities and properties are somehow synthesized out of an environment. Without quality and property, or better without quality as property (such as a signature, a specific way of marking), there would be no territory. Therefore, the setting up of a territory is always simultaneously semiotic and expressive. But functional existence is not far away, given that, by its very expressivity, every territory acts on the organization of environmental functions. The classic ethological concepts of defense, control, reproduction, and pecking order in the access to resources provide clear examples. These classical functions represent only *some of the many* possible territorial functions, which can be much more complex, nuanced, and far-reaching. Thanks to the imaginative element entailed by territory, the here-and-now can be prolonged and amplified into an "elsewhere at other times," linking phenomenology and ecology. The general organizational functions that territories perform are based on this mechanism. Functions are projected into territory, and they can be carried out whenever

For a Science of Territories

the territory is "on"—for an example, one can think about the institution of the *eruv* in Jewish communities (Stiefel 2017).

In synthesis the theoretical question that lies at the core of territory and its relationship to social life at large can be put as follows: How does it happen that the material transforms into the immaterial (Vandenberghe 2007)? How does it happen that spaces transform into relations? In traditional ontology spaces and relations are two different sets of things. But the distinction between the spheres of the material and the immaterial is weakened by the fact that in social practices these two dimensions do not simply interact but ceaselessly prolong into each other. This is what happens with every territory. Technology amplifies these prolongations and makes them more visible and perceptible, but it does not create them. On the contrary, one could define a technology as precisely a procedure to enhance the visibility of given territorial arrangements. From a territoriological perspective what matters is not the distinction between the natural and the social domains but rather the distinction between material and signifying or, with reference to a problem discussed by Henri Bergson (1889), the distinction between quantitative and qualitative, *temps* and *durée*, differences of degree and differences of nature—considering that nature is itself full of significations or, as Deleuze (1990) once said, full of *artifices*. So while as a first step it is necessary to avoid conflating territory and its physical spatial extension, the subsequent step is to take into account the constant prolongations between the different registers or layers.

In our view the concept of prolongation can be used as an integrative and a corrective to media theory. Marshall McLuhan (1964) famously advanced the image of media as sensorial extensions. One cannot conceive these extensions as if they were not mediated, McLuhan contended. Media are hardly neutral because their expressive characteristics affect the content they mediate. Such a notion was popularized as "the medium is the message." McLuhan's theory, as well as his disciples', is rather unclear when it comes to accounting for precisely how extensions work; as it tends to conflate the layers of content and expression, it ultimately becomes a reductionist theory. From this perspective the concept of prolongation is designed to resist this reductionism. Prolongation offers a notion of translation and, even better, transmutation. In the following explorations we hope to show this. In this sense the study of territories thought through the working of prolongations might help to bridge the gap between studies of human territoriality on the one hand and traditional political territories on the other. These two research areas can be recast not simply in the guise of the poles of micro versus macro territories but rather slantwise, through the differential analysis of relational prolongations, imaginative forces, and materially expressive and functional components.

Whereas the power of the notions of space and place has been amply excavated and redeemed in human geography over the past four decades (Tuan 1977; Massey 2005), the notion of territory retains an original potential that can be highlighted. Territories are always necessarily related with tracing operations and boundaries, but also with the associations and the sorts that they make possible. By comparison with the powerful and deep notions of space and place, territory appears as humble and constrained. But it is precisely by examining what constrains territory that we discover its potential. Territory exists as a bounded entity. If boundaries are a constitutive prerequisite of territory, then the analysis of territories cannot miss the phenomenon of boundary making. Through its boundaries territory enables actors to manage reciprocal distances. The management of distances, which is so crucial in ordinary social life, could be said to be the corollary of that fear of being "touched by the unknown" so vividly described by Canetti ([1960] 1984, 15) in his discussion on crowds. This fact suggests that boundaries are nothing other than critical distances, combined to shape social regularities and orders (Goffman 1971; Sommer 1967). A mundane example here is the fence between neighboring gardens. The fence helps us to create and manage a distance, but it also affords a specific kind of social interaction, one that has its own importance for the forming of neighborhood communities: talking over the fence. The activity of drawing boundaries, while in many cases implicit and even invisible, is the constitutive process of territorialization.

For a Science of Territories

Consequently, territory and boundaries should be framed as two aspects or facets of the same activity. If territorializing is a way of carving the environment through boundary drawing activities, trajectories and boundaries should be conceived as complementary rather than oppositional elements. Boundaries are not the opposite of flows but rather the moment when flows become visible, inscribed in the field of visible, socially relevant phenomena. For this reason, just as it requires a study of prolongations, territoriology also calls for a study of the visible. If drawing a boundary means drawing a line of sort—an entity materialized in a number of artifacts and signals—we have to consider that the line is also a flow, a trajectory, or vector (oriented line) that intersects or, alternatively, aligns itself with other vectors. Furthermore, because the activity of boundary making or boundary drawing is immanent and situated, there are no predestined, natural boundaries. The naturalization and absolutization of boundaries should be studied as the outcome of situated transcendent-oriented movements, practices, and discourses. In many cases justificatory practices, such as a theodicy or a nationalist narrative, are involved in this process (cf. Murphy 1990; Penrose 2002; C. Maier 2016).

Boundaries are the operations that lead to the installment of territories (we can refer more precisely to the notion of *instauration*). As we seek to show in this book, the shift from an essentialist and objectivist to an operational, interactional, evental imagination of territory can breed a sea change in our approach to the study of territories. The image of territorial boundaries as the result of contingent acts of drawing may convey the false impression that arbitrariness, or sheer will, rules over the constitution of territories. But to stress the dependence of territory on boundary-drawing activities undertaken by interacting agents employing given technologies to carry out some plans in some domain of practice of concern to them does not at all amount to saying that territories are arbitrarily constructed. Boundaries can depend on unintentional as well as intentional interactions, interactions that sometimes can be anticipated, traced, and described, even if not mapped or understood in full. Territories have histories; they are thick with temporal layering and enveloping, and their origins are often enveloped in mythologies.

Once established, boundaries become the object of an ongoing work of enactment, reinforcement, negation, interpretation, and negotiation. Boundaries are never established once and for all; quite the contrary, they are often precarious achievements, constantly reworked. Because of ongoing boundary work, territories become stratified. Stratification also means that some strata become less visible than others; some strata provide the infrastructure for others. Geoffrey Bowker and Susan Leigh Star (1999) have elaborated on the peculiar invisibility of the infrastructures of knowledge, such as classification systems. Clearly, no measure should be used to measure itself as if it were an independent magnitude—although this is in practice what often happens. So, at the end of the eighteenth century, the French astronomers Jean-Baptiste-Joseph Delambre and Pierre-François-André Méchain established the meter as the one-tenth-millionth part of the earth's meridian arc from the North Pole to the equator; however, owing to the wrong assumption undermining the metric expedition (namely, the hypothesis that the sector of the French meridian measured by Delambre and Méchain could be considered representative of the shape and measure of the whole meridian from the pole to the equator—or, in other words, a conflation of the geoid and the so-called reference ellipsoid of the planet) we now have to say that—and, correctly so—the meridian arc measures 10,002,290 meters (Alder 2002).

Boundary-drawing acts carve and attest the environments they operate on. These are technological acts that allow specific types of sign emission and processing. In their turn signs exist within a semiosphere in which acts of semiosis (following Peirce 1931) join together representamens, objects, and interpretants. The mundane acts of finding one's place on a crowded subway and of engaging in face-to-face interaction between strangers, but also the refined techniques of geolocalization and geographic information data processing, are part of the same continuum *pursued through different means*. Nation-state boundaries are also semiotic, expressive entities (M. Anderson 1996). Certainly, each territory is different and specific;

each, however, also possesses a number of comparable territory-making routines. Territories are practices—at least if by practice we understand a set of repetitions and differences that prolong from one environment to another through a set of random and meaningful variations. Connecting past knowledge to present circumstances, practice enables us to encode and decode signs, to share a meaningful environment, or, in other words, to territorialize our environments. Territorial borders thus mean nothing more than a specific deceleration of flows, a change in the magnitude of speeds. A territory always implies that some aspects slow down, whereas others speed up. The study of borders and thresholds—access, exclusion, confinement, acceptance, selection, sort, and so on—and the study of speeds naturally prolong into each other.

Because territories articulate speeds and the velocities of entry and exit, they are rhythmic at their core: they determine specific patterns of concentration and the dispersal of objects and events. Rhythms are often superposed onto one another, in which case they modulate one another, creating more complex rhythmic patterns. The stratification of rhythms corresponds to a stratification of movement: for instance, the rhythms of public transport can become a modulator for private displacements (commuters), which in turn becomes a modulator for other private displacements (customers). This reinforces the idea that territories are not fixed entities but are instead thoroughly constituted through these rhythms. Territories are embodied as series of events occurring at different paces across different locales. Inserting temporality and rhythmicality into territories is one driving theme in this book. Concurrently, however, we are also interested in exploring another face of territories, bringing to the foreground their qualitative, or melodic, aspects.

On the basis of the operations described so far, one begins to sense that territories may contribute some counterintuitive insights to the study of social space. The relation between territories and geography—amply understood as the science of space—can be specified in two alternative ways: on the one hand, territory and geography find a clear connection and common root in the earth. In the first instance both are made possible by the biosphere as a unique receptacle of life—no territory exists without *terra*, no geography without *gaia*. On the other hand, however, both geography and territoriology necessarily prolong into less contingent, more abstract considerations. If human geography in particular has over the past decades evolved into a discussion about the social "production of space" and the "politics of space"—to take two famous expressions from, respectively, Henri Lefebvre ([1974] 1991) and Doreen Massey (2005)—for its part territoriology comes with the inherent ambition to tackle all ranges of social phenomena in terms of "territorializations" that might, or might not, have an immediate projection on the land.

From ethology, territoriology retrieves the originally acoustic and musical nature of territories. For instance, the native tongue can be appraised as one such acoustic territory. Not by chance, the native tongue is also called the "mother tongue," the language spoken by the mother—and the mother is indeed the first territory for a new human creature. What is learned through the mother so constitutes a veritable home territory. Cultural and religious territories may work in a similar way: the Torah, for instance, represents the Jewish "portable territory" that has compensated for the relative deterritorialization of the Jewry from the European nation-state. Even interpersonal relations can be modeled as territorializations. Two friends or two lovers are taken in an exploration of the other as the terra incognita that, however, does not preexist as such before the encounter takes place: the meaning of a friendship, or a love, lies precisely in this open-ended aspect whereby friends coconstitute each other. These examples remind us that some territories may as well be of nongeographic nature—at least if by geography we mean the geography of the planet Earth. It is nonetheless conceivable that other geographies are possible—such as conceptual, affective geographies that have no immediate projection on the geoid.

Vitalism, Animism, and the Study of Territories

Territories are always-already folded into the life of humans, animals, and plants, and we need ways to describe and follow their continuous life trajectories. We have anticipated that our approach is characterized by a vitalist

For a Science of Territories

sensitivity guiding or better animating our studies. Before we move on to the series of studies in territoriology that occupies this volume, we should try to clarify why we are interested in animation and what it means to us. In a very intuitive sense, animation is a process that brings the seemingly inert into life. An exquisite example of animism is when a child throws an object and exclaims, "It ran away from me!" So animation is a strategy, a state of mind, or a contingency that allows for things to unfold, without reducing these things to any given static version or instant of themselves.[5] In other words, animation concerns some sort of awakening of things, and this is also where it results most connected with the spirit of territories, insofar as territories always entail formations that alert the involved actors about the nature of their own interactions. What happens, then, if we see territories as living things, albeit of a nonorganic nature?

In modern science vitalism has been uncompromisingly banished. Mainstream modern biology does certainly not appear interested in recognizing the idea that life cannot be located or assigned to some given mechanism. Such recognition would make its enterprise irrelevant. No occult properties and no metaphysical postulates can be admitted; to the extent that pure life cannot be quantified as such, to the eyes of standard science it is bound to remain one such occult property and one such metaphysical postulate. An entelechy, final causation, or intrinsic endpoint cannot be accepted in biology as, so to speak, "pulling" factors; they must always be reconstructed on the basis of partial material arrangements of molecules and genes operating on the ground. These are, in short, the tenets of molecular biology, currently the dominant approach to biology. But this also means that, perhaps paradoxically, biology must renounce life as a whole to understand its partial mechanisms. In a certain sense this is not surprising, given that all fields of specialized knowledge presuppose a foundational stratum not to be further analyzed and actually not analyzable (in the same way lawyers can never define the law in its totality; sociologists study social phenomena but don't know what society in itself is, etc.). On the other hand, in recent years in philosophy and the humanities we have seen a lot of retakes on vitalism.[6]

This is of course a different vitalism from the one that spanned the nineteenth century. It may be closer to the influence of Friedrich Nietzsche, Georg Simmel, and, to some extent, Alfred Whitehead, as mediated in particular through Canguilhem and then Deleuze.[7] In this view vitalism appears, not as a special substantive principle to be applied to a defined domain of existence or experience, but as a qualitative perspective on the totality of the world. Anthropologists were among the first to revisit vitalism, especially in its facet of animism (Bird-David 1999). Since personification happens only in and through interaction, they have suggested, animism must count as an important social skill in environments where mastery cannot be firmly exercised. Over the past twenty years, Tim Ingold (2000, 2007, 2011) has progressively outlined the contours of his proposal for a vitalistic anthropology. A similar yet distinct vitalistic overtone can also be heard in Anna Tsing's (2015) work on the matsutake mushroom, where fungal existence, with all its indeterminacy and yet inserted in the global trade, is understood in the context of "precarity as an earthwide condition," or in Marisol de la Cadena's (2015) "stories" about the *tirakuna*, or "earth beings," among the Quechua people of Peru. In parallel in philosophy vitalism has been reclaimed by some as a style of inquiry into nature. For instance, a new philosophy of nature inspired by Deleuze—who famously claimed that "concepts have an existence of their own; they are animated; they are invisible creatures" (2003, 219)—has been pursued by Isabelle Stengers (2011), Karen Barad (2007), and Jane Bennett (2010) within the frame of a movement sometimes called "new materialism" (Coole and Frost 2010).

Following Canguilhem's essay on vitalism (dating from the mid-1940s) ([1952] 1965), we suggest that vitalism can be regarded above all as an attitude of resistance to reductionism. We are thus not exploring what vitalism can say as a theory but what a vitalistic approach or sensitivity can do within one or more reference theories (Greco 2005). From our perspective vitalism is not the opposite of materialism, only of mechanism. And strictly speaking, the two are not even opposite—for mechanism, as Canguilhem puts it, is above all a method, while vitalism cannot be con-

For a Science of Territories

sidered as per se a method. Rather, vitalism is an exigency or imperative, a need manifested by life itself (even theoretical life). That is why every time we try to clarify the vitalistic assumption we end up with something vague and implicit, as opposed to the strictness and imperiousness of the scientific method. This also means that vitalism cannot stand alone. The fact that in modern science the qualification of vitalist has progressively turned into a stigma probably proves only that vitalism cannot exist as an accomplished theory. Yet it is a historical fact that vitalism has contributed no less than mechanicism to the development of modern biology. In this respects Canguilhem recalls a number of crucial nineteenth-century biologists who worked under a vitalistic persuasion. Among these one must certainly recall Jakob von Uexküll ([1934] 1957), whose notion of *Umwelt* we are going to discuss in the next chapter.

Certainly, the sheer claim that there exists a vital principle is not very helpful to advance with scientific understanding. Should vitalism be reduced to that claim, it would amount to quite a poor and sloppy position. Canguilhem seeks to show why this is not necessarily the case. Some misunderstandings may derive from an intrinsic element of nostalgia present in vitalism. Canguilhem notices how vitalism tends to appear as backward looking—for example, through the use of ancient Greek words such as *entelechy, hormè,* and so on. It is as if vitalism were looking for an original view of life, a view not encrusted with human technologies and their mechanistic, artificial workings. The problem is that such technologies include all technical tools—not only modern ones but rather those ranging from flint to computer—as well as language itself. As a consequence, vitalism remains *stricto sensu* unspeakable. If it survives, it survives as an *attitude* rather than as a principle of essence or origin. Still, as such an attitude—or even as a moral exigency, as Canguilhem suggests—vitalism may retain its importance: indeed, from our point of view, its primary service is to provide an antidote to the arrogance of determinism and reductionism.

If vitalism is a morality (an ethos) well before being a theory, its critique of mechanicism is not so much a critique of mechanical theory but rather a critique of the fact that mechanicism easily lends support to technologies that are crude, ruthless, and out of measure. What vitalism really criticizes, is the *technocratic* side of mechanicism. Ultimately, vitalism appears as an expression of the way in which life voices its own mistrust toward mechanisms or, even better, cuts mechanisms down to size. As a simultaneously epistemological and ethical position, a vitalist sensitivity suggests that (following Nietzsche) life happens with and through an inherent point of view: life is perspectival and existential; it is a measure-setting and value-setting situation. Living things do not simply conform to external norms but secrete their own intrinsic normative stance—what, before Canguilhem (1966), Simmel ([1918] 2010) used to call an "individual law" (*individuelle Gesetz*).[8] On the other hand, as Canguilhem reminds us, notions such as vitalism—or, for that matter, territory—have in turn been charged of being politically suspect, if not straightforwardly reactionary. In the twentieth century, for instance, Nazi science—especially with the biologist Hans Driesch—has endorsed a form of vitalism, thanks to an organicist parallel between the "final" or "leading cause" and the führer, the leader of the nation. Even irregular authors such as the fine essayist Roger Caillois have been accused of flirting with the radical Right's understanding of the "living community" as organic and totalitarian. This may certainly have something to do with the subsequent post–World War II disgrace of vitalistic theories. But as remarked by Canguilhem, these aberrations amount to twisted usages of notions (in fact, the Nazis also used Darwinism and genetics to their advantage).[9] It is as if, continues Canguilhem, we reproach arithmetic for the fact that bankers use it to produce social inequalities and exploitation.

The notions of vitalism and animation are proposed here not as full-fledged theories but mainly as a way of avoiding the reductionism of earlier territoriality theories. They remind us that territories should not be treated as given entities, that they are not written once and for all in genes, in nations, or in stone—neither can they, as suggested earlier, be derived from (and thus reduced to) human will or behavior alone. The actors involved in processes of territorialization—whether human or else—are *legio*, anything but dead, and they need to be handled with care.

A General Approach to Territories

Starting from the example of the Roman Colosseum as a case located across the notions of place and the city, we have in this chapter traced some sources of territorial research, identifying and very shortly mapping at least four different major fields that represent sources for territoriological analyses. Although we might have seen some more interdisciplinary approaches lately, these different fields have often been developed apart from one another. This has, in turn, fueled the development of territorial research as a series of separate fields that have tended to limit themselves by discussing only certain selected features of territoriality. The wealth of territorial phenomena and issues would, however, benefit from being kept together and studied jointly: such is the approach we have suggested throughout. Empirical research could but be improved thanks to the exercise of a comparative gaze that learns from the unexpected plurality and the many facets of territorialization. What we need is thus a more general and renewed territoriology to take care of this. This is in fact a crucial mission, both if we want to improve the weak interdisciplinary communication across different strands of territorial interrogation, and if we seek to advance territorial research as a more unified field—something we suspect that all the different traditions of research discussed in this chapter could benefit from.

In the second part of the chapter we have set up some basic key insights drawn from earlier research (including our own), which we think can form an approximate first platform for unfolding territoriology. As we have seen, giving emphasis to the social relation rather than the object invites us to avoid conflating territory with the space—or place, land, terrain, and so on—where territorialization occurs. But how is a social relation to be described and studied? This is the crucial theme that runs through the following chapters. So far we have gathered a few working hypotheses: territories are dependent on both acts of imagination and sets of materials; they are always functional, semiotic, and expressive; and, finally, they have to do with some kind of "life." The last of these is probably the most sensitive point: modern mechanistic biology, on the one hand, and vitalist philosophy, on the other, have advanced two very different conceptions of life. We have suggested that we want to borrow some insights and advantages of the latter tradition without losing the positive explanatory strength of the former—for, indeed, territoriology as we conceptualize it is to remain a scientific endeavor. Admittedly, this may not be an easy path to follow—in fact, it may well be that, before the reader can see the path at all, a few more steps in the dark are called forth.

2   Environments, Atmospheres, and Networks

In the previous chapter we have reviewed some sources of inspiration for territoriological analysis, which included mainly disciplines such as ethology, ecology, human geography, and social and natural philosophy. These broad sources in science, however, are far from being the only possible ones, and they can certainly be supplemented with a number of additional interlocutors. This is what we try to do in this chapter. Indeed, the study of territories is not to be understood as a paradigm that stands in isolation from other spatial categories and processes, nor as one mutually exclusive with respect to other approaches. As is perhaps becoming clearer, we argue for an imagination of territories that is plural and open-ended. How then do we practically situate our proposal for territoriology within a wider field of existing sociospatial inquiry? Investigating how territories relate to other sociospatial concepts and phenomena is, we believe, complementary to highlighting how, in turn, other concepts and approaches can be renewed once seen through the lens of territory. In later chapters we use territory as a structuring lens of inquiry, revisiting a number of notions coming from a variety of disciplines including biology, psychology, geography, sociology, architecture, and planning. These notions include, for instance, form, rhythm, melody, scale, and affordance. The aim of the present chapter is, however, to give our reader a first idea of how we want to situate the concept of territory in a more general landscape of inquiry. We thus set territories in relation to a few other key concepts—notably *environments*, *atmospheres*, and *networks*. We have decided to single out these notions because of the interest that they have sparked in recent literature, but above all in connection with our belief that these notions mirror genuinely important facets of territorial phenomena.

Broadly speaking, we could say that environments, atmospheres, and networks correspond to certain fundamental motifs in territories: *living*, *feeling*, and *making*. Our approach to territories can thus, for example, be differentiated from the one taken by Bob Jessop, Neil Brenner, and Martin Jones (2008). The latter have proposed a framework for the study of socio-spatial relations, which they call TPSN—comprising territory, place, scale and network. While these authors warn from privileging any one of these dimensions over the others and seek to include the possible contradictions and conflicts ensuing from the diverse articulations of the considered notions, (Jessop, Brenner, and Jones 2008, 391–94), they still posit that these four concepts should be regarded as somehow being the foundational ones for the study of social space at large. For our part we have already suggested that we probably need more notions than these to capture social life in space and time, while at the same time we do not necessarily need to regard each spatial notion as exclusive to others even when examining the same object. So to recall the opening example of chapter 1, the Roman Colosseum may as well be taken as a manifestation of a territory (characterized by the multiplicity of territorialized and territorializing effects); a place (singular, recognizable, experienced); a scale (as a local crowd collector scalable to the urban space of Rome as well as to its imperial space); and a network (of similar game arenas built by the Romans as well as by following state powers and stretching up to contemporary stadiums).

While the analytical grid set up by Jessop, Brenner, and Jones (2008) may retain a certain utility, it ultimately runs the risk of locking, instead of enabling, the imagination of new conceptual approaches as well as empirical research into social space. In this book we discuss places, scales, and networks at various moments, but for us it is not so important to establish whether these notions can be accommodated within a single framework or not. When it comes to territories, in any case, we are even less satisfied by the stipulations of the TPSN framework. Indeed, Jessop, Brenner, and Jones define territory as based on bordering, parcelization, and enclosure—a fairly traditional and reified conceptualization clearly insufficient for our purposes. A persistent underlying idea is that the territory is a kind of inert container of various phenomena: for instance, the three authors suggest that, when it becomes a structuring principle of place, territory enables the identification of places inside territories; when it becomes a structuring principle of scale, it enables multilevel government; and when it becomes a structuring principle of networks, it enables the interstate system. We hope to illustrate that the life of territories is much richer than that, and that territories cannot be captured by fixity, closure, and exteriority alone; in many cases they cannot even be captured by spatial continuity. But before we go deeper into our discussion on territories, let us set the stage by introducing the three notions of environments (or milieus), atmospheres, and networks

Environments and Milieus as Ways of Living

While the two notions of environment and milieu belong in different philosophical traditions and have evolved to cope with different sets of phenomena, it is possible that from a theoretical point of view they actually designate something very similar, if not identical. Indeed, they both point toward a level of reality that is relational instead of substantive, and compositional instead of merely additive. As such, we propose to treat them as twin concepts. Their difference, we argue, is one of perspective: with the environment observers are placed in a central position looking around, whereas with the milieu they are placed in a surrounding—perhaps even liminal—position looking toward the center.[1]

As first pointed out by Georges Canguilhem ([1952] 1965), the notion of environment is a modern one, first elaborated in physics and subsequently inherited by biology. The problem from which the notion stems is that of establishing the possibility of action at a distance in the new physical universe conceptualized by Isaac Newton. For René Descartes action between two bodies can be exercised only by direct clash, insofar as bodies are extensive and reciprocally external to each other; on the contrary, Newton admits the existence of an "ether," understood as a peculiar physical medium that conveys the action of one body on another. This is how gravitation is supposed to be transferred and exercised. For Newton the ether is between bodies but also inside them: invisible and inconsistent, it plays purely the role of transmitting forces. As such, the ether could actually be said to designate a general state mediality. The subsequent notion of field (developed by Michael Faraday in physics and much later imported into the social science) in this sense corresponds to a deessentialized or desubstativized version of the ether. For his part Albert Einstein (1949) observed that the *horror vacui* that led Newton to fill empty space with the ether was owing to the latter's belief—widely shared at his time—that the fundamental laws of physics could be derived from experience (*hypotheses non fingo*)—something Einstein himself no longer admitted.

But Canguilhem ([1952] 1965) indicates that this variant of the notion of milieu is a determinist one: it has underpinned the Darwinian theory of natural selection through adaptation and competition and has culminated in early twentieth-century behaviorism. At the polar opposite a nondeterminist notion has emerged from the tradition of human geography, as well as from marginalized currents in medicine, such as the psychiatrist Kurt Goldstein and, in biology, notably Jakob von Uexküll.[2] In this tradition (or these traditions, given that they can hardly be said to form any unitary body), animals and humans are observed essentially as in dialogue with their surroundings. While environmental determinism is an old shortcoming that afflicts geography since at least Hippocrates's treaty *On Airs, Waters and Places*, it is within geography itself that a new, antireductionist view has emerged. For instance, in Alexander von Humboldt's geography, humans are not simply on the receiving side of external forces that put pressure on them; they are genuinely creative beings who give shape to their own environment. A similar insight can be found, in an even more expanded sense, in Uexküll's environmental biology. Here it is not just humans but all animals who entertain a non-determinist relation with their milieu. As Canguilhem summarizes, the milieu "proposes solutions, but cannot impose them" ([1952] 1965, 181). Uexküll's enormously influential notion of *Umwelt* conveys the sense of such a selective and elective opening of the organism to certain traits in the surrounding world (*Umgebung*). Stimulations from the environ-

Environments, Atmospheres

ment are significant for the organism only insofar as they meet the same organism's anticipatory attitudes.

Life is inherently related to such movements whereby the animal selectively picks up only some signals from the wealth offered to it by the surrounding world and treats them as meaningful. These signals are "intentional," which means that reaction can never be explained as the simple resultant of external chemical-mechanical stimulations. What *signifies* is the whole, not the parts, and the milieu corresponds to this whole within which the animal can pose the terms of its own vital problem. Contrary to Darwinian selection, the fact that the external circumstances put pressure on the organism is only a limited case and one that signals pathological conditions or the proximity of death. During normal times the animal is *at home* in its milieu: even the paramecium floats in water "more secure than a baby in his cradle" (as Merleau-Ponty [1995, 224] phrased it). Canguilhem thus concludes that "the milieu upon which the organism depends is structured and organized by the organism itself: what the milieu can offer to the living being is a function of the latter's demand" ([1952] 1965, 195). In chapter 7 we come back to certain aspects of this co-dependent relation between the living being and its environment through James Gibson (who, much like Maurice Merleau-Ponty, was interested in the perceptions of the active body) and his concept of *affordance*.

The real environmental problem, we could say, is not so much one of causation as one of *valorization*: it concerns how the living being can attach importance and invest in certain significations that manifest themselves at the interface between its own self and the environment. Here we can also observe in limine how the issue of territorialization appears—for, in a certain sense, territories concern precisely the way in which these acts of attachment can be expressed (we explore this theme more extensively in chapter 4). But even in Charles Darwin one has to acknowledge the existence of not only competition and selection but also variation. In other words, the first environment where the animal is placed is, for Darwin, its own species. The field of each species is, so to speak, crisscrossed by a multiplicity of random variations that tend to progressively map all the possibilities inherent in that species, progressively shifting it toward new species to come. In a way it is as if each individual creature has to submit its own biological proposal to the judgment of this double environment. Consequently, in Darwin the animal can survive only if it is attuned to both the natural and the social environment. Ultimately, a species, insofar as it exists as a biological entity in transition through such an experimental and judgmental procedure, cannot but exist as an actual population or a set of such populations. The latter point strengthens the idea that there is some sort of intrinsic sociality to the milieu; that, in other words, the milieu itself provides a constant company for the animal—it accompanies it as a peculiar associate, as a socius.

Ultimately, as we have seen, both the determinist and the indeterminist view emphasize a principle of relationality as key to the notion of the environment: the location of each individual organism can be understood, and can make sense, only in relation to the ensemble of the population to which that organism belongs, as well as to the ensemble of connections among the multiplicity of consociated members as they exist in a species-specific *Umwelt*. The notion of milieu thus inherently evokes an ecological perspective, whereby elements are defined by relations. Interestingly, the *Umwelt* idea paved the way to the subsequent elaboration by Merleau-Ponty (1964) in his relentless search for a tertium quid between the subject and the object, as well as between mechanicism and vitalism. Eventually, the French phenomenologist called this complex third reality "the flesh of the world" (*la chair du monde*). In his course on nature from the late 1950s, Merleau-Ponty (1995) commented on Uexküll, remarking on the similarity between the *Umwelt* and a melody. It is a fruitful image, because melodies indeed generate a peculiar sense of time, a unity-in-unfolding (we return to this in chapter 6).

When a melody begins, Merleau-Ponty notices, all its notes are in a way already there: in other words, the whole melody is found on a single plane, so there's a sense in which not only the past generates the future but also the future generates the past. All the notes of the melody, we could also say, virtually coexist when just one of them is actualized. The *Umwelt*,

       Environments, Atmospheres

for Merleau-Ponty, is neither a force nor a substance, but as a relation it certainly has special qualities insofar as it is characterized by certain orientations. Thus, Merleau-Ponty suggests that the animal conceives its own Umwelt not as an idea but only as a "theme that haunts consciousness" (1995, 233). Perhaps the psychoanalytical notion of *archetype* and the mathematical notion of *attractor* could provide some useful characterizations of how the *Umwelt* can be present to the animal, not as an object but as a "haunting" theme. The *Umwelt* is characterized as a mode of knowing that is active. This holds not only for the relations that the animal entertains with surrounding natural events but also for those that come to be established between the animal and its territory, as well as between the animal and other animals. This is extremely important for territoriology, in that it shows how environments are naturally connected to a social-relational understanding of territorializations.

We are going to explore this trope more in depth in the following chapters. For now suffice to say that, from this point of view, Gilbert Simondon is Merleau-Ponty's prime heir. In his theory of individuation, Simondon ([1964–89] 2013) shows how the formation of a new individual (understood as a moment in the "event" and the "operation" of individuation) is always correlative to an "environmentalization." Taken in itself, the individual is an "incomplete reality" and, in fact, an abstraction. The living being is never an isolated individual: not unity but always simultaneously less and more than "one." Put differently, the individual and the milieu are two sides of the same operation. In this theorization one can detect an implicit reference to the *Umwelt* notion: for Simondon, any new individual comes with an "associated milieu" that complements the individual vis-à-vis the original whole (*synolon* or system) from which the process of individualization started. The *Umwelt* is, in fact, nothing else than the couple "individual plus associated milieu." It is well known how much Gilles Deleuze was marked by Simondon's theory of individuation. It may thus not be by coincidence if, for Deleuze and Félix Guattari (1980, sec. 11), milieus are inherently related to territories. Indeed, in their attempt toward a renewed philosophy of nature, Deleuze and Guattari argue that milieus exist in the interplay of three major forces—namely chaos, cosmos, and the earth. Not simply do milieus host action by organisms located in them, but more important, milieus are connected to other milieus by way of openness: contrary to territories, milieus have no boundaries and are caught in the constant process of being "transducted" into other milieus.[3]

The operation of transition from one milieu to another, is *rhythm*. Repetition produces rhythm, but rhythms themselves are differences, not repetitions. The rhythm is thus a *productive repetition* as opposed to a merely *reproductive measure*. Territories evolve from a specific operation that can be carried out with environments and, more specifically, with the rhythmic component of a milieu. Territories appear, Deleuze and Guattari (1980) suggest, when environmental rhythms are made expressive, when they are turned into veritable "signatures." Understood as the marking and the appropriation of a set of qualities, the signature corresponds to the inception of territory. This stage is what Deleuze and Guattari call the *pancarte*, or display signs (easily understandable, for instance, as the nuptial parades staged by certain birds or the "Keep Out" sign hung outside a private property). In chapter 5 we return to this aspect of territory by considering a series of creatures—the "little humans"—who are imagined as patrolling home territories; and in chapter 7 we indicate how the use of a shared urban equipment such as a playground can be experienced in either exclusivist or inclusive terms. Yet a further territorial stage can be attained when *style* appears: at this point the territorial act ceases to focus on reclaiming exclusive possession of anything external or trying to mark some objective conquest and turns into "self-development." Such self-development is nothing but an intensification of expressiveness and consistency—in other words, the appearance of *art* as an act accomplished in itself and detached from further purposes. A similar conception of art as an "axial inversion" of purposiveness is, incidentally, also argued by Georg Simmel in his late work; he suggested that perception loses its utility function and rather becomes productive of phenomena: "Life no longer flows through these forms to its own practical ends, but has been dammed up in them, it has so to speak transferred its power to them, and

Environments, Atmospheres

with this power (and to the extent of it) forms now operate according to their own law" ([1918] 2010, 53).

For his part Deleuze (2003) also employs the image of "the egg" (better known as the "body without organs") as a type of environment crossed by gradients of intensity, poles of potential, and thresholds of transformation, although not yet (or no longer) characterized by the precise territorialization of given organs and their respective functions. The nonorganic life discussed by Deleuze—and perhaps already evoked by Simmel—is eventually the life of concepts, understood as types of reconnaissance into unknown and uncharted milieus. Here we are thus presented with a notion of milieu that is already atmospheric in the sense we are going to discuss now.

Atmospheres as Ways of Feeling

If the environment is crucial for understanding life and how the life of any organism (indeed, of any territory) is strictly coupled with and dependent on its own milieu, the notion of atmosphere appears as an important counterpart to feelings and affects. Although philosophical aspects of feeling and affects have a very long history, the sociological-phenomenological notion of atmosphere—and the connection between atmospheres and feelings—emerged as a topic in aesthetic philosophy during the early 1990s (Böhme 1993; H. Schmitz 2016). Before then, arguably, the word atmosphere conveyed only the very literal sense of vapor sphere—that is, the fluid gases surrounding the planet. A less materialist account has since emerged, probably in connection with the attempt to take into account the more subtle aspects of sensation that the combination of light, humidity, temperature, smell, and so on generate in embodied observers. Apart from Gernot Böhme, one of the more well-known philosophers to discuss atmospheres, is Peter Sloterdijk. In his trilogy *Sphären*, developed between 1998 and 2004, Sloterdijk (2011, 2014, 2016) describes capitalist modernity as engaged in a constant production of "domes," large structured spheres in whose atmosphere purposeful social activities can be carried out and thrive. Outlining the modern technological history of bodily and societal containments, Sloterdijk highlights the historically important roles of hothouses and air-conditioning, as well as, *a contrario*, fumigation, gas warfare, and so on. On the same account he also depicts the building types of the apartment house and the sport stadium as "the two most successful architectural innovations of the twentieth century" (2016, 529). Indeed, while the apartment house works as a stackable spatial crystal, a "rigid foam body" for societal development (537), the sports stadium embodies the quintessential space for modern mass meetings and mass culture rituals.

Atmospheric production and atmospheric support seem essential in all these undertakings. Atmospheres have since become an increasingly salient and intentional part of the urban built environment (Borch 2014). We could even contend that our epoch is contradistinguished by the rise of an *atmoculture*—that is, a set of expectations and requirements about the production and maintenance of given atmospheres to accompany or guide our urban life (Brighenti and Pavoni 2017). Atmoculture can be characterized as a widespread process that places atmospheres at the center and pivot of many different urban stakes, including, for instance, the feelings of safety and relaxation, as opposed to those of anxiety and fear. During recent decades we have witnessed the proliferation of consumption-oriented spaces designed with an inbuilt atmosphere of comfort and hospitality (Bell 2007). The case of retail is particularly impressive in this respect. In European countries such as France and Sweden, large shopping mall structures had already been developed in the 1960s and 1970s. Netherlands (Rotterdam) and Denmark (Copenhagen) set early models for the pedestrianization of old inner city centers that were conducive to new ways of retail and consumption in public space. Today similar spaces have bloomed (sometimes successful, sometime struggling, to be true) into large, specialized retail areas (Gehl and Gemzöe 1996; Monheim 2003; Kärrholm 2012) as well as into new building types including lounge shopping malls, food-court plazas, urban spas, entertainment retailing, and visitor centers.

Before Sloterdijk, Margaret Crawford (1992) noted how retail already started to produce its "pleasure domes" with the department stores of the nineteenth century. Contemporary retail spaces have certainly produced larger and larger domes, while the design of feeling has been increasingly

Environments, Atmospheres

geared into such production. From the 1970s onward atmospherics—understood as atmosphere design—has become an increasingly important and studied factor in efforts of affecting the mood of consumers (Turley and Milliman 2000; Vernet and de Wit 2007; Biehl-Missal and Saren 2012; Healy 2014; Julmi 2016). The development of retail spaces can also be seen in parallel to a recent interest in the constant branding (Klingmann 2007), eventalization (Boullier 2010; Pløger 2010), mobilization (Kazig, Masson and Thomas 2017), and spectacularization (Degen and Rose 2012) of the city, as well as more generally in the sensory experience of the urban dweller as something that needs to be taken care of.

The expressive and affective components of atmospheres are crucial: atmospheres do not simply fill in space; they also play an important part in spatial and material productions (B. Anderson 2009, 80). Despite their pervasiveness, however, atmospheres remain evanescent objects: they are designed and produced in ways that often escape univocal categorizations—they are hybrid mixtures of spatial and material, psychological and social, individual and collective, perceptual and affective, and objective and subjective components. Atmospheres are both part of an experience and part of the experienced, while the list of actors participating in an atmospheric experience is potentially indeterminable, or yet to be defined. In general, as recognized by both phenomenological literature (Böhme 1993; Runkel 2016) and affect theorists (B. Anderson 2009), atmospheres imply collective and individual sensory experiences and moods related to the peculiar aspects of light, air, scent, and visual patterns capable of inducing certain moods and attitudes. But these aspects cannot be easily reduced to simple metrical or territorial dimensions. In opposition to territories, atmospheres lack constitutive boundaries. This fact adds to the fuzziness of the notion and may also explain why a good chunk of atmospheres literature gives the impression of turning around almost nothing—often reduced to the petitio principii that "atmospheres matter." What is it exactly that atmospheres are made of and how to capture analytically these components synthesized within an atmosphere? Arguably, what is most difficult to account for in detail is how different scales or level of importance interact and how each atmosphere materially encompasses heterogeneous things including "mundane interventions such as the dimming of lights as well as threats of violence or impending meteorological events" (Gandy 2017, 370). Thus, while atmospheres might have relevant social, cultural, and political impact, they remain notoriously hard to pinpoint down.

How can we further distinguish territories from atmospheres? If a territory can be described as an affective and to some extent valorized relation between actors who imagine one another and can project a possible social intercourse between them, an atmosphere can, as Andreas Philippopoulos-Mihalopoulos has suggested, be seen as *"the excess of affect that keeps bodies together; and what emerges when bodies are held together by, through and against each other"* (2015, 90). Whereas territories can be seen as attempts at holding a certain entity or process accountable for some purposes, atmospheres are the excess of bodily interactions and can as such not really be held accountable for anything. They might be associated to a certain territory, but they do not in the same sense have a direction (intentional or unintentional) toward the production of a certain effect, meaning, or value. Still, territories and atmospheres might intersect and contribute to the reciprocal thriving. For Sloterdijk, for example, human dwelling has since always strived to produce atmospherically conditioned human "islands" (Thrift 2009, 124). From primitive shelters, homes, villages, and urban walls to modern domes, stations, malls, cars, and so on, a continuum can be identified from the perspective of anthropotechnical spaces. Atmospheres are thus intimately connected with architectures and nonhuman bodies, and as such they are inherent products as well as producers of our society. Architectural modernism is related to atmospheres in terms of comfort design and indoor climates in the new building types of the nineteenth century and onward (Sloterdijk 2005, 2011). Contemporary engineered atmospheres can thus be seen as part of the modernist spatial project of territorializing the whole globe (Serres 1995, 2011).

Atmospheres can never be held by territories and vice versa, and although they might draw from one another they are not bound to one another. In fact, atmospheres, like rhythms, might often help territories to transform and even to move. In early architectural theory (Gandy 2017, 365; Forty 2000), as in market theory (Kotler 1973), atmosphere was related to design and thus to the idea that atmospheres were possible to produce and move between different places. If atmospheres, however, are produced in the moment by the excess of affects between present bodies, then it should also follow that they are impossible to produce or reproduce with any exactitude. Instead, atmospheres are ephemeral, unruly, and capable of producing change even in the most standardized environment. While atmospheres may be aimed for in design, the sheer number of elements and actors involved and the relations they generate may often induce sudden, unforeseen variations in meaning and outcome. But this is also the reason why atmospheres easily come to be absorbed into territorial associations: for instance, an atmospheric perception of "creepiness" may easily induce the territorial association of "dangerous place" or similar tags that can be easily circulated even at a distance. The atmosphere might thus be one of the reasons why territorial associations are so mobile, and why they cannot always be pinned down to the specific locale they are supposed to refer to.

Networks as Ways of Acting

From atmospheres and feelings we now quickly move on to a seemingly more tangible topic, networks and different modes of making and organization. During the 1990s, in the context of a historical period of relative international stability and the rise of the new digital communication media, network talk became pervasive. Networks have been recurrently portrayed as generating a new type of social action, one supposed to be irreducible to territoriality and in stark contrast to it.[4] But the absolute distinction between territories and networks does not seem very well placed to us. In fact, networks can be understood as a specific type of territory in which access points and speeds are hierarchically arranged, ideally to the point of closing all access ways except a number of elected ones. If we think about mobility infrastructures, we can notice that a fast lane is something that already complements a territory with a network-type character; similarly, subway stations and highway gates function as hubs that regulate the access to a given territory, which they also turn into a network type. Arguably, the distinction between territories and networks is scale-sensitive. For instance, the answer to the question, "Is a street a territory or a network?" depends on the scale at which we observe the street: if we look at it as it appears on a map, then it is certainly very similar to a network; but when we actually walk down that street, we can also appreciate it as a territory.

Territories and networks might thus relate to each other in different ways: under certain respects and capacities, a territory might be seen (and practiced) as a network, and conversely under certain conditions a network might be seen as a territory. A territory might take the shape of a network that, from a perspective of its geometrical form, might be continuous, like a railway or subway net. But a network can also be spatially discontinuous, like a system of parking places within a city. A network is, in this sense, a system for logistics, and the city can, as Gabriel Dupuy has showed in *Urban Networks–Network Urbanism* ([1991] 2008), be studied through the development and management of its different networks, each exhibiting its own specific territorial features.[5] It suffices to recall information and communication technologies, roads, and sewage canals to have an illustration. Another different, yet related, view on spatial networks and logistics can be found in space syntax and in Bill Hillier's configurational theory (Hillier and Hanson 1984; Hillier 1996), which sets out to describe and quantify how different urban spaces of a similar quality (for example, interior spaces, exterior spaces, isovists, convex spaces, axial spaces, etc.) relate to one another. These descriptions are then both categorized in different ways (as spatially integrated, intelligible, etc.) and associated to specific urban functions. In short, it is a theory that analyzes and categorizes various kinds of spatial networks or infrastructures to territorialize them in different ways.

But the notion of network does not always suggest a specific geometrical form or even a system of uniform entities (whether water drains or axial lines); it might also be used to describe something seemingly formless. In the latter sense a network does not necessarily look like a "net" but can be described as a specific mode of organization or, perhaps better put, a spe-

Environments, Atmospheres

cific mode of making or acting: it is a set of connected and heterogeneous actors. These actors might change in terms of form and spatial location, yet as long as they remain connected, they still belong to the same network. From this point of view, a network is the specific effect produced by the connections that define it (which also is one of the main points of actor network theory; see Latour 1999a, 2005; Mol 2010). Looking at a territory from such a network perspective means that one needs to include all the different kinds of actors that together make the territory effective, the actors connected through the territory, and those from which the territory to a certain degree draws its power. For instance, a specific parking lot, observed as such one territorial network, might depend on the connections between a heterogeneous number of actors—including signs, parking meters, parking regulations, wardens, cars, and governing agencies of various types. If cars or wardens change, as long as there are new wardens and cars to take their position in the network (in other words, as long as connections remains stable), the parking lot network might still remain in effect. By seeing a territory as a network we might thus highlight some of its aspects, such as the logistic activities that serve, support, and reproduce the territory.

Historically, networks have been opposed to tree structures (Deleuze and Guattari 1980). "Flat" and open-ended networks have been seen as inevitably critical of hierarchical tree structures (Torisson 2017). But if it is true that the network, from a geometrical perspective, might look somehow "formless" (at least, in classic Euclidean space), this is because, as a mode of organization, it can take on many different geometrical forms, including that of the tree. In practice, as a system of associated entities, the network can assume any formal shape, from a highly stabilized tree shape, through a ring shape, to a grid shape, and so on. In this sense the network is not really opposed to the tree. Rather, we should say that the topological features of a network cannot be matched with Euclidean geometry (Law 2002). The reason is that a Euclidean object is destabilized by deformation and deterioration, whereas a network object is destabilized only by detachment and disconnection. In the previous chapter we observed that a territory must never be confused with the space where it takes place. In a similar way we must also argue that a territory can never be confused with the network that stabilizes its effects. The network is defined by its associations and connections, and, as such, it necessarily leaves all other aspects in the shadow. True, a territory can find its stability in the connections that to a certain extent constitute it, as well as in its material and geometrical form, but it can also find its stability in other modes of acting. John Law and Annemarie Mol's work has, for example, pointed to fluidity as one such mode of acting (1994; De Laet and Mol 2000; Law 2002).

A strong network might be incompatible with fluid stabilization, but a territory is perfectly compatible with it. Stabilization through fluidity occurs when a certain effect can be sustained even though both geometric forms and network connections are changing. In a fluid topology the actors related to a certain territorial effect might be replaced, as long as they are not replaced too quick or all at once and, more important, as long as there remains some kind of family resemblance between the object as it looks before and after the replacement has been done.[6] Fluid entities are thus never dependent on one aspect alone (such as an obligatory point of passage or entry point, etc.) to sustain their effect. In fact, each single part of the territory can be replaced. Two different states of a fluid territory might thus have no actor in common at all, providing that there are states in between that have actors in common with both.

A specific territory might thus remain a certain stability even through quite severe changes. My home might, for example, remain the same home over decades, even as I rebuild it and even if connections and relations that once seemed crucial are cut. As long as it does not happen too quickly and abruptly and as long as the changes are not too radical, the home can keep on thriving and in the end actually become stronger through change. This is because, as we have seen, fluid stabilization works very differently from network stabilization: whereas the latter favors firm and recurrent (even obligatory) connections, the former increases with the number of actors who come to be associated with it. The more the actors I associate with my home, the easier I might find home both within and outside the perimeters of my dwelling. If we look at different territorial types or sorts, they might thus often spread precisely through fluidity (Kärrholm 2007, 2012). For instance, a bathing place is a sort of territory that can spread easily and can take on many guises, precisely thanks to its fluidity. By contrast, an IKEA store also benefits from a certain fluidity but is probably more dependent on network stability, in that it necessitates a number of obligatory connections to be sustained; otherwise it will no longer count as an IKEA store at all but become merely a furniture store.

All territories depend on a series of different modes of organization acting for their stabilization. So far we have discussed the network as one of at least three different modes that might help to stabilize a territory. We could continue along this line and find other modes, but we think these suffice to make our point clear.[7] A territory can be viewed through different modes of acting, modes that require their own ways of measuring. Networking can be seen as one among these modes.

A New Topology of Territories

Living, feeling, and making (or acting) are strictly related to what territories do. This is why there are several similarities between territories, on the one hand, and environments, atmospheres, and networks, on the other. We have quickly reviewed these notions to ascertain how various territorial operations can be better understood and qualified. We have proposed that environments, atmospheres, and networks can become interlocutors of territory; in other words, there seems to be various family resemblances spanning across these different notions. While we seek to avoid conflating them, and while we don't specifically aim to provide a single framework to formalize their relations, we highlight the various interweaves and crisscrosses between them. Environments, atmospheres, and networks are thus important places from where we can understand certain aspects of territories and how they act. In fact, all three tend to be intentionally or unintentionally co-produced with or through territories in different ways.

Environments, atmospheres, and networks provide very rich insights into social life as it unfolds in space. On the other hand, the aspect of temporality remains relatively in the shadow. This is why in the next chapter we turn toward the problem of how to capture the temporal dimension of territories. Once the temporal aspects of territories are taken into consideration, we believe that more life can be added to territories than is usually granted by, or that can be investigated through, the notions of environment, atmosphere, and network alone. Indeed, in the subsequent chapters we also consider two additional dimensions that we think can help us understand territories more thoroughly—namely, morphogenesis and animation.

One final consideration concerns the issue of power and power relations. In extant literature territories have been described mostly as power constructs, in terms of jurisdiction, spatial control, and so on. In this vein Robert Sack (1986) has advanced the thesis that territories are, at bottom, strategies to induce people to behave in certain ways; Richard T. Ford (1999) has documented the legal construction of the notion of jurisdiction and the rise of "jurisdiction thinking" as a peculiar spatial fiction in law; David Delaney (1998) has illustrated the legal territorialization of race in the history of the United States; and Charles Maier (2016) has proposed a long-term historical account of how modern states have developed and organized territories as "decision spaces." This facet of territorial life is of indisputable importance. But in this book we seek to advance a slightly different take on territories. We assume that power dynamics are always-already ingrained in territorial compositions and that, in this sense, territories work as mediators of power. But while the inception of territorial relations can never wholly abstract from the issue of power, we add that, by also addressing the fact and experience of perceiving, feeling, and acting, it is possible to attain a richer and more nuanced picture of the multifaceted social undertaking of territory. In practice territories are mediators not only of power but of social life at large. And while it is certainly possible and relevant to analyze social life *sub specie potestatis*, additional considerations may open up new insights.

3   The Multitemporality of Territorial Production

Scholarship on human territoriality has traditionally been keen on empha-
sizing two principal dimensions of territories—namely, *space* and *power*.
From this point of view, territorial phenomena would come about as strategic attempts to exert control on given spaces—that is, using space as
a means of power (Sack 1986). Territoriality has also been linked to the
claiming of space, so territories have been regarded as spatial objectifications
of specific assertions; as we have anticipated in chapter 1, territory has thus
been defined as the arrangement that ensues from a set of requests (Malmberg 1980). In the study of territorial formations, time and temporality
have been relatively marginal. In fact, the process of territorialization has
always been about time as much as about space. We believe that territoriology should also engage in a careful consideration of the temporality of
territories. Regarding territories as events, as territoriology invites us to,
inherently draws the researchers' attention on their rhythmical formative
dimension, considering territories temporal as much as spatial modulations
and envelops—that is, as time-spaces.

In this chapter we go deeper into the question of how time functions
in territorializing processes. By doing so we aim to strike a fairer balance
between the spatial and the temporal dimensions in our understanding of
territorial phenomena. In particular, we underline the *plurality* of temporalities that are co-present in each process of territorialization. In a wider
sense territorialization can perhaps be described as a process in which
time and space are used as a means of not only control but also measure
and expression. Certainly, Peter Merriman (2012, 21) has argued against
the idea of time-space as an a priori measure of social phenomena, stating
that the unfolding of events, movement, and change cannot be reduced

to predefined sets. While we in part agree with him, we also suggest that territorialization could be seen as a way of *producing* time and space as much as a way of *using* them as means of measure and expression. In other words, *timing* and *spacing*—rather than time and space—are the structures deployed by social actors to stabilize events and territorialize them as well as, ultimately, territorializing themselves in those events.

Our aim is thus to investigate time as a measure of territorial becomings or, more precisely, the multitemporality and simultaneous presences of territorial production. Because we are particularly interested in the temporality of the present, we delve into an exploration of its richness. We believe the present is a specifically rich time as well as a generous time. To highlight how the present is a time of fruition for territorial undertakings of all sorts, we play with the two senses of the word *present*—namely, (1) the here-and-now and (2) a thing given to someone as a gift. Thus, we entertain with the idea that time presents us with a present that is always a surprising, albeit often excessive, *gift*. If time gifts us with something, the present can be said to constitute its most genuine outcome. We suggest a three-fold articulation of the temporal present, describing three *facets* of the present. These facets or forms of present time should not be understood as in isolation from one another. Every empirical situation contains simultaneously, to various degrees, all three forms. In other words, these forms of present can be regarded as analytical traits to grasp a range of differing actual situations. It is also quite likely that there are more presents than those discussed here. In this sense our current exploration is not meant to be reductionist; rather, it is proposed as a preliminary inquiry into a more rounded theory of temporality that might be suited for social-spatial and territoriological studies.

In the first part of the chapter, we articulate the three facets of the present to be examined in depth. We draw inspiration from the philosophy of Gilles Deleuze, especially his 1969 work on the logic of sense (better, the logic of *meaning*) as well as other authors in social theory such as Georg Simmel, Alfred Whitehead, Walter Benjamin, and Furio Jesi. A few illustrations are also sketched to help visualize the discussed notions, before moving to a more extended case study in the following section, where we hope to show how the three presents may enrich our lexicon and understanding. The peculiar case of the collector John Soane guides the discussion in the second part. In particular, we reconstruct the establishment of his house-museum as well as, more generally, of the house-museum as a peculiar type of building. Notably, Elizabeth Grosz (2001) has argued that utopian architecture cannot be understood apart from its specifically temporal dimensions. In light of this our discussion revolves around the process of specialization: the production of a specific new *sort* of territory and building type, the *house-museum*, within a specific urban context—London of the eighteenth and nineteenth centuries. The nature of the case also allows us to focus on the changing material infrastructure of territorial stabilization as well as the slow, dynamic, and multitemporal processes inherent to it. Time might not always, as we shall see, go together with space, but like space, it is certainly dependent on movements, becomings, and acts of "making present." This is because territorialization is integrally about making time and space *present*, turning them into a venue of attention constantly conductive to new events. This we could of course already see in our first introductory example (in chapter 1), where we showed how the Colosseum, as a more contemporary territory for different species of plants, also made a series of dramatic historical events present to the informed observers.

Aion, Kronos, and Chronos

The first present we want to discuss is Aion. We symbolize it with the Greek letter α (alpha). Aion is probably the most difficult temporal notion to explain, yet arguably not the most difficult to understand. Properly speaking, we say it is the linear yet atopic present of the eternal becoming. Definitional attempts, however, might mislead us into thinking that α is a logical abstraction. Quite the contrary, we believe, it is a most concretely immediate, even mundane—although disembodied—experience, notwithstanding the fact that its applications might turn out to be counterintuitive. Aion is the endless infinitive line of the instant. In *Process and Reality*

Whitehead calls it "feeling" ([1929] 1978). A feeling is, in Whitehead's parlance, the manifestation of a relational "engagement" of an actual entity or actual occasion with reality. "An actual occasion," explains Whitehead, "never changes, it only becomes and perishes" ([1933] 1967, 204). Arriving and going is what the actual present understood as becoming does. What is peculiar of the endless infinitive line of the instant is that it does not move forward *without concurrently moving backward*. In *The Principles of Psychology* (1890), William James uses an interesting analogy to describe how the past and the future, in this way, are always mixed in with our present: "The practically cognized present is no knife-edge, but a saddle-back, with a certain breadth of its own on which we sit perched, and from which we look in two directions into time" (qtd. in Heft 2001, 178).

This is perhaps also why α looks so unfamiliar from an everyday understanding of the temporal flow. Using an expression that features prominently in Lacan's inquiry into the unconscious, Deleuze writes that the instant *manque à sa place*—it lacks from its proper place. The point is that, precisely, the "place" of the instant cannot be found anywhere. Insofar as it is *atopon*, without place, α is ipso facto incorporeal. The instant, in other words, never corresponds to a state of things or the succession of states of things. In the memorable opening page of his treaty, Deleuze connects aeonic time to the adventures of *Alice in Wonderland*, as she magically changes size:

> When I say "Alice becomes larger," I mean that she becomes larger than she was. By the same token, however, she becomes smaller than she is now. Certainly, she is not bigger and smaller at the same time. She is larger now; she was smaller before. But it is at the same moment, by the same stroke, that one becomes larger than one was and smaller than one becomes. This is the simultaneity of a becoming whose characteristic is to elude the present. Insofar as it eludes the present, becoming does not tolerate the distinction of before and after, or of past and future. It pertains to the essence of becoming to move and to pull in both directions at once: Alice does not grow without shrinking, and vice versa. (Deleuze 1969, 9)

Multitemporality

It is relatively simple to understand why the instant cannot but "move and pull in both directions at once." Certainly, the instant wants to go. Yet, since it can never be located, its vanishing and withering away remains inherently elusive vis-à-vis all attempts at spatial determination. This is why Deleuze writes that the instant, qua the only purely nonspatial element of time, eludes the present. More than a *present*, the instant could be said to be a *presence*, as not merely a phenomenological, experiential effect but as a peculiar ontological constitution. Aion has a *preposterous* nature: quite literally, the coming instant is simultaneously "pre" and "post" any single phenomenon. Deleuze's book contains a fascinating exploration of the series of paradoxes generated by the peculiar simultaneity of becoming. For the French philosopher, α is the time of the event. An evental time is such that the event does not correspond to the state of thing that it effectuates, for the event is aeonic and incorporeal.

In this sense, we suggest, α is also a time "by subtraction," a present whose proper operation is *countereffectuation*. The notion of countereffectuation becomes clearer by comparison with the operations carried on by the other presents. For now let us content ourselves with saying that the aeonic present is a *momentum*—not the things that happen but the very truth *that* they are happening. In a musical register α equates to pure improvisation, an absolute yet absolutely mundane type of abstraction that, for instance, jazz players and listeners praise so highly. As the existentially momentous aspect of time, α best reveals itself in all those peculiar experiences that exceed and simultaneously punctuate the everyday. The existential experience of the city is full of similar sensations. At a gig or concert, for instance, the audience tends to produce unique instants that have the effect of, so to speak, amplifying the world while eschewing its actuality. In a similar way collective celebrations of New Year, and more precisely the very moment when the New Year replaces the old one, is an important and often ritualized aeonic moment in many cultures.

Not by chance, the experience of the momentous present is often remembered as a dreamlike or hypnotic state, as a unique and distinctive bubble of existence that is just as impossible to define as it is undeniably self-evident (a "firstness" in Peirce's [1931, sec. 1.302] sense). While usually associated with a sense of fullness, instants are, in fact, better understood as incredibly void and hyaline. The power of α is not fulfillment but emptiness—potency instead of power. Aion presents us with an incorporeal time of the pure event, a perspective from which corporeal things are already gone and simultaneously yet to happen. Literature offers important testimonies of this. In Victor Hugo's *Le dernier jour d'un condamné* (1829), for instance, the man sentenced to death declares, "Je ne suis pas préparé, mais je suis prêt [I'm not prepared, but I'm ready]" (Hugo 1829, sec. 21). Photographs can similarly conjure up the aeonic present: suffice to recall the comment by Roland Barthes in *Camera Lucida* about the 1865 photographic portrait of the failed conspirator Lewis Payne: "He is already dead and he is going to die" (1980, sec. 39). Aion is thus a *divergent* present. Similarly, Deleuze (2001, 28) points to a scene from Charles Dickens, who describes the sudden care people show for a disreputable man, just because he is dying. In a way they are caring, Deleuze suggests, for *a* life rather than for this specific life. It is an in-between moment, a presence where the becoming of *a* death also brings a becoming of *a* life. One does not enter the desingularization of death without a concurrent desingularization of life. Aion is thus the present caught as *Jetztzeit*, now-state (as opposed to *Gegenwart*)—or what in quantum physics is called *eigenstate*.

The second present to be introduced is Kronos, which we symbolize with κ (kappa). In ancient Greek the verb κραίνω (*kraino*) is a quite complex verb, encompassing several different significations. In our hypothesis the truth about κ is somehow encapsulated inside a semantic triangle that comprises the following denotations (we are selecting among several more): (1) to accomplish, fulfill; (2) to reign over, govern; and (3) to come to an end, terminate, result in. Kronos is not a chronological but a chronic time. It is chronic in the sense in which certain medical conditions are said to be chronic: they come and go but never pass. From this point of view, κ seems almost the antithesis of α: whereas the latter eschews the present state of things, the former can never supersede it and is constantly riddled with it. Insofar as its inner logic is mythological rather than historical, κ is probably the most difficult temporal notion to understand. Indeed, its structure is pre-Olympic. Kronos as Cronus, the Titan of the Harvest, lives before the establishment of order—the reign of Zeus—yet his presence is incipient and even immanent to that order. For all the disorderliness of $\varkappa$, no order could be conceivable without it. So here we have a sense of a coming power that can be prepared by bringing struggle and disorder to an accomplishment. This is precisely what Titan Cronus does.[1] Cronus embodies that type of accomplishment that makes the order of sovereignty possible. Some important remarks in this respect are made by Deleuze in one of his lectures on cinema. Deleuze (1984; our translation) notes orally that $\varkappa$ is a very excited time: "It is the time of generations that clash against one another, which overturn one another. It is a savage time. It is really a savage time; I mean an unleashed time, an undomesticated time. . . . I'd nearly say that what belongs to the myth is such a savage and undomesticated time. In other words, a time of the abyss from which successive generations come and in which they struggle against one another—it is a terrible time, a time of terror, a time without foundation, a groundless time of terror and struggle among the gods."[2]

Kronos is the time of struggle between generations, and, probably, the very notion of generation is a chronic notion. In his course Deleuze makes explicit reference to Jean-Pierre Vernant's ([1965] 2007) hypothesis that the function of mythology is to link explanation of origins with justification of hierarchy. Origin and sovereignty are, in other words, the two poles of each myth, two poles that inevitably enter into tension. Cronus the accomplisher, the one who revolts against the father and thus fills that gap that enables the instauration of a new sovereignty, is also the figure that best expresses such tenseness. For Cronus the rebel reproduces indeed the same son-eating scheme adopted by his father. The origins remains bloody, and the order that it can be founded on is also necessarily bloody—this is the dirty birth of law (Brighenti 2006b). The assertion of sovereignty is always an assertion of chronic temporality. All revolutions, insofar as they are expression of a new constituent power, begin by suspending the old time and instituting a new one: that's why, as recalled by Benjamin ([1940] 1968, 261) in his

Theses on History, the revolutionaries of 1789 fired at the clocks in towers to stop ordinary time and install a new calendar. In itself suspension can hardly be a fruitful time. In this sense, we should say, the chronic present is a specifically barren time. Not by coincidence sovereignty, particularly as theorized by George Bataille (1967), appears as grounded in wastefulness or, as Bataille says, useless expenditure (*dépense*).

Mythology is not, in any case, a thing of the past. On the contrary, there is definitely a present of mythology—nowadays and always. Such is the thick, viscous present of *subversion*. Kronos is the ominous present of revolution, understood as an effective principle of ordering without acceptance of any possibly realized order. More precisely, following Jesi, we should distinguish between *revolution* and *revolt*, recognizing in *κ* the present of the revolt:

> I use the word "revolt" to designate an insurrectional movement that differs from revolution. The difference between revolt and revolution does not lie in their goals. Indeed, they can have the same goal, such as the seizure of power. What distinguishes the revolt from the revolution is, rather, a different experience of time. If, on the basis of a relatively common understanding of these two words, the revolt is a sudden insurrectional explosion, which can certainly be inserted into a larger strategic design but which by itself does not entail any long-term strategy, and if the revolution is, by contrast, a strategic complex of insurrectional movements which are coordinated and oriented towards certain distant final goals, one could say that the revolt is an actual suspension of historical time. The revolt suddenly introduces a temporality in which everything that is done has value in itself and for itself, regardless of its consequences and its relations with the complex of transience or endurance which makes up history. ([1969] 2000, 19; our translation)

The time of revolt is a time of critique and endless *mise en question*; it is a time that does not proceed, that does not flow—a stagnant time of subversive suspension. Suspended yet not empty (in this, neatly distinct from Aion), *κ* is in fact filled, crowded with words, arguments, objections, undertakings, deeds, and things. In such full present of the revolt, words, deeds, and objects cannot be judged according to external criteria or requirements—"everything that is done has value in itself and for itself, regardless of its consequences." The reason is that it is *in* Kronos that criteria are being set up. That's why *x* looks like a groundless, abysmal present. German philosophy seems to have entertained a special liaison with this temporal conception. Not by coincidence, chronic time appears in the reflections of key authors, including Johann Wolfgang von Goethe, Georg Simmel, Walter Benjamin, and Carl Schmitt. One important *fil rouge* resonating with chronic temporality can be found, for instance, in Goethe's notion of the Ur-phenomenon (*Urphänomen*), or original phenomenon. Indeed, the notion of Ur-phenomenon makes sense only in relation to the idea of an "individual law"— that is, the singular point where a mere actual entity becomes the expression of a law, which however is valid only in that single instance. As explained by Simmel,

> We usually place the general law of things in a certain way outside of things themselves: as partly objective, in that its timeless and spaceless validity [*zeit-und raumlose Gültigkeit*] makes it independent from the chance of its material entanglement [*materialen Verwirklichung*] in time and space, partly subjective, in that it is purely an object of thought and does not appear to our sensuous energies that will always perceive but the particular, never the general. This separation is what the concept of the Ur-phenomenon aims to overcome: it is the timeless law itself, but in a temporal observation [*das zeitlose Gesetz selbst in zeitlicher Anschauung*]—the general immediately accessible in a particular form. (1913, 57)

Chronic time is no less contradictory and no less tense than a law happening only once. As a rhetorical figure of *hapax*, it designates a peculiar, nonindifferent condition. For his part, in his early treaty on eighteenth-century German *Trauerspiel*, Benjamin (as we also noted in chapter 1) developed a notion of "origin" (*Ursprung*) designed to stand in opposition to an idea of "beginning." The origin is not in the beginning, Benjamin claims, insofar as the former is not simply what was there before us. Instead, the origin is in the present tense; it is right in the middle of the thing: "Origin, although a thoroughly historical category, nonetheless has nothing to do with beginnings. . . . The term origin does not mean the process of becoming of that which has emerged, but much more, that which emerges out of the process of becoming and disappearing. The origin stands in the flow of becoming as a whirlpool. . . . Its rhythm is apparent only to a double insight" ([1928] 1974, 226).

In a destabilized historical vortex, however, things cannot flow but in a disorderly, unsettled, accident-ridden way—here is another image of chronic time. Actually, it is not even correct to call it a flow, for a flow would presuppose a certain smoothness, but in x nothing is smooth; everything is contested, clash-prone, controversial, exceptional. That is why the notion of x inevitably connects to Carl Schmitt's (1932) idea of sovereignty being established at the limit between rule and exception. Sovereignty, in Schmitt's famous formula, manifests itself only in the possibility of voluntarily decreeing the upholding of ordinary (founded) law. We should not forget that Benjamin had precisely Schmitt's (1922) *Political Theology* in mind (besides Hegel and Marx, of course) when he started elaborating his idea of "dialectic at a standstill." "A historical materialist," Benjamin would later state, "cannot do without the notion of a present which is not a transition but in which time stands still and has come to a stop." A materialist—as well as a believer—cannot do, for the messianic time is precisely a similar suspension "pregnant with tensions" ([1940] 1968, 262).[3] Perhaps, if Benjamin hesitated all his life through to either become a Marxist or a Zionist, and eventually became none, it is because he saw so well that the historical can never get rid of the mythical and that power can never be founded as such. This is also the leading theme in his earlier cryptic essay on the critique of authoritative violence, "Zur Kritik der Gewalt" ([1921] 1999).[4] A fullness such as the one of chronic authoritative violence is a double presence that also, inevitably, produces a double absence.

There is an ongoing struggle to assert *when* is the present—that is, to answer the question, "When are we?" For we know that, far from being a given, what we call "contemporaneity" is something that must be produced. Kronos is a time of clash and revelation that opens up when a radical interrogation on contemporaneity is vociferously raised. It is a "pregnant" present of dissatisfaction and discontent. The attributes of animosity and clash, however, do not necessarily refer solely to the large-scale, visible struggles of politics. Instead, we should also consider all the "tiny catastrophes" of the everyday as manifestations of $\varkappa$. As well put by Siegfried Kracauer, "we must rid ourselves of the delusion that it is the major events which have the most decisive influence on us. We are much more deeply and continuously influenced by the tiny catastrophes that make up daily life" (1978, 252). It is in this sense that the temporality of $\varkappa$ encompasses an array of mundane practices that entertain a specific relation to time-spaces and measures, such as collecting. Not by chance was Benjamin himself a fond collector; not by chance was his mythical urban explorer, the flâneur, a peculiar collector of urban memories, like a vertical probe cast deep into the sedimented urban strata:

> But the great reminiscences, the historical shudder—these are a trumpery which he [the flâneur] leaves to tourists, who think thereby to gain access to the genius loci with a military password. Our friend may well keep silent. At the approach of his footsteps, the place has roused; speechlessly, mindlessly, its mere intimate nearness gives him hints and instructions. He stands before Notre Dame de Lorette, and his soles remember: here is the spot where in former times the *cheval de renfort*—the spare horse— was harnessed to the omnibus that climbed the Rue des Martyrs toward Montmartre. Often, he would have given all he knows about the domicile of Balzac or of Gavarni, about the site of a surprise attack or even of a barricade, to be able to catch the scent of a threshold or to recognize a paving stone by touch, like any watchdog. ([1927–40] 1999, 416 [M1, 1])

A watchdog, a creature guided by the soles of his shoes, the flâneur lives in a kind of "addictive" temporality. Jean Baudrillard (1994, 22) made a distinction between accumulation, described as inferior, and collection proper, where objects are allegedly more clearly distinguished from one another. But, we suggest, the distinction is never settled and never ultimately clear: not unlike art making itself, collecting is in fact always entwined with the addictive drive toward accumulation. In this sense collecting raises a question of measure that chronic time cannot solve and yet cannot help but keep asking. Usually, collecting is interpreted as a neurotic-obsessive attempt at keeping everything under control. But while this view may capture some aspects of the collector's practice, the story of great collectors, such as Soane, seems to reveal that, instead, collecting is an operation always and constitutively carried out at the limits of control. That is why collections are always fragile creatures on the verge of collapsing into chaos and can exist only insofar as they are kept together by a body-to-body engagement of centripetal and centrifugal forces. Chronic time remains, per se, immeasurable, just as aeonic time. From this point of view, $\varkappa$ and α—the subversive and the countereffectual present—look alike: they remain measureless. Where does the possibility of temporal measures come from?

The answer lies in the third type of present, Chronos, which we designate with χ (chi). As opposed to Kronos, Chronos is the cyclical present of chronological return. Schedules, calendars, plans, and all other means of rational temporal organization make sense only as properly chronological endeavors. As organized time, time *tamed* thanks to organizational devices, χ is the—only apparently simple—present of *effectuation*. As such, it stands in opposition to α, the time that countereffectuates and liberates. Chronos is time productive of measure, for a measure can be defined only by a unit, and a unit can be defined only by a return—the homogeneous return of the minute, the hour, the day, the year. As opposed to $\varkappa$, χ is reassuring time, time that flows, sequential time: scheduled, predictable, stabilized. But we should not be misled and overlook the fact that χ also harbors its specific oppressions and obsessions: deadlines, to mention just one example, are the deadly production of chronology. The example also makes us attentive to the fact that it is χ that provides the link between time and morality. Through chronology the present becomes "ought"; it becomes moral time, as well as psychic disorder, for there is a special affinity between χ and the neurotic attitude. The endless return of chronological cycles is a tiresome, burdensome, exhausting return. That is why nostalgia for the great freedom and the great emptiness of α, a nostalgia for countereffectuation, cannot but punctuate the chronological present of effectuation.

The origins of χ are probably pre-Hellenic. The image of the swirling serpent, often spiraled around a shining egg or biting its own tail, seems to be Egyptian. The serpent is a very ancient symbol strictly associated with chthonic gods and rivers. These are local gods of the earth. Since the late antiquity the ouroboros, the snake biting its own tail, is employed to evoke the seasonal aspect of time. In his masterful work on the Orphic tradition, the classical Greek scholar Martin Litchfield West observes,

> The Orphic scheme of an aboriginal watery abyss (Oceanus and Tethys?), from and within which is born an eternal creator in the form of a winged serpent (Chronos) paired with a female counterpart (Ananke), can thus be related to ancient Egyptian mythical antecedents. . . . The serpent form of Chronos may have its origins in Egyptian fantasy, but in Orphic poetry it took on a symbolic significance which justified its retention and elaboration. Chronos was represented, we are told, as a winged serpent with additional heads of a bull and a lion, and between them the face of a god. (1983, 189–90)

The "Egyptian fantasy" evoked by West is, probably, a reference to the Egyptian god Apep, or Apophis, the celestial devourer of the sun. For his part Carl Gustav Jung (1956) discussed the mercurial serpent as an archetype of psychic transformation. Curiously, it seems that χ is more ancient than ϰ, yet also more modern. In other words, the three-fold partition of presents we are proposing contradicts the usual imagery about cyclical time as a conception that contradistinguishes premodern and archaic cultures, as opposed to the linear time characterizing modern and Western cultures. In reality, if χ is the type of measured time that makes the notion of linear history possible, we should acknowledge that it is entirely premised on the existence of cycles. All rational schedules and organized rhythms are produced chronologically, but there could not be any chronological time without cycles. So, in χ, the homogeneous connection of the past to the future is obtained thanks to the prolongation of a single, uniform present. Future can only be a future *present*. In Benjamin the traces of χ are observed through a peculiar historical *décalage*, which renders them in a crystallized state: "In 1857 there was still a coach departing from the Rue Pavee-Saint-Andre at 6 A.M. for Venice; the trip took six weeks" ([1927–40] 1999, 431 [M7, 9]).

The theme at play here is logistic temporality. Logistics includes a vast array of techniques and know-how entailed in the establishment and maintenance of efficient networks to sustain transport, distribution, and communication. Today logistics has become central in the organization of contemporary capitalism. Across the world a new geography of places, mobilities, connections, and commodity flows is being increasingly designed according to logistic imperatives. The bottom line of logistic time is that, chronologically speaking, nothing can be in two places at once. Consequently, the transport and delivery of goods and persons to a certain place at a certain time must be structured and calculated according to a chronogram. Chronos is thus the great present of organized governance. Following the classical analysis by Michel Foucault ([1978] 2004), the modern endeavor of governance consists in an attempt at controlling human beings and things using an array of technical and mathematical means. For instance, statistical curves define quantitative increases and decreases relative to a population that can be traced from the past and projected into the future, but only thanks to the deployment of a protracted, cyclical present that is going to section, sort, and arrange the data. If the modern state can govern its population by numbers, and if corporations are increasingly doing so themselves, it is thanks to the working of χ, which closes the errant and swinging course of ϰ. In summary figure 3 encapsulates the dynamic relationship between the three presents discussed so far.

The Gift of John Soane

The architect Sir John Soane's house in London was, at the time of his death in 1837, a veritable conglomerate of different room and building types. A building or room type is a territorial formation one can call a "territorial sort": "territorial" since a so-called type always territorializes a certain

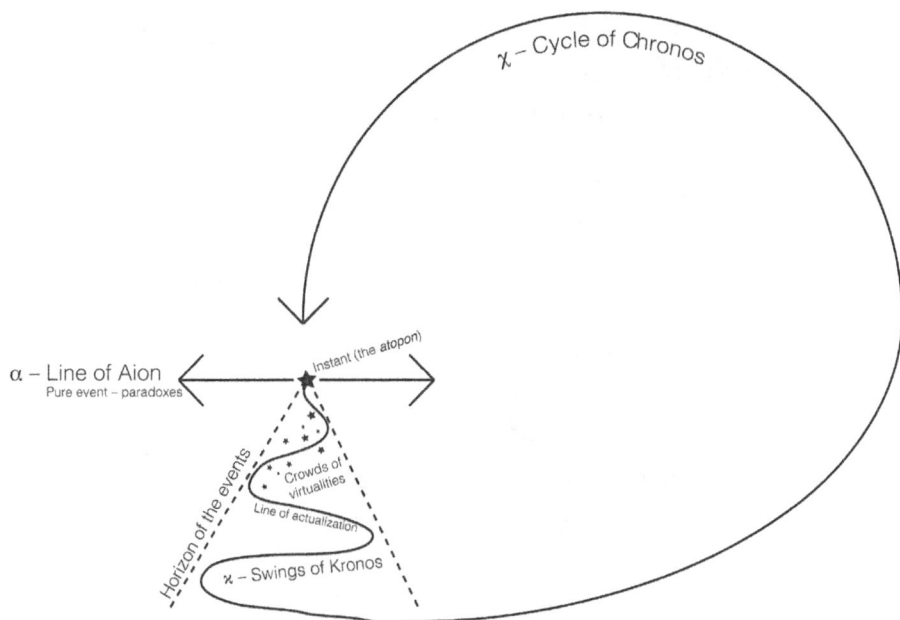

3. A diagram of the three presents. Created by the authors.

space with a certain meaning and intensity through associations to other territories, and "sort" since it is not defined by an obligatory set of actors (like prototypes, stereotypes, etc., might be) but must be seen as a more fluid order of stabilization, where crucial effects are sustained even as its parts are transformed or replaced (Kärrholm 2007, 2013). Soane's house can indeed be seen as complex formation of different, fluid territorial sorts of changing intensities. Helene Furján has, for example, noted that it was simultaneously "a domestic residence, an expression of cultivation and taste, a museum and archive, a space of amusement (a collection of faux period rooms and a theatre of effect and atmosphere), a teaching collection and apprentice's studio, an architectural office, a model townhouse, a cenotaph and, finally, a public monument" (2009, 90).

Despite that, one could argue that among these types, one was more salient and dominant than the others—namely, the house-museum. The legal document for the establishment of the Soane house-museum was settled in 1833 by an act of Parliament and came into force after John Soane's death in 1837, when the house was vested in a board of trustees (Dorey 1999, 154). In descriptions from the 1820s and 1830s, Soane's house was categorized as "a house and a museum," but the act of 1833 declared it simply a museum (Elsner 1994, 157). As such, Soane's mansion is possibly the first example of the building type, or territorial sort, known as house-museum (Young 2007, 60). Our question is how and when could such a hybrid, uncertain territory be stabilized? Through which steps and according to which temporal coding have the multiple presences of the house-museum been produced? What are the forms of presents involved in the making of Soane's house?

John Soane bought a townhouse at 12 Lincoln's Inn Fields in 1792 (fig. 4), much helped by the money that his wife, Elizabeth Soane, recently had inherited from her father. The house was from the beginning also a working studio and full of Soane's collections (see fig. 5). After becoming a professor in architecture in 1806, Soane "began to arrange the books, casts and models so that the students might have the benefit to access them" (Watkin, qtd. in Dorey 1999, 150). In 1807 he consequently bought the adjacent house, number 13, to expand his collections and construct a proper museum area. The building of this museum area in 1809 (Feinberg 1984) can perhaps be seen as the first official attempt to open Soane's house to the public; it started a steady stream of more or less irregular visits from scholars and students. In 1824 he extended his museum further after buying number 14. The first guidebook of the museum was published during Soane's lifetime, in 1827, whereas the first official opening hours seem to have been established just after his death, in 1837. Today the museum counts more than a hundred thousand visitors per year (Knox 2009, 44).

After providing such basic information about this curious enterprise, we can now go through the three different presents, using them as tools for investigating some of the temporal aspects of this process of territorialization. To this aim a useful driving question is when did the building become a house-museum? Of course, it could be argued that it was one already in 1809: "From the moment Soane made the decision to link his

4. The main entrance to Sir John Soane's museum, Lincoln's Inn Fields, London. Photo by and courtesy of Jesper Magnusson.

5. The dome in the Sepulchral Chamber. Photo by and courtesy of Jesper Magnusson.

office to his house through a museological space, to the moment he made a gift of all its spaces, scenes, and spectacles to the public, it remained a hybrid being, one that could never be entirely private again, and conversely one that, as it became increasingly public (or dedicated to a public stage), could never be free of the private" (Furján 2004, 76).

Another possibility would be to claim that the museum was born at the moment when Soane realized that he did not want any of his sons to inherit his home, but that it needed to be institutionalized and "left to the public." Soane's second son was sent to prison for debt and fraud in 1815 and later that year verbally attacked his father in two anonymous articles. Soane's wife died just after reading them, while Soane framed the articles and hung them on the wall with the inscription, "Death blows" (Knox 2009, 33; Darley 1999, 24). A third option would be to set the birth of the house-museum to the year 1833, when the legal issues around the museum were settled by the English Parliament. A fourth option could perhaps be in 1837, when official opening hours were first introduced, and the museum opened to a wider public.

These questions of birth hint at the many different presences of the house-museum itself. Many are the different temporalities to take into account. The process definitely started much earlier in Soane's life, when he received a scholarship from the Royal Academy and left London at 5:30 a.m. on March 18, 1778, for Italy and his Grand Tour, not to return to London until two years later. Throughout his life he longed to get back to Italy but never did. In many ways his house seems to have become a compensatory testimony to that wish. John Soane's house cannot be seen as a domestic ideal (which otherwise is common among architect's houses on display). It also sits uncomfortably with a traditional museum space. From the beginning it was a machine for the production of architectural ideas (Furján 2009, 107), an assemblage of fragments, a miniature world, or, perhaps more specifically, a spatiotemporal Grand Tour neatly packed, displayed, and enacted in the middle of London. Soane's territorial project can be grasped only by taking into account the rich production of spatialized temporalities and presences that crisscross and overlap in his vision. As an architect, Soane was always interested in the deconstruction of classical rules and forms, and the displays at his house can be seen as an inspiration to that aim (cf. R. Middleton 1999, 35). The Grand Tour was in its day a vast undertaking in terms of time, space, and expenditure, and Soane's place at Lincoln's Inn Fields can in a way be described as the Grand Tour itself compressed inside the walls of an urban townhouse. One can experience the house "as a model tour, or as a tour through a model" (Furján 2011, 28), a compression of time-space but also, as we shall see, a territory of simultaneous presences that can teach us about the role of temporality in the conjuring up of territorial sorts.

In the implementation of the house-museum, there is one presence that the museification of Soane's house cannot do without, the present of Aion that eludes the present of states of things. Because of its aeonic quality, territorial production does not conform to Baudrillard's distinction between *accumulation* and *collection*: both procedures are essential here, and the one is neither inferior nor superior to the other. In fact, accumulation (perhaps even more than collecting) is about being in the present, about celebrating the interstitial qualities and the parallel becoming of the now with the becoming of the past and the future. It is an unplanned opening in both directions that reconfigures simultaneously the past and the future. As hinted at earlier, collectionism is grounded in a specific form of territorialization. On the one hand, it entails an addictive thrust toward increase and expansion; yet, on the other, it spins around a specific rhythmicality of acquisition. Between these two forces lies its pure, aeonic eventality.

The folding of the Grand Tour is a remarkable aeonic achievement; the aeonic presence in Soane's place also becomes clear in those ongoing moments of potency, when the owner-dreamer reassembled his material claims, buying new objects, adding new spaces, selling his country estate, and so on. In 1824 he bought the Egyptian alabaster sarcophagus of King Seti I, outbidding the British Museum. This moment of acquisition plays an important role in the founding of the museum (see fig. 6). The sarcophagus seemed to immediately have posed questions about the nature of John Soane's house. Are a mansion's spaces grand enough for this sort of piece?

6. The sarcophagus of King Seti I. Photo by and courtesy of Jesper Magnusson.

Because the question must be answered in the negative, the sarcophagus initiated the redoing of the household offices into catacombs and a sepulchral chamber (Knox 2009, 34–36).[5] From a strictly architectural point of view, Soane's place is neither properly a house nor properly a museum, and yet, as soon as we observe its becoming (as a house-museum), we realize that—just as Alice cannot grow without shrinking—it cannot become a house without concurrently becoming a museum and vice versa. In a similar way it cannot become public without, as Furján (2009) noted earlier, also directing and reminding us of its private origins. Territorial production thrives on the presence of Aion, the interstitial moment of possibilities and virtuality, a double bind that tames the has-been in the light of the to-come. At the core of this collecting and exposing enterprise, there is a purity of becoming that is the great emptiness of the instant. It is through such an empty present, through the charm and potentiality of the yet-not spatialized instant of α that a history of the territory slowly establishes itself, reproduces, and changes in unpredictable ways.

Multitemporality

Second, we detect the presence of Kronos. After buying the sarcophagus and finally turning domestic chambers into public exhibitions, Soane held a three-day party with almost nine hundred invited guests (Darley 1999, 25). This party was giving body to the moment of acquisition, one of many tiny revolts in the evolution of the museum. The sumptuous exaggeration of the feast was clearly a manifestation of sovereignty. But the sarcophagus was not just a moment of potency; it was also a revolting moment that brought an end to the domestic quarters of the basement. In a similar sense Soane's fight with his sons must also be seen as a revolt—indeed, as a chronic (and antichronological) moment par excellence. The house-museum rests on a fight between generations, the revolt of the sons against Soane as a father, the revolt of Soane against his sons (the disinherited), but also the revolt of Soane against the social expectations of parenthood and generational succession, as he eventually left his sons and grandchildren without economical support or inheritance, investing all assets in his own museum—including a mausoleum for his wife and her dog.

One of the first chronic moments along these lines can be found already in Soane's strange manuscript *Crude Hints towards an History of My House in Lincoln's Inn Fields*, written in August and September 1812 (and published in 2015). The house at 13 Lincoln's Inn Fields was being rebuilt during the summer of 1812 and thus was partly in ruins. Possibly inspired by this, Soane imagines a future narrator, the Antiquary, speculating over the ruins of Soane's not yet built house: What was this place that now lies before us in ruins? Was it a burial ground, a prison, a convent of nuns, a heathen temple, or the palace of an enchanter? The imagined moment of his future house in ruins has its aeonic qualities, as it produces a presence or "now-state" that opens for the rewriting of history and future in one blow. But it must first of all be seen as a chronic moment of destruction, birth, and suspense, where the nature of what Soane's house will be and eventually has been is not yet settled. In 1812 Soane was starting to realize that neither of his two sons were going to follow in his footsteps and become an architect; instead, they had both proven to be disappointments, both in terms of profession and marriage (Dorey 2015, 5). This can also be seen in the last paragraph of Soane's

Crude Hints, where the Antiquary summarizes the state of affairs that now lies before him: "What an admirable picture to show the vanity and mockery of all human expectations—the man who founded this place fondly imagined that the children of his children would have inhabited the place for Ages and that he had laid the foundation of an establishment which would daily gain strength and produce a race of Artists that would have done honour to their Country:—Oh what a falling off do these ruins present—the subject becomes too gloomy to be pursued—the pen drops from my almost palsied hand" (2015, 32). In Soane's vision his house thus lies in ruins, both figuratively and literally. This was, however, only a foretaste of the final and catastrophic moment of the "death blows" that followed a few years later.

To a certain extent the violent break between the father and the sons can be seen as the very founding stone of the home-museum. Soane emerges as a new Cronus, "the son-eater," revealing the "dirty birth" of the institution (cf. Brighenti 2006b). The infamous origin is chronically made present by the framed cursing letters of the son, which for years also were venomously hanging on the museum walls.[6] It is a revolt against an existing order that gave birth to an uncanny territory that stood across different and mutually incompatible spaces, such as the private-domestic and the public-urban. The presence of a chronic temporality is evident in the fetishism of the unsettling moment—in the form of the narcissistic three-day party and the even more so posting of the two letters, or in Soane's preposterous manuscript from 1812—but the production of the museum also depends on a thousand additional tiny revolts, for example, the ones brought about by every new object or space that breaks the flow of time by questioning the established order. The present of x is impregnated by the chronic megalomania of the founder as it swirls in the fullness of things accumulated and deeds accomplished.

The third presence, Chronos, is perhaps the one most often associated with the process of territorialization. The cyclical recurrence of χ makes itself heard in many different voices. If we yet again take the sarcophagus of King Seti I, a most costly and grandiose purchase, one might ask if the museum was turning from an Italian into an Egyptian fantasy. In fact, we find that the museum is manifesting itself as a coalescence of uncoordinated fragments that cannot be totalized in any way (hence, again, a chronology riddled with chronic aspects). But one of the most important rhythms of Soane's new spatial order started with his formal announcement on January 6, 1812, that students were welcome "to his house the day before and the day after his lectures to inspect the drawings and other collections" (Dorey 1999, 150). We know that, at some point, the place was open at Thursdays, which testifies to the installment of a hebdomadal, predictable rhythm. After 1837 the museum was then open three days a week, from April to June, and two days a week from February to March, and from July to August. This went on until the 1920s (Richardson 1999, 52).

In a related fashion new guidebooks of the house-museum were constantly printed. Starting with a description that Soane commissioned John Britton to write in 1827, new guidebooks were written by Soane himself and published in 1832, 1833, and 1835 (the latest one also with a translation into French). As Danielle Willkens (2016) has shown in her investigations of these descriptions, no fewer than twenty-one different editions were subsequently published by different curators between 1840 and 2014. While these different rhythms of "making public" may look like minor details, in fact they are quite important in that they reveal how, by linking up to a chronological present of scheduled procedure, a given process of territorialization may acquire a specific identity. Just as the rhythmical acquisition of objects is the measure of the Soane the collector, the constant updating of guidebooks, the regular and recurrent visits of students and scholars—and later of a general public of visitors—is the measure of Soane the curator.

As all territorial endeavors, the production of a house-museum is not something done once and for all, but an ongoing venture. Soane is perhaps best known as an architect who worked with complex spatial interiors, light, mirrors, and openings (see fig. 7). It has also been said that Soane's greatest quality was his way of designing interior spaces (R. Middleton 1999, 29). In the case of John Soane's house-museum, we are dealing with a formidable labyrinth, neatly packaged in a uniformly designed box, where the inner

7. The Breakfast Room at 13 Lincoln's Inn Fields. A series or mirrors and openings allow glimpses from adjacent rooms and museum spaces. Photo by and courtesy of Jesper Magnusson.

complexity of the picturesque landscape stands in sharp contrast with the uniform exterior—especially if we compare it with the plans for the greater extended museum (which was never completed), comprising Lincoln's Inn Fields from number 12 all the way to number 16 in a symmetrical and palace-like facade. To be in the presence of the museum is a multimodal adventure—a gift of time as much as a gift of space. Soane worked with the presenting of times and spaces from far away (like ancient Greece or Egypt) through his exhibitions and with less distant times and spaces through his architecture, anticipating the next room or moment of the tour through the use of mirrors, vistas, and perspectival openings between floors. His architecture was always as much about time as about space. Soane, in this sense, worked with the contrasting practices of distraction and absorption, of passive reception and active participation—a theme much later investigated by Benjamin and Kracauer and usually more often attributed to the twentieth rather than the nineteenth century (Furján 2004, 73–74).

Three Gifts of Time

The presence of different forms of "present" in Soane's project is revelatory, we believe, of something more general about territorial production. From the suspensive and generative crack in private space induced by Aion (α), through the association of the Grand Tour and the cluttered accumulation of objects and spaces, to the sometimes violent revolts against societal demands and the domestic order that contradistinguish Kronos (κ), finally stretching to the rhythmical return of exhibited objects visitors, opening hours, funds, new guidebooks, and directors, under the regime of Chronos (χ), Soane's house-museum provides us with a vivid illustration of the multitemporality inherent to territorial phenomena. In this sense Soane can be used as an intriguing case to back up our claim about the requirements for a general science of territories. As stated at the outset, territoriology needs to attend temporality no less than spatiality—that is, both the spacings and the timings that give way to territorialized space-times. Territorializations are always time-space territorializations. They are expressed through spatiotemporal borders that, however clear they might be seen from a certain perspective or situation, to some extent always are fuzzy and multiple.

As we have seen, the plurality of temporalities co-present in each process of territorialization is precipitated in the complexity of the present tense, or the time of *presence*. In this chapter we have explored the present as a time of richness. The three forms of present we have called Aion, Kronos, and Chronos are the veritable presents (that is, gifts) of the present. The present is a gift insofar as it embodies a kind of majestic realization. Whether we like or dislike the megalomania of the gesture, Soane's gift cannot be separated from the material grandiloquence of its presence, especially considering that his place probably never became what he had in mind. This also means that his house-museum as we can see it today may no longer be aeonic or chronic enough. With all due differences, looking at Soane's house today is a bit like looking at Simon Rodia's Watts Towers. Both are testaments to the exuberant if obsessive genius of their creators. If we insist on the theme of the gift, it is because we believe that the fullness of the present cannot be reduced to any prearranged scheme, of either a calendar-celebration type or of a clear-cut conflict type between opposing parties or generations. The gift of the present lies in its very overflow. In many cases we literally don't know what to do with such abundance of life that unconventional figures such as Soane make us encounter. In anthropological theory, especially in Marcel Mauss's ([1924] 1950) classic yet endlessly inspiring take, each gift is always filled with *hau*, the spirit of the giver that surveils the exchange to sooner or later settle the score. The spiritual presence that looms large over the given gift, the present gift, is of animistic type. The gift can thus even become a *Gift* in the German sense of the word, a poison. The house-museum was in fact not a wholly welcomed gift, not for Soane himself, who perhaps rather would have founded a family of architects or artists than an institution and a museum, and not for some of his contemporaries. In fact, in an article from 1837 in the *Civil Engineer and Architect's Journal*, the gift was called a mockery as well as "a most notable piece of show and delusion—a gift wherein the donor evidently consulted his own vanity more than anything else" (cited in Furján 2011, 160).

Certainly, the gifts of the present are not always *wanted* either. In this sense there can be an excessive abundance in the temporal present—as the Soane case illustrates. This is why we have insisted on the tension between aeonic emptiness and chronic fullness. The activity of collecting, we have suggested, is largely played out in this domain of tensions. The present, we have argued, raises an issue of measure that cannot be solved in either Aion or Kronos. The mediating role of Chronos is essential. It is the present of the latter that enables measure and control, or mastery, over the presence and temporality of territories. On the other hand, however, the needs of expression in both the spiritual-existential and the political sense cannot be deduced from, reduced to, or granted by any chronology. Soane's dream and, ultimately, his gift to us lies in making us aware that territorializations that entail time and space become means of not only measure and control but also expression and transformation.

4   Morphogenesis and Animistic Moments

In previous chapters we have suggested that territories can be understood as social formations and social acts. We may now attempt to specify what is a social formation by looking at how it is shaped, with which materials, and through which acts and deployments of which energy. Formation must here be explored as the result of form-taking processes, or what is also called *morphogenesis*—literally, the generation of forms. To begin with the problem of form taking is one that crosscuts the domain of physics, biology, psychology, and sociology. All these disciplines seek to capture in various ways the coming about of forms. Of course, this does not mean that domains are all alike, nor that forms are always established in the same way, in the same sequence, with the same materials, and the same acts across different domains. In fact, there are important distinctions between formative processes that take place in nonliving matter, living organisms, psychological systems, and social ensembles. It is necessary not to conflate or confuse these domains. Nonetheless, it may still be fruitful to adopt the working hypothesis that morphogenetic processes represent an order of reality endowed with a certain degree of inner consistency and that, consequently, it is possible to learn something about form taking in general by combining insights from these different fields. As put by biologists Gerald Webster and Brian Goodwin, morphogenesis is an "intrinsically robust" process (1996, 233).

Clustered objects, social collectives, and territories all appear to have forms. We often recognize sets of objects, human groups, and territories on the basis of the overall shape of their formal appearance. Are we facing a single problem concerning form and form taking? Where do forms come from, and what do they aim at? How should we conceptualize the boundary and the limits of a form? Within which limits do changing forms remain recognizable as correlative to certain social, spatial, and material entities? How do social relations and social forms encounter territorial relations and material forms? How could, ultimately, the problem of form illuminate the science of territories? Venturing into these questions, in this chapter we seek to suggest some speculative ways to approach the problem of form, form taking, and formations. As we have seen, territorial production can be regarded as a way to give form to social arrangements. Territories are, in this sense, materialized social programs. The problem, of course, lies in finding the right balance between form and process in the interpretation of territories. In structuralism—probably drawing from the antique Platonist tradition—the notion of form was regarded as superior to the processes through which it could be revealed or, in various ways, made present. By contrast, since the 1960s, a whole generation of critics of classic structuralism has foregrounded process. So territories have come to be closely associated with strategies and plans to control space, while the territorial form has increasingly come to be seen as a passive moldable product, an inert means of human desires. For example, in environmental psychology scholars criticize research interested in the form-taking aspects of territoriality, more specifically territorial markings, and advocate more focus on social interaction, identity, and affective attachment (e.g., Altman 1975; Brown 1987; Bonnes and Secchiaroli 1995). When it comes to studies explicitly interested in form, whether in social theory or urban morphology studies, form has often been regarded as no more and no less than the outcome of the interlocking of different agents and structures (see Archer 1995, 2013; Newman 1973; Hillier 1996; Caniggia and Maffei 2001; Conzen 2004).

Privileging either form or process as given, however, is not enough to advance knowledge of social life in space and time. Our attempt here is not so much to revisit the previous elaborations, as much as that of bringing new voices into the conversation on morphogenesis. Following authors such as Gilbert Simondon and René Thom, we are keen on highlighting the phenomena of pregnance, animation, and expression inherent in the life of forms. In particular, we draw from the critique of the hylomorphic model first set out by Simondon in the mid-1950s as a strategy to circumvent both classic determinism and radical indetermination. Simondon ([1964–89] 2013) was arguably the first to investigate individuation as a problem of energy rather than merely a problem of form in the classic sense. For us the shift from morphology to morphogenesis entails precisely tackling the problem of form as the result of a combination of forces within dynamic systems. This is the reason why we are interested a specific episode in the history of forms, which we call the "animistic moment" (Kärrholm 2016). We believe that a conceptualization of the animistic moment may help us to gain insight into the power held by forms and, relatedly, the sociomaterial life of territories as they are shaped, stabilized, and mobilized again.

We usually treat form and process as separate, as if a discontinuity existed between them. But as Maurice Merleau-Ponty (1995) has argued, following the biologist Edward S. Russell and the psychologist Arnold Gesell, there is in fact a radical *continuity* between the form of the organism, on the one hand, and its action or behavior, on the other. In a way action continues and supplements what the organic forms have already partially achieved. For instance, Russell (1945) documented a continuity of restoration processes in animal structural and functional relations that spans wound healing, case reparation in larvae, and nest reconstruction in birds. We believe it is important to admit that every new form is, in a sense, a *metanoia*, an act of conversion: it calls for a special moment of epiphany or revelation. We can borrow again from the biology of the living creature, particularly the work of Adolf Portmann (1990), to suggest that form is an essential concern for not only biological but also psychological and social life. Notably, the sociality of form is not simply external (i.e., concerning relations between different organisms) but also internal (i.e., concerning relations within the physiology of a single organism), and it is not only intraspecific (i.e., occurring in the sociation of creatures belonging to the same species) but also always interspecific (occurring in the sociation of creatures of different species). Furthermore, the requirement of interspecificity can be extended to address the fact that social life associates entities that can be both living and nonliving and that the very consociation of living creatures always passes through nonliving entities. In other words, social life, in its unfolding, incorporates bits and pieces of different nature, animate and inanimate, contributing to a single becoming of morphogenesis, prolonging and exploring formative series.

The Mystery of Appearances

At first sight the notion of mystery should not play any legitimate role in science. To positive science, mystery features as no more than a provisional residual category to be overcome as soon as possible. On closer inspection, however, mystery might retain an important heuristic role. This, at least, is what we suggest in the following pages. Indeed, mystery breaks with our intimate, natural familiarity with forms—which the mathematician René Thom (1988, 1991) claims to be inborn in our species. The apparition of form—or, how form is formed—does not cease to be surprising (*thaumastòn*), and, despite the panoply of studies of morphology in the most diverse disciplines ranging from physics to biology, from psychology to sociology, scientific understanding has not yet entirely subsumed form to exhaustive explanation.

If we look back at the beginnings of modern science, we could say that the Early Renaissance tradition of *natural magic* represented a first protracted attempt to come to grips with form making. According to Marsilio Ficino, for instance, "the works of magic are works of nature, and nature is their ministry" ([1469] 1987, 145). If magical operations can be naturalized, it is because nature is imagined as a deeply connected domain of action. In his commentary on Plato's *Symposium*, Ficino reasserted cosmic sympathy as grounded in the existence of an intimate communication among all entities: "Because all the parts of the world are the work of a single author and members of the same machine, and reciprocally similar in being and existence, they are tied together thanks to mutual charity" ([1469] 1987, 54). As we shall see in more detail, well beyond the Renaissance tradition, the apparition of individuality can be represented as one such *natural-magical* process, irreducible to a simple coming together of appropriated qualities—or "emergent properties," as they are called with current scientific jargon. What we describe here as the "moment of animation" offers a possible way to cope with the natural-magical mystery of forms as well as to advance toward a more radical appreciation of formation.

In the twentieth century two towering figures in zoology and mathematics approached the topic in a most original way, which in our view is not thoroughly at odds with the Renaissance tradition of natural magic. We would like to quickly recall their contributions here, albeit in a summary and imperfect way, for their cogitations represent a major source of inspiration in our subsequent analysis. For the zoologist Adolf Portmann, animal self-preservation cannot be reduced to the preservation of living functions. On the contrary, it necessarily requires the preservation of the *richness* of forms. There is always something superfluous, gratuitous, in forms: "Each plant and animal, no less than ourselves, must be experienced as an incomprehensible way of being which is grounded in the mystery of reality" (1990, 155). While mystery is certainly not the aim of science, it remains its beginning and constant spur. The expression "mystery of appearances" thus means that, in the first place, forms cannot be successfully reduced to functions. Animals develop forms of life that cannot be explained in terms of strings of physical-chemical molecular events. In biology the apparition of a *natural form* is determined by the animal becoming a visible entity, equipped with a nontransparent surface. The form as a visible, adiaphanous (nontransparent) surface of the animal is the natural correlate of the existence of a *viewing eye*, to which Portmann attaches extreme importance. Certainly, the viewing eye does not create the surface, insofar as it does not act directly on it; yet every formed surface presupposes a viewing eye and is actually made to serve it: "The surface's display is a part of the presentation of self of a living being. To be sure, the perceiving eye plays no role in the life-realm in which patterns and designs first arise from these newly constructed forms; but, in that same life-realm the possibility of perceived beings already exists—and that potential leads to the further promise of an enrichment of living relationships which grows out of the existence of those patterns and designs which uniquely characterize distinct individuals" (1990, 25).

Portmann thus inscribes the social relation between the viewing eye and the visible body into the very essence of the living form. Living forms are made to be seen; they are physiologically developed to serve communication between organisms or even to join organisms into a different type of "matter," which might be called the *element of the visible* (Brighenti 2017). Visibility, or inscription into the visible, is described as a potential to be actualized. Actualization is, in fact, what occurs at the surface of the body. This means that the boundary of the individual creature is not a point of closure but a surface of communication, a kind of territorial space where relations of visibility are articulated. The bold theoretical move undertaken by Portmann consists in locating the *inwardness* of the animal precisely on its surface: "Indeed, the inwardness of the living thing is a non-dimensional reality which is spatially located neither in a spatial inside nor in a center. Rather, an active 'medium' or 'midst' is present within the entire animal. . . . The more powerful inwardness, possessing as it does a consciousness, is ever more and more able to sense the appearance-aspect of the organism. The boundary of the organism becomes the organ of this inwardness; the very outermost speaks quite particularly of the very inmost" (1990, 26).

A theory of surfaces inevitably leads to an appreciation of the individual as *always-already* more-than-an-individual. Each individual form a living creature may assume is purposefully constituted through the prism of a social relationship. This is what we might call a "social program"—or even, perhaps, a "social dream"—namely, the idea of possible associations to come, together with the idea that the organism will always live through these associations. That is arguably why form is endowed with such a highly vital value, and it is certainly the reason why a science of territories as social enterprises needs to tackle in depth the origin and becoming of forms.

For his part, in his later oeuvre, the mathematician René Thom (1988) launched the project of a *semiophysics*, or "physics of meaning," that attempts to bridge the material and the semiotic domains. In Thom's conception form is neither just a given nor a mere attainment of life. Instead, it is more akin to a *credo*, in that a specific "investment in form" is made by the living matter. The painter Franz Marc, in a wonderful aphorism that plays with

Nietzsche, noted down his working program: "From the Will to Power there will arise the Will to Form [*Aus dem Willen zur Macht wird der Wille zur Form entspringen*]" (1915, sec. 26).[1] Such "Will to Form" allows us to understand better why, as we have seen with Portmann, form possesses value *in itself*: the creature makes an energetic and existential investment into it. Form is, thus, not simply valuable but in a sense the *source* of all possible value: it is, precisely, what confers value to the other elements of the living experience—hence also its "animistic" aspect. Forms, Thom argues, are not only *salient* and visible but also *pregnant*, imbued with forces they condense or capture. The phenomenon of pregnance is something that keeps manifesting throughout forms, in the sense that forms receive and emit informal pregnancies (or pregnances). That is why Thom is to be regarded, together with Gilles Deleuze, as one of the latest heirs—as well as a profound innovator—of the vitalistic tradition in philosophy. Each form represents a maximal deployment of possibilities previously enveloped (folded, or even trapped) in a given local state. In striking similarity with Simondon ([1964–89] 2013)—yet probably unaware of such connection—Thom speaks of a "structural germ," or formalizing seed carried along by singular events: "When we have a germ of a function, we can always plunge it into a family that is its maximal family. Such an analytic germ engenders a family that is the family of all its deformations. Thus, it engenders something *qualitatively*, by its own structure. The universal deployment is simply a way to 'deploy' all intrinsic information that lies enclosed in a singularity. In my view a singularity of an application is always something that concentrates a global structure inside a local structure" (1983, 27; our translation).

Form always appears as interlocked with deformation: indeed, form and deformation compose a single narrative, thanks to the mediation of peculiar qualitative moments or events, called *singularities*.[2] The adventures of form are generated through operations of folding (concentrating) and unfolding (deploying) such singularities, which in the earlier passage Thom designates as movements from the local to the global and vice versa. The specific movements that emerge from such singularities and reach back to them constitute the ongoing play of form and deformation. Here it

Morphogenesis and Animistic Moments

may also be worthwhile to remark that another word for "deformation" is *metamorphosis*—literally, the overcoming of the current form. In this sense the study of form cannot be carried out in isolation from the study of an informal counterpart that flows through the space of forms and enables their deployment—a deployment that can always be renewed and pushed further. Stressing the peculiar "unity" of form and the overcoming of form, in his last work Georg Simmel writes, "Life as immediately experienced is precisely the unity of 'being formed' and 'reaching out or flowing beyond form,' which manifests itself at any single moment as destruction of the given current form" ([1918] 2010, 15).

Forms are not free-floating or always easy to undo, though. While metamorphism marks an important acknowledgment, it is not per se sufficient.[3] Forms exhibit what Thom calls "structural stability," which makes them recognizable even through a series of deformations, at least until a major change takes place that brings a form *beyond itself.*[4] In this sense *catastrophes* are singular points where the structures defining a form undergo a sudden and total breakdown. The relation between continuity and discontinuity becomes crucial. On the one hand, form presupposes discontinuity, in that each form appears bounded and severed from its background or its surroundings, persistent through time (as a *Gestalt*). On the other hand, however, form also presupposes continuity, in that each form is but a temporary achievement in a more general process of generalized catastrophic metamorphosis. The latter point is particularly striking in the case of living and social forms. Here morphogenesis does not simply concern the first instantiation of a living individual or a social formation but accompanies its whole life. Forms appear in successions, and morphogenesis is an ongoing facet of social territorialization. The insight that forms are intrinsically correlated with metamorphosis is another way to make explicit that the domain of life (whether organic or not) is the domain of metastability or dynamic equilibrium.

Metamorphosis and Investments into Form

Morphology, understood as the science of living forms, was inaugurated in the late eighteenth century by Johann Wolfgang von Goethe ([1790]

1983) with his essay on plants transformation. The German poet held a strong belief in the unity of the whole vegetal domain (and, probably, the whole living domain), which he expressed through the notion of *Urpflanze* (Primal Plant). His famous saying, "Alles ist Blatt" (Everything is leaf), must be taken as conferring to the word *leaf* a special, enlarged meaning that does not match the common understanding of what a "trivial" leaf is. What Goethe calls *leaf* is, in fact, the metamorphic yet unitary element of vegetal existence (in Thom's words, not a salience but rather a *pregnance*). The insight encapsulated here is that vegetal life moves from one form to another through continuous contractions and expansions of a unitary vegetative module, the capital-B *Blatt*. Goethe thus establishes the conceptual couple of *Gestalt* (form) and *Bildung* (development), or, in other words, the intertwining of the static form and the dynamic formation of biological beings. In a famous page of his *Journey to Italy*, he notes, "In view of further understanding, that much may be shortly stated—namely, it has risen in me the idea that, in that organ of the plant that we usually call the leaf, lies hidden the true Proteus, who can flow through and reveal itself in all forms. From each side the plant is always but leaf, united in such an inseparable way to the coming germ that one cannot think of one without the other" (1817; our translation).

Making reference to the mythological figure of Proteus, Goethe gives emphasis to the coessential relation between form and transformation, simultaneously pointing to something unitary and persistent across the transformational vegetative series. Along a similar line, in the early nineteenth century, the French zoologist Étienne Geoffroy Saint-Hilaire advanced a monistic interpretation of living forms, according to which animal forms are obtained via the subsequent unfolding of a single anatomical buildup. He called this the "principle of the unity of organic composition of all living creatures" (1830, 48). Working jointly, the principle of analogy (analogy of functions across different species) and the principle of connections (connection of anatomical parts, or the chain of pieces present within each specific anatomical buildup) seamlessly lead through the transformations of all zoological forms. Geoffroy's method for the analysis of skeletal anatomy could be said to resemble a zoological origami, where organs know no transpositions of, but only magnifications and miniaturizations by folding and unfolding. For Geoffroy the organization of vertebral animals can be brought back to a uniform type of organization with many intermediary degrees. In this process, he remarks, "an organ is rather diminished, deleted, annihilated rather than transposed" (1818, 405).

The fact that morphology as a science flourished in the nineteenth century is per se an interesting fact. Two connections, in our view, stand out. On the one hand, the bourgeois philosophy of liberal individualism needed form as a stable, individualized phenomenon to valorize the individual being, elected as the foundational element of social and political order. On the other hand, the naturalist evolutionary view, which culminated with Darwin, introduced a radically dynamic regard on the biological form (just as, in the following generation, Pierre Janet and Sigmund Freud introduced a radically dynamic regard on the human psyche). From a Darwinian point of view, species are inevitably transformative formations. Darwinianism, in other words, inserted species in a fluctuating dynamic medium produced by random variations and slow yet incessant global morphological drifts.

In the 1910s the Scottish biologist and mathematician D'Arcy Wentworth Thompson ([1917] 1945) undertook a wide-ranging study of living cells and tissue growth. In Thompson's eight-hundred-page summa, the animal shapes are deducted from geometric—as well as, we may say, *geodetic*—necessities. The conceptual geometrization of form is aimed precisely to move "from the conception of form to an understanding of the forces which gave rise to it" ([1917] 1945, 720). Mathematical models accounting for the homologies between different forms enabled the Scottish scientist to capture each form as a peculiar "deformation" or "permutation" of another. Indeed, Thompson observes,

> in a very large part of morphology, our essential task lies in the comparison of related forms rather than in the precise definition of each; and the *deformation* of a complicated figure may be a phenomenon easy of comprehension, though the figures itself have to be left unanalysed and

undefined. This process of comparison, of recognising in one form a definite permutation or *deformation* of another, apart altogether from a precise and adequate understanding of the original "type" or standard of comparison, lies within the immediate province of mathematics, and finds its solution in the elementary use of a certain method of the mathematician. (723)

As anticipated earlier, transformations appear to be limited within certain biological boundaries, which Thompson defines as "lines of constraint": "It is clear, I think, that we may account for many ordinary biological processes of development or transformation of form by the existence of trammels or lines of constraint, which limit and determine the action of the expansive forces of growth that would otherwise be uniform and symmetrical" (737).

Despite the fact that, as we have just observed, the kernel of morphology lies in a conception that ties form to transformation, curiously, the morphological idea of form also seems to be inevitably connected to the idea of *right* or correct form, or what we may call *orthoform*. Despite their contingent and even transient nature, forms often appear to contain a sort of normative dimension. This dimension is correlative to that *credo*, which we have designed as "investment in form"—namely, the fact that, for the living matter, forms assume a value in themselves and must be protected as such. A fortiori, this hypothesis can be corroborated by considering how deformations have such a deeply emotional and psychological resonance. Deformation is the domain of not only physiological but, above all, psychological trauma. Since the early twentieth century, psychology and psychoanalysis have advanced important insights in this respect. In the psychoanalytic tradition, for instance, Carl Gustav Jung worked out a notion of the *archetype* that shares resemblances with some essential features of the living form, as identified in particular by Portmann. For Jung an archetype is not simply, as it is usually defined, a stable, persistent or even "iconic" image; rather, the archetype appears to him as an active force that "can seize hold of the ego and even compel it to act" (1956, 66). The archetype seems to reside in a form that strives to preserve itself at all cost; containing a normative imperative, it constitutes a veritable orthoform. At the same time, especially in his work *The Psychology of the Child Archetype*, Jung connects the archetype to the type of nonrational thinking that can be retrieved in both mythology and the free associations so frequent in therapeutic settings: "The archetypes appear in myths and fairy-tales just as they do in dreams and in the products of psychotic fantasy. The medium in which they are embedded is, in the former case, an ordered and for the most part immediately understandable context, but in the latter case a generally unintelligible, irrational, not to say delirious sequence of images which nonetheless does not lack a certain hidden coherence" (1940, 100).

The complexity of archetypes that appear in myths and dreams therefore derives from their being simultaneously *both* normative orthoforms *and* constantly inserted in transformative flows. This may seem contradictory—how can something that actually and factually changes come to generate an axiology? Interestingly, on this specific point Jung refers to the French psychologist Janet (and not to his mentor, Freud). A coetaneous of Freud, Janet (1889) had inquired into a type of neurosis he had called *psychasthenia* (literally, "mind weakness"). Specifically, psychasthenia clinically manifested as a psychic obsessive-compulsive disorder that, ultimately, entailed a dissolution of the patient's psychic forms. Mental illness is explained by Janet as the loss of a normative orthoform to be evoked. Janet has become famous especially for his analysis of the lower psychic faculties, such as psychological automatisms. And Jung refers precisely to Janet's phenomenology of neurotic states as entailing a "lowering of the mental level" (*abaissement du niveau mental*). Myths, Jung believes, were formed in a "primitive state of consciousness," which existed in a condition similar to the one described by Janet (Jung 1940, 103). But rather than saying—as Freud (1913) did—that "primitive" peoples resemble neurotic patients, Jung (using Janet) argues that certain states manifested, to various degrees, by neurotic and psychotic patients actually open up to a universal psychic formation that is the archetype and that, a fortiori, makes those nonrational states pop up in the most diverse settings. From our perspective, while Jung's theoretical position may read as quite idiosyncratic, it at least creates the possibility of looking for an explanation of the origins of the normative dimension of forms.

Besides that, relatively less known is the fact that the later Janet (1929) developed a much more rounded theory of personality that thoroughly engages the issue of form. Specifically, Janet conceived of personality as a dynamic process unfolding not only at the (conscious and unconscious) individual level but also at the social and historical levels. Starting from the corporeal grounding of personality, which he had established since his early studies on automatism, Janet aimed to develop a "complete psychology," bridging the gap between *formation* and *action*. In Janet's view such a gap could be filled only by taking seriously into account the formative power of human social existence—namely, the fact that "what makes personality is society" (Janet 1929, 14). From the perspective of the psychologist, society is evoked as a kind of ambience, a milieu or environment. This does not correspond to the image usually entertained by social scientists, who regard society as more akin to an object or process to be explained (the environment being conceived in this case in material or ecological terms). From both perspectives, however, a consideration of the relation between form taking and the environment in which formative enterprises unfolds remains essential. This is where Simondon enters our discussion.

Following the important insights by Portmann, Thom, and others, in the previous section we have attempted an appreciation of *form* as a type of *boundary* and, more precisely, a movable boundary. In this respect, in the late 1950s the French philosopher Simondon ([1964–89] 2013) carried out a masterful analysis of formative processes, which he called *prise de forme*. In Simondon the genesis of forms coincides with the genesis of individual beings, a process he defines as "information" (literally, "putting into form"). Starting from an apparently minor example, the humble activity of brick making, Simondon builds a powerful conceptual case to highlight the limits of the Aristotelian model of the relation between form and matter.[5] In the classic "hylomorphic" (form-and-matter) model drawn from Aristotle, a substance is produced as the result of the coming together of immaterial form and unformed matter. By contrast, Simon-

Morphogenesis and Animistic Moments

don asserts that *individuation*, the process of becoming an individuated form, is an operative principle independent of any specific substance. (Thom also argued that morphogenesis is largely independent from the nature of the "substrate.") Because, in hylomorphism, matter is regarded as merely passive and form as uniquely active, the model fails to account for the series of technical preparations and the operations that, functioning as necessary mediations, make the encounter between form and matter possible at all. Simondon's aim is precisely to account for such operations (and, indeed, he seeks to introduce a theory of operations he calls "allagmatics"). The individuation of a brick through modeling cannot occur without a specific phase transition (79) that unfolds within a system (see fig. 8). Simondon thus explains, "To be modeled does not mean to undergo arbitrary displacements, but to order one's plasticity according to specific forces that stabilize deformation. The technical operation is *mediation* between an inter-elementary entity and an intraelementary one. The pure form already contains certain gestures, and the primary matter has the capacity to become; the gestures contained in the form meet the becoming of matter and modulate it" (42).

The stabilization of deformation is an actual case of what we call territorial stabilization, and which Thom referred to as structural stability. From this perspective a form can be stabilized thanks to an operation of mediation, while mediation itself may proceed from either one of the two end points of the process. Simondon calls such end points, respectively, molding and modulating. Instead of being imprinted by an active agent onto a passive one, form is thus observed as "taken" by a force that acts up another forces.[6] In other words, "it is as *forces* that matter and form are put in each other's presence" ([1964–89] 2013, 44). Such is the nature of the moment of *prise de forme*: a veritable capture of forms. This is why, as anticipated, forms can also be regarded as boundaries; they represent a *limit* in the event of the actualization of a given (systemic) potential of energy. In this sense the brick mold is only an extreme case of a more general operation, just as, at its polar opposite, is the modulator—that is, the device that enables the variation of the properties of a periodic waveform with a signal con-

8. Brick making in Ahmedabad. Photo by and courtesy of Amit Srivastava.

taining information. The technological continuum from the brick mold to the wavelength modulator tells a single story of morphogenesis: "The mold and the modulator are extreme cases, but the essential operation of form-taking is achieved in the same way; it consists of the establishment of an either durable or non-durable energetic regime. To mold is to modulate in a final way; to modulate is to mold in a continuous and perpetually variable way" (47).

Once form is thought of as a capture, we also might expect that, at a certain point, it will be liberated, given back, perhaps even redressed. Capture, so to speak, does injustice to force. Tragic as it is for its consequences, the structural collapse of a building is one such instance of liberation (Stoppani 2012). More generally, in the vitalistic tradition the moment of *liberation from form* plays an essential role in morphogenesis at large. In *Twilight of the Idols* (*Götzen-Dämmerung*), for example, Friedrich Nietzsche famously expanded on what he calls "the psychology of the artist," remarking the specifically *perverse* and *seductive* operation carried out by the artist: "He enters into any skin, into any affect: he constantly transforms himself" (1889, 197). A conceptually similar (yet ethically divergent) image of the artist as the "custodian of transformations" can also be found in Elias Canetti (1975). The importance of the vitalist tradition lies in its insistence that, in life (be it biological, psychological, or social—perhaps also nonorganic), there is something that cannot be reduced to visible form. In the words of Georges Canguilhem ([1952] 1965), the living cannot be downgraded to a special type of form-producing causal mechanism. Form is a purposeful accomplishment, but at the same time "out there" (as well as "between us") there is much that is not formal and not causal. Whenever we perform formal analysis, we tend to systematically discard the question of the *origin* of the current forms. To a large extent scientists tend to take forms for granted because they are more interested in questioning their correlations and variations. But the properly morphogenetic question cannot be ultimately eluded, for the genesis of form is not something that existed before forms were formed, just to be superseded by current forms. On the contrary, a formation is a type of protracted internal communication that lies in the genesis of the individual entity. Genesis should be understood as, not the historical beginning, but the living, persistent origin—what Benjamin ([1928] 1974) called *Ursprung*, or source. Genesis continues in the current forms. Genesis is life itself, to the extent that life consists precisely in the constant attempt to expand the beginning from the center (or, as we see in chapter 2, from the milieu).

If individuation is a process that continues through the by-now-individuated (or relatively more individuated) individuals, two aspects deserve special attention. First, the temporal dimension of individuation is a kind of present continuous state, of protracted, thick present—as well as, perhaps, also a suspended one. We can refer to the chronic present discussed in the previous chapter. Second, given that an individual can still undergo further individuations, individuation is not an all-or-nothing phenomenon. Rather, we have a phenomenon that occurs *in degrees*, and these degrees are also energetic levels. Such degrees of individuation constitute, in themselves, a principle of limitation: the process of individuation is always a local enterprise, and there cannot exist a global individuation. The grounding of individuation is phenomenological, related as it is to the absoluteness of the (phenomenological) here-and-now. This is what Alfred Whitehead ([1929] 1978) used to call "presentational immediacy." The here-and-now also inherently functions as a principle of limitation, of preservation and restraint against the immediate overcoming of present forms: "The individuated being exists here and now, and this here-and-now prevents the coming of an infinite number of other here-and-now[s]" (Simondon [1964–89] 2013, 255).

On the other hand, the vital, metamorphic, elusive element of force that flows through forms (Thom's *pregnance*) and that can never reside in the here-and-now itself is what we might call its *value*, its *worth*. Pregnance as value-worth reveals the nonlocal part of the life of forms. Thanks to value-worth, there is not "just a form," but there can be a "just form."[7] The orthoform—or, again with Jung, the archetypal form—makes it possible to think about deformation and metamorphosis as engendering specific operations of (cognitive and affective) *meaning*. This is essential when

Morphogenesis and Animistic Moments

we turn to social and territorial arrangements. What is important about territories is that they are bounded. Boundaries, however, are not trivial entities. They are not just offsets; rather, they always entail points and moments of "critical" change or phase transitions. Critical boundaries are the place where a set of differential qualities coexists in a conflictual state and simultaneously the place where such a conflict is temporarily stabilized. Thus, stabilization understood as a threshold of criticality *is* the form itself—it is what we usually call "the object," or a formation. In many cases it is because we cannot stand the formless that we repeatedly precipitate into forms.

The Formation of Individual Collectives

A study of social formations informed by morphology and territoriology must then lead to an analysis of individual collectives. At first, the very expression, *individual collective*, reads as a *contradictio in adjectum*; in fact, collectives can and do have their individuality, their proper degree of individuation. Accordingly, we need to develop notions of individuality and individuation that are insightful enough to see this. Individuation is the result of an act of inscription of a form into a domain or "element," which we call "the visible" (Brighenti 2017). An individual object—as well as a corresponding subject capable of perceiving it—is the result of an operation carried out in an environment or, more precisely, of an operation carried out *with* an environment—what we may call a "medial operation." From this perspective the difference between object and environment is not an ontological difference but a difference between two different modes of inscription into the visible. The act of inscription creates the unity, but no unity is possible without a form. In other words, no morphogenesis is possible without a milieu.

The individual itself is not the opposite of the environment but its correlative creation. The individual, in other words, functions as an environment of individuation. One of the greatest contributions from Simondon lies in the idea that, just as the individual derives from a process of individuation, the environment too is the product of the operation of individuation. To reiterate, the environment is a correlative production to the production of the individual. That also explains why the environment is never a virtual field that may preexist forms. The individual-environment represents an unbreakable couple—one cannot have one without the other. The individual and the environment, we may gloss, are perspectives on a single reality, a reality of topologically and energetically variable formations. Just as with Janet and Portmann, for Simondon too the individual is not isolated, to the extent that, in its evolution, it retains a protracted bind with a nonindividual environment.[8] This way the social dimension is always-already present in every individual—just as, similarly, extraterritorial aspects are always present in the territory. Relations produce boundaries, boundaries produce relations, and the repetition and stabilization of these relations and boundaries produces territories. In its turn form is the continued critical limit between the individual and the environment.

When we face a collective social, spatial, material entity, such as a crowd or a city, the issue of *form* can be approached in terms of *formation*. Each formation entails, we may say, a two-fold operation. On the one hand, it entertains formal relationships with the parts that enter its composition; on the other hand, however, it subjects those parts to a synthetic moment that institutes, by discontinuity, an additional dimension of existence. Formation lays out a new space of existence: $n + 1$. We might even say that by crossing a singular threshold of consistence, each new formation may take up a new kind of existence. A veritable ontogeny is at stake in formation (Massumi 2009). Thus, a continuation of objectual individuation is taken into new dimensions and prolonged to further degrees. Consequently, a collective entity emerges, takes place, happens—it looks more like an event, or what Whitehead used to call "actual occasion," than an object. Correlatively, we need to redefine our notion of object as something much more dynamic than previously imagined: it may not be by chance that, as we try to dig into these processes, we are also pushed to undo our vocabulary that encapsulates so many preconceptions and are recurrently led to struggle with words. Such an idea also fits with the notion of "concrescence" as elaborated by Whitehead ([1929] 1978). Each collective entity is

Morphogenesis and Animistic Moments

a new form—but what else is a form if not a formation, a morphogenesis in existence? Morphogenesis is formation understood as *prise de forme*. Form is the adventure of the point that becomes line and generates its many counterpoints that slow it down and redirect it through the many spaces of an element. Form-taking activities unfold in an element capable of setting up interrelated objects, subjects, and environments. New forms are thus defined by relationships with previous forms, in the sense of continuation as well as of catastrophe. Formal social analysis is the modeling of such relations and, as such, is grounded in topology.

As hinted at earlier, formation can be said to possess two faces: on the one hand, it is a collection; on the other, an emergence. *Collection* defines a proximity of elements in an element (e.g., critical distances among the parts), while *emergence* creates a differential moment that occurs once those critical distances are overcome (e.g., a critical turn happens through the correlations among the parts). With emergence the previously existing dimensions are superseded, and a new dimension (n + 1) is laid out where the individuality of the collective entity begins to exist. At the same time emergence constantly liberates or unleashes a number of collected elements back to the milieu (n − 1): it is an unfinished undertaking that cannot be thought of as a merely additive task or as an achieved unity. In fact, emergence is simultaneously additive *and* subtractive or, as we may also say, evolutive and involutive at the same time. In mathematical terms it is a catastrophic moment—given that, per Thom, "every discontinuity in phenomena is a catastrophe" (1991, 28). Thanks to emergence, form entails formation (form taking), and formation entails transformation (metamorphosis). Certainly, individuality is *quantity* (n = 1), yet it does not make sense without a set of *qualities* and *properties* ready to enter novel combinations. Individuality occurs when a set of free-floating, nonindividual qualities are individually appropriated within a given domain. An appropriated quality is not a quantity but rather a *formal* property: formal properties are the memory of the catastrophic moments an entity has gone through to become what it is and continues to become.

What is the role of the existing parts caught in a formation? A formation is not simply a summation, which resonates with the holistic idea in social science that a society is not to be reduced to a collection of individuals. A form might be decomposable into traits or entities, but it is at the same time also a nondecomposable whole, an supplemental effect produced as a temporal settlement through a catastrophic (discontinuous) leap (where catastrophe entails subtraction).[9] Every formation has its individual parts, but it also subjects these parts to a relative deindividuation to attain the unit. This movement is in some sort a formal one yet is meant to feed the new, upcoming individuation in a nonformal (pregnant) way. Each new settlement is obtained by relatively unsettling previous arrangements; emergence liberates sets of qualities that start wandering and can be appropriated by upcoming formations. Properties emerge not out of material composition but out of organization within an excitable medium whereby differentiation and asymmetry appear.[10]

With Thom's notions, however, form represents a type of salience, premised on the discontinuity between form (figure) and background; formation, on the other hand, is better appreciated as a type of pregnance, given that pregnance addresses the process of *emanation*, *investment*, and *impregnation* taking place in the continuity of a medial element. As Paul Valéry once said, "The background is but an impure form" (1957, 1437). Whereas salience visibly establishes the foreground, pregnance invisibly ensures the ongoing commerce between the foreground and the background. Such a "commerce" is a way of speaking about life. Saliences are extensive, whereas pregnancies are intensive. Pregnancies are not localizable entities: while inherent in forms, they constitute the nonlocal factor that drives from one form to another—or, one could also say, the social factor capable of producing catastrophes in extant forms. In this sense, for Thom, and contrary to what happens in field theory, there is no preexistent virtuality independent of the existent forms or objects themselves. To put it differently, our approach to morphogenesis aligns with an immanentist perspective. The medial element is not a passive environment, a meaningless background, but an active propagator of discontinuities—an "excitable

Morphogenesis and Animistic Moments

medium," as Webster and Goodwin (1996) call it. *Emergence*, as we have defined it, can happen only in one such medial element. That the medium is alive: the claim of natural magic was nothing other than this.

Walls and Their Humans

Our inquiry is driven by the search for a nonreductionist gaze onto social arrangements and their materialities. If we subscribe to a vitalistic sensibility, it is especially insofar as it stands at the polar opposite of reductionism. Of course, we need to develop a type of vitalism that does not turn into a resurrection of occult qualities. The latter was the reason why classic vitalism has been unreservedly banned from modern science. With this caveat, and in line with works such as W. J. T. Mitchell (2005), Jane Bennett (2010), Tim Ingold (2011), and others, we still believe that the vitalistic perspective may offer an important lesson, shaping a special sensitivity to attend the *revelation* of forms. Observed in this way, the issue of form cuts across the domain of living matter and spans beyond it. The collaboration of saliences and pregnancies in the emergence of a collective entity—or, the collaboration of saliences and pregnancies in emergent processes of individuation—reminds us that, biologically and socially, *meaning* is a sort of *blessing* or even *bliss* bestowed on certain forms, capable of receiving or accepting certain pregnancies through formative processes.

Formation, we argue consequently, is best addressed as a special event of animation. In this sense meaning is intimately related to what might be described as an "animistic moment." Such animistic moments differ from the traditional way of understanding animism. Whereas animism is generally seen as the idea that objects or entities have a soul or some kind of spiritual essence—that is, that they are living figures—the animistic moment denotes a specific invested and energetic becoming that keeps the process of de/reterritorialization alive. It is a way of establishing a circulation between two heterogeneous energetic fields. The animistic moment does not describe a stable state of life as achieved after the process of individuation but a way of keeping the question of life itself alive. We know that the animal is, quite literally, the *animate*. The identification of a specific domain of animal existence presupposes that nonanimallike individual objects are correlatively regarded as inanimate. The boundaries of the domain of animation, however, are not easily drawn, and it is certainly not biology that can determine the province of animation.

History is full of examples of animistic strategies: from Cyrus stopping his march against Babylon to destroy the Gyndes River as a penalty for his drowned horse, to Sicilian farmers expelling, drowning, and hanging statues of saints as punishment for a dry spring (Frazer [1906–15] 1959, 46). Edward P. Evans (1906, 175) tells us how the great bell of Uglich was expelled to Tobolsk, Siberia, for ringing the signal of insurrection as the Russian prince Dmitry of Uglich was assassinated in 1591. The church bell was not allowed to return until four hundred years later, in 1892. Animism also has a long tradition in the history of architecture and the built environment (Frascari 1990), and an undercurrent of animism can be easily spotted throughout the nineteenth and twentieth centuries in the production, design, representation, and use of the built environment.

Especially since the 1850s animistic rhetoric was used mostly in the many vivid descriptions of haunted houses ("dead yet alive") found in the Victorian ghost stories (Marcus 1999). The same theme can also be found as a central motif in realistic novels such as Victor Hugo's *Les travailleurs de la mer* (1866) (Vidler 1992, 19–20). Other examples include the malicious or disobeying utensils and objects in the novel *Auch Einer* (1878) by the German philosopher Friedrich Theodor Vischer (Papapetros 2005, 16–17) or even the becoming alive of whole city districts, like in Gustav Meyrink's description of the Jewish ghetto in Prague in the novel *Der Golem* (1915). Although animism has been used mainly in demeaning ways by modernist artists, more positive and encouraging usages can also be found. John Ruskin was, for example, not a stranger to granting agency to buildings, writing of "living architecture" ([1849] 1880, 153) in his *Seven Lamps of Architecture*, and of buildings demanding sympathy or buildings watching over us (177; see also Marcus 1999, 118, 254). A more design-oriented use of animism can be found in Le Corbusier and his reappropriation of the Vitruvian man. Since both *Le Modulor* and the plan of *Ville Radieuse*

Morphogenesis and Animistic Moments

encapsulate idea of human-made spatial formations as extended versions of the human body (Vidler 1992, 75), the city resulting from the application of such principles will necessarily be a "living" city.

In short, the recognition of the animation of the world points to the outer limits of our rational control of it, as well as to its revelatory impact. The animistic moment is a moment of animation. To better understand the role of such moments, we need to go beyond the list of examples reported here and look more closely at how concrete relations unfold in specific cases. In the following we thus look at two examples of the materialization and animation of territorial boundaries. The first example relates to the architectural construction of brick arches and walls, while the second relates to urban warfare and the demolition of urban walls. We tackle more extensively the issue of walls in chapter 6, especially in conjunction with rhythms. Taken together the two urban architectural examples evoke different perspectives on territorial re/deformation and the—creative or destructive—always-inventive shifting of sociomaterial forms.

One of the best modernist examples of an animistic moment—*metánoia*, or leap of faith in relation to a form—can probably be found in the architect Louis Kahn, who is well known for his animistic architectural language, famously expressed in his dialogue with a brick reported in the film documentary *My Architect* (2003). Here Kahn describes how he asks the brick what it wants to be and how the brick answers that *it wants to be an arch*. In his dissertation Amit Srivastava (2009) describes in detail the very moment when this Kahn-brick was produced. In 1964, when Kahn was working on building the Indian Institute of Management he came to inspect the building site and, disappointed by the result, realized that he needed to get to know the material conditions better. He went down into the construction pit to work with the bricklayers. This is where he constructed what was later called the Experimental Arch.[11] During this process Kahn negotiated with the brick, deciding possible ways of interacting with it—such as how it should overcome holes in walls, how certain brick bond details should be arranged, and so on. From that occasion in the pit, there emerged the Kahn-brick (a Kahn-brick-architecture) but also a brick-Kahn (the brick-architecture-Kahn). What we see is as much a new formation and territorialization of the brick as it is of Kahn himself as an architect of brick buildings (see figs. 9 and 10).

Kahn's way of expressing his dialogue with objects has been much criticized and even mocked. Kahn's own anagogic rhetoric was, however, not a particularly good description of his achievements. Rather, his brick dialogue can be interpreted as an attempt to "communicate the experience of an active and symmetric exchange with materials" (Srivastava 2009, 236). In fact, Kahn was producing specific agencies rather than demasking essences: "The Experimental Arch was completed not as an exercise of translating abstract paper drawings onto real but inert material forms but instead as a 'continuous happening' resulting from ceaseless and dialogic encounters with the material" (Srivastava 2009, 218). What Kahn ultimately produced was thus not the essence of brick architecture but something that nurtured the plurality of architectural forms and the heterogeneity of social institutions (including the brick makers). In the end his processes of dedifferentiation can be seen as strategy of invention. It is not a reduction of architecture into a single order but a creative reassembling of materialities, the production of a specific architectural style of making—and a case of an animistic moment.

Formation through an animistic moment addresses individuation in the deepest sense, because animation always embodies a crisis in the established order of things, in the status quo. To enter an animistic moment is to treat things as more than things, which subsequently also makes us aware of the fact that we are not just individuals but always also more than individuals: as we animate an object, the object animates us (Stengers 2011, 188–89). Our relation to the object, in other words, enables us to access the domain of a number of previously unknown participations. Contrary to what is held by modernist thinking, animism is not groundless superstition but a type of engagement or skill that can be employed "in situations when we cannot control or totally predict our interlocutor's behavior, when its behavior is not predetermined but in 'conversation' with our own. . . . We do not first personify other entities and then socialize with them but personify them, *as*, *when*, and *because* we socialize with them" (Bird-David 1999, 78).

9. The Experimental Arch. Photo by and courtesy of Amit Srivastava.

10. The Indian Institute of Management, Ahmedabad. Photo by and courtesy of Amit Srivastava.

Thus, the animistic moment initiates a process of deindividuation as well as, simultaneously, a kind of rebirth of the individuation process, where the individual and its associates are co-produced. Simondon ([1964–89] 2013) calls this realization a "transindividuation." In the process what is living and what is not living are bracketed and remain undetermined. Animism can, in other words, be seen as a way of producing a monster not yet fully defined or categorized, an entity of which some parts are open but some other closed. During such ongoing struggle the virtuality of potential energy is sustained in the actual state and denotes a situation of becoming, an ongoing process still saturated by indecisions and possibilities (Eriksson, 2010, 529). The animistic moment corresponds well to the description of an intense (metastable) situation of formation—a yet-to-find-its-form, a yet-to-come that can take on situations and shapes, even though at a later stage it might prove impossible to live or endure them. In this sense the animistic project is not a morphogenetic process in search of possible states or of the limits of those possible states—as Philip Steadman (1983, 2), for example, would have it. Even though the process eventually and temporarily might end up in a stable form (as for Kahn's famous brick architecture) it might, from the perspective of a specific temporal situation, seem improbable, even impossible (but still bricks cannot talk back!).

Animation, as we have defined it here, is intimately related to "facialization," as theorized especially by Deleuze and Félix Guattari (1980).[12] The facialization of either a human or a nonhuman leads to the production of an interiority. But such an inwardness is, as Portmann (1990) also argued, located on the boundary, on the threshold of the creature—it is a property of a system of territorialization. The production of an interiority of the other produces simultaneousness—not just of the face-to-face situation but of interiority and exteriority in coexistence. The exteriority becomes unified through the contemporaneity (and synchrony) of the interior and thus "comes to life." The staged performativity of the exterior is not an expression of an interior; rather, it produces its own interior. Here is where we rejoin Simondon's claim that "the living individual is contemporary to itself in all its elements, contrary to the physical individual" ([1964–89]

2013, 28). Whereas living forms are autopoietic and *continuous* systems, in nonliving objects *discontinuous* breaks exist between past and present states. An object, like a crystal or even a text, grows slowly; some parts might be of last year's work, others of last weeks: these objects are temporally layered. The living creature, on the other hand, has an interiority that makes all its parts contemporary to itself. Our intuitive sensation of the existence of a present results from this. This interiority or inwardness is, as Portmann has enlightened us, present at the surface—a surface that is also milieu. From this perspective the natural magic of the animistic moment appears as a special negotiation on threshold points, where the formation of surfaces becomes a force in itself, a moment that through a temporary ignorance of given categories and borders focuses on relations and pregnancies to let them spark a new process of individuation, new interiors, new life forms, and new territories.

The type of animism present, for instance, in the Kahn-brick clearly appears as a struggle for receiving and accepting certain pregnancies through ongoing formative process. In terms of territorial production (the territorial strategy and association of the Kahn-brick), this struggle and co-formation of the territory and its milieu also entails the production of an orthoform—that is, a meaningful territorial sort endowed with boundaries. The Kahn-brick is a brick transformed; it is of course still a (kind of) brick among (other kinds of) bricks, yet the Kahn-brick is nothing short of an invention (emergence of a novel individuality). Entities of different potentials are put together (the molded clay, Kahn, and the bricklayers and their traditional molding craft, etc.), but there is also something new that comes to life, an individuation more than a mere addition of previously existing entities: a territory that in turn keeps on proliferating into Kahn-walls, Kahn-architectures, and so on.

The critical formation of a territory seems to call for an animation that, as shown earlier, becomes apparent in artistic and creative moments. In fact, the animistic moment might always strive for some kind of invention (with Tarde, the social logic is both a logic of repetition and one of invention), but this invention must not always be a constructive one. The animistic moment can also play its part in destructive processes and might thus pop up during moments of threats to security. Common everyday instances of territorial associations taking form might, for example, be expressed by statements such as "the streets have eyes." In these cases human and nonhuman actors are in a state of formation and cannot (yet) be separated or known from each other: "What is that lurking in the shadow? Is that a friend or a foe, or is it just a mailbox?" These kinds of animistic moments, pervaded with threats and warnings, can also take on a more enduring dimension. Thomas De Quincey, for example, recounts that Constantine chose Constantinople instead of Rome as his capital city not because of economic advantages but because Rome "*could not be depaganised. Too profound, too inveterately entangled with the very soil and deep substructions of Latium were the old traditional records, promises, auguries, and mysterious splendors of concentrated Heathenism in*, and *on*, and nine times *round about*, and 50 fathoms *below*, and countless fathoms in upper air *above*, this most memorable of capital cities" ([1847] 1897, 303). The relation between Constantine and Rome was a living one—actually, a struggling one—where the emperor eventually yielded.

Finally, to illustrate the correlation of formation and deformation, we end this section with a contemporary example of how the animistic moment can also contradistinguish territorial formations of warfare. Bricks and walls, we learn, can come to life through greater catastrophes than Kahn's delicate and ambitious experiment. In his book on Israel's territorial colonialism, the architect Eyal Weizman describes the territorial strategies and tactics of the Israeli urban warfare known as "swarming" or "infestation" (2007, 185–91). In an uncanny echo of postmodernistic literary theories, modern military swarming techniques have been developed since the late 1980s as battlefield strategies that involve a series of small, loosely coordinated, and semiautonomous military units instantly (that is, catastrophically) overwhelming a certain territory. Swarming was further developed during the Israeli attacks on Palestine, for example, in Balata and Nablus during the early 2000s, as a reinvented—or even *inverted*—battlefield. An Israeli general said, "We interpreted the alley as a place forbidden to walk through, and the window as a place forbidden to look through, and the door as a place forbidden to pass through" (qtd. in Weizman 2007, 198). Where then can one walk, look, and pass then? New spaces of movement and visibility were produced through taking up holes, digging tunnels, and developing instruments that carve and see through walls, all of which enabled the military to fight their war through living rooms and hallways, turning domestic enclosed spaces into accessible circulation spaces. Not just soldiers, but whole vehicles were placed or taken through private homes. In response Palestinian fighters similarly resorted to the same techniques and included domestic spaces in warfare territories.

Similar processes of de/reterritorialization lead to a transformation of the urban battleground, conceiving the city as "not just the site, but as the very *medium* of warfare" (Weizman 2007, 186; see also Virilio 2004). The city comes to life, but this time as *monster*. New forms, new pregnances, and new values are hence evoked and enacted. Walking through walls became part of a territorial formation producing new meanings and opportunities for the military through an aberrant reconfiguration of the battleground. From the perspective of the civilians, the territory really at stake was their home. In the Nablus Kasbah, where more than half of the buildings had between one and eight violent openings in their walls after the battle (Weizman 2007, 196), the application of territorial swarming begs questions: Which walls might come alive, and which may not? Which walls "have eyes"? Which walls might explode into my living room the next moment? These became compelling questions of territory, of life and death—a reminder that territory is ultimately always about life and death, about social coexistence and its limits. This is a painful moment of animation, put on hold. The animistic moment might be a strategy of formation, but it might also be a situation that we suddenly have to face where order breaks down, meaning and orthoforms disappear out of sight, and agency becomes hard to distribute—moments when we have to look for new faces and new coordinations to come. Just as the animistic moment can be full of promises, it may as well manifest as an existential threat—it always puts something at risk.

Territories, Forms, and Formations

In this chapter we have started from a concern for territorial production as a lens to capture the process of social formation, venturing into the theory of morphogenesis. Our leading hypothesis has been that, just as we need to stabilize territories, we also need to stabilize forms. Territories involve precisely the production and stabilization of associations and boundaries— that is, of forms. Such relationship between territory and form is perhaps never more alive than in moments of animism. Interestingly, formative (developmental or morphogenetic) processes cut across the domain of living matter and span beyond it into the domain of what appear to be inanimate matter. This is why morphogenesis is a pivotal domain for the study of sociomaterial collective formations.

Seeking to contribute to a renewal of the vitalistic take on morphogenesis, we have advanced three points. First, we have briefly recalled the Renaissance tradition of natural magic, to approach form as a peculiar mystery. Speaking of mystery, we have clarified, does not entail giving up the scientific ethos; instead, it invites us to develop a nonreductionist, encompassing type of science. To begin with, the mystery enables us to break with the natural precomprehension of forms. This is particularly helpful to focus on the dynamic dyad of form and transformation that, as we have seen, constitutes a single continuous process—while at the same time also recognizing the special importance of certain forms (orthoforms) that resist deformation (or receive deformation only as a discontinuous catastrophe). Meaning, we have remarked, is a blessing bestowed on certain forms to the detriment of others. The genesis of forms can thus be regarded as an origin in the middle of things, a living center that persists at the heart of each formation.

Second, we have approached forms from an energetic and relational perspective. The domain of form—and of living forms in particular—has been consequently observed as a quintessentially social accomplishment. The morphogenetic perspective applied to social theory helpfully enables us to crosscut the individual-collective divide. We have observed formation as

Morphogenesis and Animistic Moments

a two-faced operation of collection and emergence of properties. The social dimension of forms leads to a special consideration of the environment where individual forms coalesce. It is precisely at the interface between the individual and the environment—that is, in the *social* space—that the phenomena of animation and facialization occur. In this context animism can be best approached as not a belief but an operation that occurs in precise, punctual moments, with crucial morphogenetic import. It is in this sense that we have observed the formative process as a special event of animation. Ultimately, we have suggested, animistic moments represent the immanent blessing of meaning as well as the looming curse of meaninglessness.

Third, we have suggested how the animistic moment, for better or worse, plays a crucial role in the production (and destruction) of territorial orthoforms. The animistic associations might very well be one of the reasons that led territorial scholars to abandon the issue of territorial form in the first place, but in our view such rejection was both too quick and too absolute. In fact, territorial formation often proceeds through animistic moments, although this might be forgotten afterward. The animistic moment is a struggle of life and death, posing the question of what might take life and what might not. This fact becomes evident if we look, as we have proposed in the previous section, at the mundane example of walls in the context of architecture and urban warfare. As apparently humble materials, walls become nonetheless an integral part of social formation and the afforded possibilities of expression.

To conclude, the notion of formation emphasizes that every form is, in fact, a specific (more temporary or more durable) resolution of unstable ensembles of elements (a condition of metastability) or constellations of pregnancies. Because new life forms (including social forms) appear only thanks to the work of pregnances, the *formal* analysis of forms (such as the mathematical, statistical, or topological ones) is not per se sufficient to fully appreciate social life. Here we encounter an intrinsic limit of twentieth-century social theory. An enlarged inquiry into the relations between saliences (visible forms) and pregnances (vital values) remains the crucial question to deepen our understanding of the sociomaterial life of territories.

5 Domesticity and Animation

In this chapter we continue our inquiries into the role of animation in territorializing processes. More specifically, we focus on the notion of domesticity and the home space to look at how multiple borders are constantly produced in the process of territorial formation. As we hope we have made sufficiently clear in earlier chapters, to ask, "What is a domestic territory?" equals asking, "Which are the territorial expressions of domesticity?" By setting our analysis in the regime of the expressive, we inherently attempt to clarify the forces that shape territories. Expressions always result from forces, and the forces expressed by domestic territories in particular are a mix of material, biological, and psychosocial factors, architectonically captured and encapsulated. The domestic domain thus appears as a complex equation that ultimately results in the recognizable phenomenological experience of domesticity. Because expressions are always singular and unique, territoriology entails a veritable *Stimmung* analysis. *Stimmung* (in German—voice, vocation, tendency, special mark, tone of feeling, or mood) is the term employed by Georg Simmel ([1913] 2007) in his philosophy of landscape to address the tension between unity and composition that contradistinguishes each given landscape. Simmel defines *Stimmung* as a "carrier of unity" across the collection of elements contained in a landscape. As such, the notion shares resemblances with the old Latin idea of the genius loci. Both conceptions, as we shall see, speak of a vision of space as radically heterogeneous, made of intensive, discontinuous, unique, and *living* locations.

In the first part of this chapter, we develop the idea of domestic expressions further, touching on notions of dwelling, homeliness, and the unhomely. In the second part we go through a series of anthropological sources and cases of how the home has been animated in mythologies and folk-tales across the world. In the third part we discuss how these animations, seemingly appearing at the limits of control (and sustaining this state of liminality), actually play a crucial role for the ongoing production of the home—they are indeed a way of keeping the question of home alive.

Inquiring into Domestic Expression

In the case of domesticity, we have to consider that uniqueness somehow sits with typification. Domestic territories are recognizable and recognized as such, despite the fact that they may differ greatly in terms of their material buildup and relational arrangements. Home is unique but simultaneously also typical; it as such always has both its *kronic* and its *chronic* (or, perhaps better, chronological) moments. Whereas uniqueness is not transferrable by definition, the typical is recurrent and frequent. In this sense frequentation is the proper not only spatial but also *temporal* dimension of home, its constitutive *rhythm*. Home is a frequented territory; it is appropriated, incorporated, and in the end produced as a singularized unity and a non-exchangeable place. Yet it also borrows its strength and stability from territorial associations to other homes as well as appropriations made by other parts of the family (home comrades), neighbors, friends, and so on. In a sense a home is always a complex territorial conglomerate, and although it is co-constituted by and with the world outside of the home (Steinbock 1995, 182), liminal borders and zones between home and nonhome do not just surround the home but are written all over the territorial conglomerate. These interrelations between what Anthony Steinbock (1995, 255) calls the "homeworld" and the "alienworld" (the nonhome) are also what deepens the home as a home. The home is nothing like a fort; instead, it thrives on liminal encounters (Turner 1982), and it is thus no wonder that the study of threshold rites has a long history (Trumbull 1896; Van Gennep [1909] 2011; Turner 1969; Bourdieu 1972). Homemaking and domestication are part of social and cultural relations in multicultural societies (Boccagni and Brighenti 2015) and have bearings on both the private and the public spaces of the city. In this context domestication is seen as something that alludes to the taming of the world (Mandich and Cuzzocrea 2016, 225), involving the making of a home space either inside or outside private dwellings (Koch and Latham 2013).

The typification of domestic territories is usually mirrored in the fact that the definition of domesticity tends to be elaborated in customary legal terms. The domestic is, in a sense, the quintessential space of customary law. Home is the space of implicit law, a basic law of repetition, and a force of reproduction. But radical legal scholars such as Roderick Macdonald (2002) have revealed how the domestic realm can also be a space of legal inventiveness and change. For her part the anthropologist Mary Douglas (1991) has placed a certain organizational and even institutionalizing concern at the basis of the idea of home. Yet approaching domestic territories through an analysis of forces, as we are suggesting, means looking for further explanations that necessarily stretch beyond the domain of custom, law, rules, and institutions. Contrary to either legalistic or organizational definitions of home, in this piece we approach domesticity as a phenomenon grounded in an ongoing negotiation with the limits of control and in a series of experiences that come to term with such limits. Most important, limits are not merely neutral layouts or fault lines. On the contrary, they embody a living phenomenon, signifying precisely the concretion and concentration of forces that express the domestic.

We can find a vivid illustration of such a clash of forces in Sigmund Freud's (1919) famous essay on *The Uncanny. Das Unheimliche* in Freud's title is a nominalized adjective that cannot be easily translated. Literally, it signifies the unhomely, yet it encompasses the unfriendly, untamed, weird, and frightening. Freud himself wants to go beyond a simple equation of the uncanny and the unfamiliar. Instead, he suggests that the uncanny is the emotional tone that marks the inadvertent, sudden *return* of repressed psychic contents. Far from being unfamiliar, the unhomely is in fact the all too familiar, as it corresponds to an original psychic component, which has undergone superegoic submission—so that it now appears in an estranged guise, generating anxiety. From this point of view, the domestic is not the opposite of the uncanny; rather, it incorporates it. Famously, for Freud home is also the territory where the Oedipal drama is consumed. A specific dimension of return cannot be severed from the production of unhomely feelings. In an interesting anecdote Freud recounts an autobiographic experience of spatial uncanniness resulting from getting lost in a foreign city and continually returning to the same street despite his best efforts to escape the place. If the city itself was not familiar to Freud (it was not a homely space in the first place), what really provoked the unhomely feeling in him was the recurrence of unwanted returns to the same place he was trying to avoid or escape from. Such returns certainly signal a lack of mastery of sort—geographic or psychic.

More generally, these considerations seem to lend support to our argument that the unhomely is not the opposite of home feeling. On the contrary, home inevitably contains its own hidden dimension of always-present creeping estrangement. Between home feeling and the unhomely there is no direct opposition but rather a small difference, often activated by barely perceptible changes of light. Our argumentative strategy thus proceeds in this direction. Instead of identifying home space with the register of the familiar, we emphasize how home necessarily includes both the familiar and the unfamiliar, as well as their constant negotiations carried out in a region at the limits of control. What the uncanny evokes is the existence of strangeness inside familiarity or, even better, the strangeness *of* familiarity—an invisible, deep crack in the regime of the familiar that suddenly, for unclear reasons, becomes visible and inevitable. Inhabiting home necessarily entails similar moments when home loses familiarity, and spatial, organizational, and legal mastery can no longer be firmly established.

Scholarship on the cultural and phenomenological meanings of dwelling has provided crucial insights into the practice and the imagination of inhabitation, especially if we look at the phenomenological tradition that derives from authors such as Martin Heidegger ([1951] 1971) and Gaston Bachelard (1957). Whereas Heidegger contends that dwelling is a prolongation of the original gesture of building and entertains a special relation with the theoretical side of existence, Bachelard relates home to a feeling he calls *être abrité* (being protected). For Bachelard to develop a study of *habiter* (inhabiting or dwelling) means in the first place to develop a phenomenology of protected intimacy. Not only persons and bodies but the unconscious itself is *logé* (lodged). Home holds an integrative power that brings together its material features and the immaterial components of memory and imagination. That is why Bachelard designates his approach as "topo-analysis," a peculiar mixture of psychoanalysis and spatial analysis that he conceives as a tool to penetrate deeply into the meaning of lived spatial experience. In the last part of this chapter, we come back to the imaginative and commemorative power of home, to establish a firmer connection with the phenomenon of animation. In any case an interesting point on which Bachelard insists is that the feeling of protection can be created by very different material setups. In our view this idea does not necessarily downplay the role of materiality; rather, it is a matter of ascertaining the specific linkage that exists between the materials of the house and the forces of home. The most precious indication that comes from phenomenology to our present discussion is the nonreductionist stance that contradistinguishes an adequate approach to domestic territories.

During the twentieth century philosophical approaches to homeliness and the unhomely have echoed across the social sciences and architecture. Notably, in architecture the concept of home became important in the, often phenomenologically grounded, critique of modernist housing during the 1970s and 1980s. The distinction between home and house was much stressed, for example, distinguishing homelessness and housing problems as two different things: one might have a house but not feel at home in it; one might have a home but no house (Dovey 1985; Wikström 1994). Creating shelters or houses might be a territorial strategy, but insofar as it is not subsequently appropriated and associated as a home, it might seem more like a way of institutionalizing people than of "giving them a home," something that never can be done by an external part (Steinbock 1995, 233). Although often related to strategies and tactics of owning, renting, or squatting (i.e., of a more intentional territorial claiming), a home is produced through dwelling (Latimer and Munro 2009) and can be primarily described as a complex process of multiple territorializations through the expression of feelings. Homeworlds thus intersect to form complex relations as the spatial-temporal borders and the threshold of the home changes. That is why, as noted earlier, a territoriological analysis must encompass phenomenology but also span beyond it, to include the larger ecological, material, and systemic dimensions in which domestic experience is inserted. The aim of territoriology is also to advance toward an understanding of the *life* of home, not reduced to either biological or imaginative production. One way to advance such an inquiry is by focusing on the unhomely domestic phenomenon of the elusive others living with us.

The Elusive Others Living with Us

The history of cities could be recounted as a story of parasites. In the case of the United States, for instance, Dawn Day Biehler (2013) has reconstructed an interesting history of pest control (notably, flies, bedbugs, German cockroaches, and Norway rats) as a branch of urban governance. What emerges from this and other similar studies is a cultural conceptualization of pest animals as crowds and swarms that must be managed biopolitically—that is, as living aggregates. This is also typical, to take another example, of pigeons (Escobar 2014; Jerolmack 2013). Pests and stray urban animals alike are regularly treated as anonymous populations of parasites usually to be searched, confined, or destroyed (Holmberg 2015). From a theoretical perspective, Michel Serres (1980) first envisaged a whole philosophy of parasitism, revealing how the parasite embodies a general economic phenomenon—namely, the tendency to appropriate resources before they are directed elsewhere (e.g., taking the cow's milk before the calf). Parasitism can thus be generally conceptualized as consumer-resource interaction grounded in a halfway collection that interrupts the previous link between the source (energy) and the receiver.

If we move closer to home territories, it is not difficult to find parasitism. Traditional houses have always been afflicted by pests. These are essentially defined by the fact of being out of control inside a space supposed to be placed under a general management (such as the customary law discussed earlier). In other words, houses have always been complete ecologies with many uncoordinated actors living within them. But our argument is that the ecological view needs to be complemented: such is the ambition of territoriology. We insist that home cannot be understood as a merely organizational diagram, as it inherently evokes a spiritual notion. The ecological perspective is useful, in that it highlights how relationships always revolve around resources, but it remains partial. We also need to take into account that home is populated by not only pests but all sort of *presences*. From the Latin *lararii* (domestic shrines for statues representing the deities of the family) to the Japanese *kamidana* (household Shinto altars), home presents itself as a territory of spirits, in many cases ancestral spirits. Home exists as not only a stock of resources but also a community of homely spirits. It is inhabited by not only the living but also the dead. In many civilizations across the globe, at the intimate core of each house is a small temple (*edicula*), a sacred and isolated place where the ancestors are requested (and enticed) to reside.

More generally, we are facing various sorts of spiritual crowds, as either pests or spirits. The word *crowd* is apposite here, insofar as crowds are social formations that cannot be forced into an individual-based or person-level order (Brighenti 2014a). Crowds are swarms and populations that can only be figured collectively. Anthropology teaches us that the home is populated by peculiar crowds positioned vis-à-vis the regular human inhabitants of the house. These crowds are, so to speak, located at the thresholds of humanity: they are humanoid crowds. More specifically, in this section we would like to examine the particular manifestation of the little humans. Such miniature humanoid creatures are well attested in traditional mythologies and folktales in different civilizations. Ethnographic information is also available on this phenomenon.[1]

In central Asia, for instance, the anthropologists Grégory Delaplace and Rebecca Empson (2007), collecting and comparing in particular two stories from different parts of Mongolia, have documented the presence of little humans (*jijig hün* or *ongon*). In both cases a daughter-in-law rids the house of one such little human, but in one case it causes the family of the house to prosper, while in the other it inadvertently causes the death

Domesticity and Animation

of her natal family. Both cases use the little human to tell about becoming part of a new family and the progressive, more or less successful integration of the daughter-in-law into her new home. There are a couple of very interesting aspects that characterize the relation between ordinary human inhabitants and the little people. First, a matter of individuality: the little humans are a kind of multiple creature. Perhaps, this fact is not unrelated with their very smallness, as if reduced size operates as a deindividualizing factor. We are thus once again led back to the idea of a population or spiritual crowd, instead of individual members with proper names. Second, a matter of visibility: not only are the *jijig hün* not very visible in general, but their visibility is selective in a meaningful way. They can be seen only in glances, not continuously—with the eye's tail, so to speak. In both stories the only human who can catch sight of the little humans is the daughter-in-law—that is, a new bride and little more than a girl who is in need of acceptance at her new in-law's family. In this sense the selective visibility of the little humans emphasizes status differences within the home. The daughter-in-law is representative of a special class of beings "who can see with their eyes" (*nüdeer yumüzdeg hün*), which also includes infants and horses—arguably, particularly sensitive creatures.[2]

Another country where the little humans are recorded is Japan. An excursus into this country can be mediated by the sort of contemporary mythological storytelling encapsulated in *manga* and anime productions. Studio Ghibli's 2010 anime *The Secret World of Arrietty*, in particular, tells the story of an encounter with the invisible "small people" inhabiting human houses. The anime itself is based on a 1952 novel by the British writer Mary Norton. But the original term employed by director Hiromasa Yonebayashi is *karigurashi*. In his commentary Aaron Gerow (2010) usefully explains,

> The Japanese word in the title, *karigurashi*, refers first to living through borrowing (*kari* 借り = borrow; *kurashi* = living). But the phonemes "kari" can also refer to hunting (狩り), which is played out in the film through Pod's hunts for things to borrow, and the figure of Spiller as the primitive huntsman. Borrowing then becomes a more active, if not aggressive

endeavor, one that eventually becomes embodied in an Arrietty who refuses just to move away once discovered by Shō, and seeks out a more positive, negotiated existence. Perhaps this makes her more like the Miyazaki *shojo* heroine, always on the cusp of adulthood, learning to take command. But the "kari" in "karigurashi" can also refer to "temporary" (仮), as if not only their residence, but also the states of being of the little people are provisional. In fact, I think the real emotional center of the film, the beautifully evoked small story of the love between Arrietty and Sho, is that much more powerful because it is transitory from the start. (Para. 6)

The karigurashi are thus pictured as tiny people who make their living by borrowing (or hunting) small scraps of sugar and bread (but also, according to their needs, nails and paper) from human kitchens. Later we discuss various aspects that emerge from the specific meaning of the term, as interpreted by Gerow, notably the characters of temporariness, parasitism, and hunting.[3] For now we content ourselves with noticing how the karigurashi might be remindful—at least to some extent—of the *koropokkuru*, the minute creatures known to the indigenous Ainu people of Hokkaido. Like the *jijig hün* and the karigurashi, the *koropokkuru* are known to be exceedingly shy. A legend relates that they have become practically invisible since the time of a mythic accident involving a young Ainu man who captured a *koropokkuru* girl. The condition of the *koropokkuru* is, however, remarkably different from the karigurashi, in that the former appear to have constituted an entire parallel people. They are said to be not only small but also coarse and primitive and living in pit dwellings—to the point that some anthropologists conjectured they could have existed as an extinct native people side by side with the Ainu themselves. In any case what is interesting is that the relation between the Ainu and the *koropokkuru* is based on gifts and offerings—a point to which we shall return later.

In Russia the house spirits are known as *domovoj* or *djäduschka domovoj*. They were often associated with fire and made their home where there are ovens and fireplaces. Henry Clay Trumbull tells us how blood sacrifices in the form of meat were buried under the doorstep to please the *domovoj*.

Domesticity and Animation

This was done during the annual Death Week, which was a festival marking the beginning of spring (Trumbull 1896, 19). Gunnar Landtman recounts that, in Belarus, a rooster was sacrificed to the *domovoj* during the building of a new house. The rooster was buried on the spot of the new building, often in the corners of the house. Sometimes a rooster was also cooked to mark the initiation of a new fireplace. As a later reminiscence of these blood sacrifices, human nails and hair were sometimes placed in different cracks in the corners of a house (1922, 18–19, 27).

Moving farther west, similar phenomena are known in the Mediterranean area. In southern Italy, for instance, the tiny creatures known as *monachicchi, monacicchi, monacelli,* or *munaceddi* are a common presence.[4] In a memoir of his forced stay as a political exile in a small village in southern Italy during the 1930s, *Cristo si è fermato a Eboli* (Christ stopped at Eboli), Carlo Levi ([1945] 2013) vividly describes *I Monachicchi di Grassano* as follows:

> They are tiny, little creatures—merry, airy creatures running here and there. They delight themselves with procuring all sorts of annoyances to Christians: they tickle sleeping men under their feet, lift the blankets from the beds, throw sand grains in the eyes, upturn wine glasses, disguise themselves in the air currents to better shuffle all the papers; they drag laundered suits to the ground and filth them, pull the chairs from beneath women's bottoms, hide things in the most unpredictable places, make milk curdle; they pinch you and pull your hair, buzzing and hissing like mosquitoes, and by night entangle the horses' hair and tails. (138; our translation)

As can be noticed from the list of their preferred mischiefs, these characters are deeply ingrained in the global physical (falling, shuffling) and biological (fermenting, rotting) processes that affect the household. The Neapolitan version is known as *munaciello*. In her *Legends of Naples*, Matilde Serao (1881) collects a story that is probably not very old, although it is purportedly set in the late fifteenth century. The munaciello was a dwarf man, son of a forbidden love between the daughter of a bourgeois family and a young man from the lower classes. He was hanging around in Naples dressed up like a monk because his mother had sought refuge in a monastery. The poor creature was insulted, persecuted, and vilified, and news spread about his supernatural powers. Serao, who was particularly sensitive to the topic of urban transformations, locates the munaciello's actions specifically in the inner city of Naples, in the narrow alleys of the popular neighborhoods where the underclass dwell. A series of further accidents continue to be attributed to the action of the munaciello, who returns in spirit after his death. Although in the earlier part of his career, the munaciello seems to be more of an urban dweller than a domestic ghost, a shadowy outcast wandering in the dark alleys, in his afterlife he is defined more in terms of accidents in the domestic economy:

> Whenever the good housewife finds the larder's door opened wide, the lard's package broken, the oil's jar upturned, and the ham bitten by the cat, it is surely the malice of the *munaciello* that has unlocked the door and caused the mess. Whenever the absentminded maid lets the tray fall and the glasses crash into a thousand splinters, it is the pert spirit who made her stumble; it is him who badly hits the gentle young lady's elbow, who pricks the finger of the knitters; him who makes the broth overflow from the pan and the coffee from the *cogoma*; him who makes the wine turn acid in the bottles; him who makes the hen languish and perish; him who uproots the parsley, yellows the majoram, and crunches the basil's leaves. (172–73; our translation)

While the pattern is similar to the *monachicchi*, the Napolitan version contemplates heavier damages, probably mirroring the tough living conditions of the inner districts of large cities in modern times. But the effects of the munaciello can also be favorable. Just as in central Asia, the munaciello can hardly be seen except by young ladies and children, and those who catch sight of him should better keep the episode secret, for they can be rewarded with a lot of luck and wealth.

In Scandinavian folktales the little humans are known as *tomtar* (*tomte* in singular) or *tomtenissar*, a kind of house deity named after the domain where they reside (*tomt* in Swedish means "house lot," "plot," or "building site"). Tomtar are related to Russian *domovoye* (pl.) but are perhaps more often related to nature and the land than to the fireplace (Landtman 1922).[5] Tomtar are quick-tempered, melancholic, vain, old-world creatures in gray clothes who guard (the order and prosperity of) the house and farm (Hyltén-Cavallius 1863, 206). Their form is quite elusive. Although they often take the form of old men of the size of a four- to six-year-old children (see fig. 11), they can take on a number of different shapes, such as that of old or young women or younger warriors. Sometimes they are described as having one eye like Cyclopes; sometimes they are without a head; in the first-known Swedish depiction of them from 1555, they look almost like small devils (Magnus 1555, 127). They can appear as animals, such as toads, sheep, calves, or seals, and at times they can even take the form of dead things such as tree logs or houses (Hyltén-Cavallius 1863, 204; Landtman 1922, 2–3; Schön 2006, 17–19). Tomtar live on the premises of houses or farms (and they are, in contrast to *munacielli*, primarily rural creatures) but often reside in one of the more hidden spaces, such as hearths, barns, or sheds; under the floors; or in attics. Landtman (1922, 9–23) has suggested that the origins of *tomtarna* (pl. definite) are the natural deities (*vättar*, *troll*, *skogsrån*, *underbyggare*, *bäckahästar*, and so forth) of Scandinavian folklore—the ones responsible for house lots and all that happens there. Although they are most commonly found in connection to homes, tomtar have also been known to reside in such places as ships, churchyards, mills, mountains, islands, trees, springs, and so forth.

In the 1360s Bridget of Sweden wrote about tomtar as a kind of God, *tompta gudh*, and—without in anyway questioning their existence—forbade peasants to pay them the tithe, the tax that should go to the church (Ehrensvärd 1979, 6). From the sixteenth century the description of tomtar as deities or God became less common, and they were often referred to as *tomtenisse* or *tomtegubbe*. But tomtar as creatures "other to," or even in opposition to, Christianity was never abolished, and tributes were paid to them well into the twentieth century. Usually this was done during important events, such as harvest times, birthdays, and certain holidays, especially Christmas. The tribute was often paid in the form of food (preferably porridge), liquor (*brännvin*), tobacco, and even in new clothes.

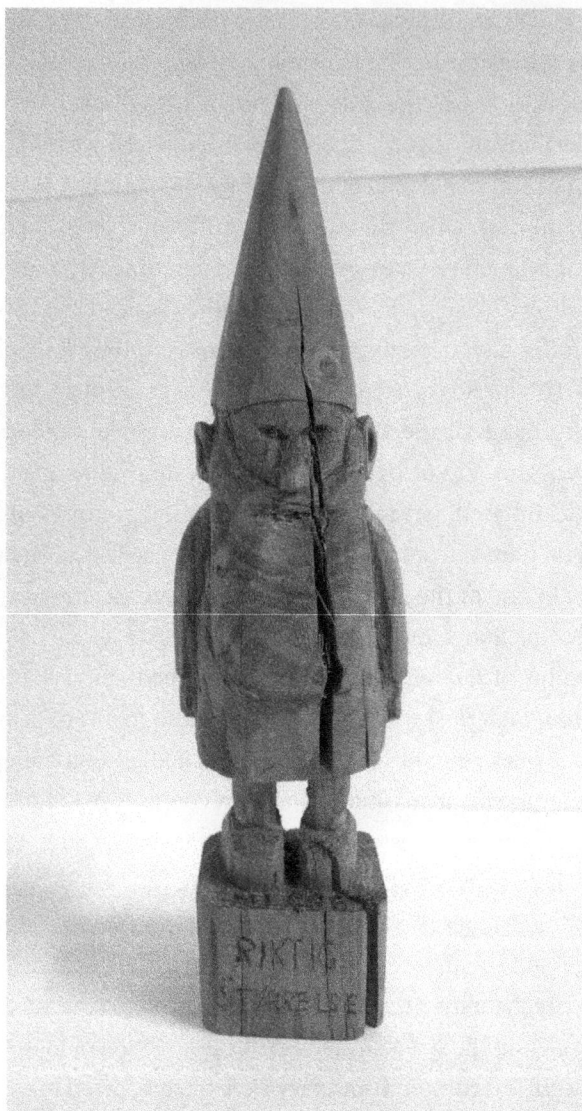

11. A wooden sculpture of a tomte. Made for the exhibition *I sagans värld* (In the world of the saga), 1983–84. Courtesy of Karlsborgs Fästningsmuseum, Sweden.

There can be no doubt that tomtarna were territorial actors. They took care of farms and animals and protected inhabitants from misfortune, thus belonging to a category of Scandinavian creatures called *råde* (which translates into the one mastering, managing, or caring for). A relative of tomtarna is also *rågubben*, who dwells at the border between different farm territories (in Swedish this border is called the *rå*), guarding its sanctity (Landtman 1922, 13). Tomtar thus guarded farms against evils and mishaps, patrolling the territory. In Swedish there is also a verb, *tomta*, which refers to the practice of walking around without doing anything in particular. But just as much as tomtarna protected territory from outsiders and threats, they guarded the behavior of the inhabitants and thus came to play an important part in the co-production of the territorial order of homes. They were said to punish farmers who mistreated their animals, and they were also used to threaten children so that they would not misbehave. Tomtar could also play a part in temporal regulations, especially in relation to working hours. Farmers were not to work in the barns after eight o'clock in the evening during wintertime, nor to make sound during the night or wake up too late in the morning, as this would upset tomtarna. These rules often had a practical function, as they were minimizing the use of lanterns in barns and sheds, where things could catch fire, as well as securing a night's sleep and a day of work (Schön 2006, 93–95).

Tomtar also played their part in interterritorial relations. It was not uncommon for them to steal bread or even livestock from other farms, and there are also stories about regular fights between *tomtenissar* of different homes and farms (Schön 2006, 59). Tomtar were sometimes used as marks of bad behavior. A bad family was believed to have an evil tomte (one that, for example, took the milk from cows or sucked the blood out of livestock), and people who ran into luck or fortune might be accused of having a tomte. The tomte was thus an important part in the production of discipline, from self-discipline to the raising of children, the handling of animals, and even the social relations between farmers.

Tomtar can perhaps be described as animations of the territorial rules and associations of homes. As noted earlier, the territorial production of the home does not work like a light switch—that is, when the house or dwelling becomes a home remains an open question—and neither is there any definite answer to the question of when a house gets its tomte. Some stories claim that the tomte is there from the beginning or that it arrives as soon as the first corner stone is laid. Others claim that the tomte arrives when the first layer of timber is put in place, when the first oven or fireplace is built, when the first fire is lit, or when the first meal is eaten (Landtman 1922, 31). Other stories inform us that farmers have to bribe the tomte to get it to their farm (or, alternatively, to get rid of it) or even go through certain blasphemous rituals (Schön 2006, 32–36).

In contrast to the Mongolian examples examined by Delaplace and Empson (2007) or the Italian munaciello, the visibility of tomtar does in general not depend on who is seeing them, although they often remain invisible to humans.[6] Much like the wild animals, they tend to see us before we see them. In short, tomtar can be seen as disciplinary figures (although they are of course themselves also the subject of a domestication: domesticized natural deities). They are actors who allow for the forming of regular customs and rules, a rhythm of appropriation rituals, including not just the main spaces of the house but also its peripheral annexes. Tomtar help in coping with catastrophes, either as active helpers or as scapegoats. Through their ability to produce mishaps as well as feelings of fear or unease, they give the unjust or the unhomely a face and a name, explaining the unexplainable.

Patterning Relations and the Limits of Control

In the previous section we have collected a number of ethnographic examples concerning the little humans and their domestic emplacement. Admittedly, these cases are far from systematic, and their overall anthropological significance might remain open to differing interpretations. Certainly, we do not claim for any conclusive evidence. Nonetheless, we believe that they provide for a richer understanding of the expressions of domesticity. To begin with we have defined the little humans as elusive others to stress how they are characterized by an attitude of avoidance, if not bafflement, vis-à-vis the regular inhabitants. As we have seen, there are differences

Domesticity and Animation

as to how the little humans relate to humans. For instance, whereas the karigurashi try to live a separate, fleeting existence, the *monachicchi* and the tomte engage more actively with humans in their everyday domestic life. Also the former are contradistinguished by three interlocked yet notably distinct if not contradictory elements: borrowing, hunting, and existing temporarily. It is an interesting triad that speaks of the temporality and orderliness of the house.

In general, it seems as if the little humans are parasites. They take or crave for food and drink such as milk and porridge and also liquor and tobacco, but in their own peculiar ways they also engage in securing supplies for the future, both for themselves and the household. It is in this double role that they become a part of the household itself. It is particularly striking to compare the condition of little humans to human-animal relationships. For instance, in a fascinating ethnography of monkey capture in Delhi, Ajay Gandhi (2012) has remarked how, while simians are seen as food thieves (and thus captured and encaged), they are in fact also inserted in an important ritual chain of food offerings: "A person received *punya*—a diffuse, cleansing merit from God—by feeding monkeys. People bought fruit and placed it where monkeys gathered. Through this *dan* or gift, volatile energies were harnessed for one's protection. . . . The menace that monkeys embodied—removing clothes from laundry lines, invading kitchens in search of snacks, rifling through papers in offices—was mirrored by the function of feeding. One sought to placate an unstable being through a ritual of supplication" (2012, 45, 52).

Although the little humans are not always helpful or friendly, and in fact, as we have seen, they can easily ruin the household, strictly speaking they cannot be characterized as enemies, in the sense that it is difficult to envisage any direct confrontation with them. Precisely their elusive nature contributes to prevent such a clash. Indeed, elusiveness might be an important dimension from which the experience of domesticity can be observed. Rather than a position of struggle or war (declared against other types of pests), what we have to do with here is a more subtle relation of antagonism cum complicity, if not ambivalent alliance. As in the human-simian case described by

Gandhi, between stealing and offering there is an actual mirroring, albeit an inverted one. True, the tomte can steal livestock and demand a tribute of food or drink, the *munacicchi* can make milk curdle, and the *jijig hün* can make family members perish. But simultaneously, a sense of striking similarity cannot be denied between us and them. In fact, the little humans look almost like us: these humanoids are practically a double of humans.[7] The problem is that, contrary to human socialization, it is impossible to subsume the little humans under a firm normative order. Even various animal species can be tamed, but the little humans cannot. Certainly—and, it seems, especially in the *tomtenisse* version—the little humans are susceptible to a sense of honor and thus, a fortiori, a rough, legalistic scheme of sort (notably, a vendetta or revenge code). Nonetheless, the position of these creatures in the domain of law remains marginal and tangential.

Probably, this fact can be explained with reference to their crowd existence. Of course, the little humans do not always move about in crowds. But except for certain specific literary renditions, they tend to form a nameless, faceless population that can be recognized only by its uniform, forming a distinct yet collective category or class of beings.[8] As hinted at earlier, the crowd effect has to do with the little humans' unruly nature. In many cases the tiny creatures are perceived as unwanted but unavoidable presences; in other cases they are even regarded as securing the (sometimes unmerited and extraordinary) prosperity of the house. Regardless of whether they appear more as a welcome presence or one only reluctantly accepted, the tiny creatures hint at a series of playful and funny, and at the same time threatening and uncontrollable, aspects of home territories (neither fortune nor misfortune, as we know, can be planned). Precisely in this sense, they are revelatory of the expression of domesticity. Home territories cannot be fully planned, owing to both a plurality of actors and a weak determination of boundaries. Just as the house is not severed from its outside, its surroundings, and the alienworld, so its inner order cannot be severed from its own immanent disorder.

It is through thresholds and borders that the homeworld and the alienworld are produced, not as two separated domains but as porous and

Domesticity and Animation

multilayered territorial conglomerates. This is also the idea we have suggested to retrieve from Freud's notion of *Unheimlichkeit*. The control of the home emanates as much from its nooks and crannies, its hidden spaces (Korosec-Serfaty 1984). These in-between spaces allowing for overlapping and unprogrammed uses (cf. Bettelheim 1950, 117) are vital for the home, as they provide places of play, adventure, secrecy, shelter, security, accumulation, and affluence. The little humans can be seen as a figuration of this relation, playing a fundamental role in the proper temporality of the house. The places they attend are places endowed with a peculiar character (in fact, a peculiar *Stimmung*). They are *folds* where life can be stabilized, allowing for at least a partial planning of the home; for the storage of food, drink, and tools for future use; and for things to be saved as well as lost and forgotten (Korosec-Serfaty 1984, 317). The house is not a home, yet its spatial and material structure is of course important to dwelling. It sets bodily relations, and it co-produces possibilities of visibility and invisibility, stability, and transformation.

During the modernist era, especially post-1850, the home was increasingly reduced to become "exclusively a place for eating, sleeping, raising children and enjoying leisure" (Forty 1986, 101); above all, it became a place devoid of work (Forty 1986, 99; Rybczynski 1986). During the nineteenth and twentieth centuries, the functional borders of the home—that is, the activities and room types placed in or outside its borders—were also continuously changing. In the Scandinavian countries, as in many other places of modernization, rooms and functions that formerly were located outside the dwelling itself, like places for food, bathing, laundry, latrines, and so forth, now moved inside the dwelling. New technology also meant that some room types became superfluous; their functions were no longer needed or could be integrated into other rooms. This decrease in secondary spaces outside the home proper continued slowly throughout the twentieth century. During the 1930s and 1940s, storages in cellars decreased, as refrigerators and freezers became more common and fresh food could be bought all year round. Activities once performed in the home were executed in other neighborhoods, cities, regions, or even countries (sites of production formerly in the home might, for example, have moved to the other side of the world).

During the modernization and urbanization of the twentieth century, when places of work and storage were increasingly outsourced, and the nooks and crannies of the home disappeared, the little humans, such as tomtar, also vanished. Domestic spaces became increasingly designed as spaces of circulation, often devoid of cellars and attics, and characterized by enhanced visibility and transparency. But the territorial importance of transitional, interstitial, and hidden spaces where the encounter with the little humans becomes possible, remains. Possibly, there is also a modern dream of attics and cellars, not because of a Bachelardian urge for the verticality of dwelling but because of our need for a more multifaceted temporality, a polytemporality that also allows for new formations and animations to emerge in the domestic realm.

Many little humans lost the battle against modernization, but not all of them: the Icelandic parallel to tomtar, the *huldufólk* or *álfar*, seem to be an exception (Árnason, Hafsteinsson, and Grétarsdóttir 2007). These creatures live in rocks and are believed to take a horrible revenge if disturbed by modern development projects such as new roads across their land: "Every year hidden people make the news in Iceland in connection with building projects taking place near their homes. Projects run into trouble, machinery breaks down mysteriously or workers suffer injury . . . in cases of what some might refer to as elfish terrorism" (211).

Similarly, Marisol de la Cadena (2015) has recounted how, in Peru, the *tirakuna*, or earth beings, almost undefinable creatures tied to the territory and the soil, have become active actors in the land struggle conducted by the native Quechua people since the 1980s. Perhaps the little humans can be appreciated only with a touch of animistic sensitivity. They are practical actors in the domestic territory, but they are also milieus, environments of the domestic itself. They form a living atmosphere of the domestic, where agency becomes contested and, in many cases, evaporates. As we have observed, stories concerning the little humans also often take place in the kitchen, in the vicinity of the stove or the fireplace. This is hardly a coincidence, given that these are the places where the element of fire is located. The life of fire—a domesticated yet always dangerous creature—is of the same animated order as the life of the little humans and no less than the shadows of the cellar and the dust of the attic. One could not understand much about domestic fire and shadows reducing them to mere "actors." All sorts of physical and biological processes affect domestic territories. These are natural processes, yet a distinct perception of aliveness is also present in them. Where does this mess come from? It's natural, but it's magic: it is natural magic, a secret domain of animation. Today the elective domestic spaces of secrecy have moved into cupboards, balconies, and computers or to externalized spaces such as rented storage spaces and garages. Consequently, we have new kinds of animation games both similar and different from the little humans. The animistic moment—that is, when the things "come to life"—is today as always a mundane experience. Computers might die or behave erratically; stored things pile up and grow almost organically; just like the unwanted life of spiders, mice, and silverfish, dust brings forward its formless mode of existence.[9] As we know, computers, parasitical animals, and large quantities of accumulated things can threaten the integrity of the house as well as the physical and especially mental health of its inhabitants.

In this sense the presence of dust and parasites, just as the little humans, has to do with the expression of tiresomeness that affects home in its relentless yet doomed search for order and control. Hannah Arendt famously opposed labor to work, associating the former to the household and the second to the workshop. It is not only a matter of spatial demarcation, though. Labor corresponds to the endless effort of reproduction and maintenance that, by definition, is cyclical and can never be accomplished. Labor has no output; it involves no evident product, no oeuvre. This is why the classics held such a contemptuous view of labor as being specifically a slavish activity: "to labor meant to be enslaved by necessity"; "it is indeed the mark of all laboring that it leaves nothing behind, that the result of its effort is almost as quickly consumed as the effort is spent" (1958, 83, 87). So the domestic inhabitants are certainly ecological actors in a complex system, but they are also *subjected* actors. The domestic realm is the realm of private property, but in the first place property subjects the owners to its own maintenance against decay. Each distraction, each slip of the eye—which is inevitable, just as labor itself—animates the household to an independent *unheimlich* life.

Homes, Borders, Encounters

Our hypothesis is that the ways in which the little humans can be encountered and interacted with reveal something important about domesticity itself and its proper expressive regime. In particular, the formation of home is an ongoing attempt, never settled once and for all. Home territories are not so much domesticated territories as they are territories where domestication occurs as a sustained and incomplete attempt. The domestic would not exist without the process of domestication to which tame animals, the newborn, and ultimately also adults must be subjected. The role of food is quintessential in domestication—also considering that food figuratively stands for a more general issue of access to resources. Food transactions are at the core of a general domestic economy, and they are the place where parasitism manifests. The little humans, as we have seen, steal food, just like mice and other parasites. But their condition evokes more closely that of the newborn baby as well as, to some extent, that of every new member of a family group. All these subjects, in many respects, rely entirely on the regular members for feeding. As Serres (1980) first stressed, parasitism essentially defines a condition of radical nonreciprocity, and that is arguably why, from a moral point of view, the figure of the parasite looks so troubling to us. Spatial occupation of domestic territories inherently raises the question of moral legitimation. In fact, most of our efforts in house management are aimed at asserting some sort of reciprocity, perhaps precisely because in this respect the little humans are not easy to come to terms with.

Food is energy, but also morality. Indeed, in all the stories we have studied, food is always both an object to be stolen and an offering to be served. This way a spiritual meaning comes to be ingrained in the whole economic cycle. Domestic economy is always more than economy: through offerings to the little humans, it bears a religious significance. The existence of such a minor, domestic religion (very different from official state religion) marks the fact that the expression of domesticity is written not only in the domain of activity but more specifically in the register of *presence* (and, as such, also connected to *grace*). Domesticity is perhaps above all about recurrent presences or gifts. It is about food on the table, a night in bed, and the reencounter with family members and objects of affection; it is about the manifold ways in which home can reoccur and through this very repetition establish a "same." Food thus has a potentiality to induce both ties and ruptures in domestic negotiations (Counihan 1999, 156–60). Here is also why animated moments with little humans are important: in their double role of parasites and family members, they confirm both the value and the meaning of home. They help in the domestication of specific unhomely events, but at the same time they keep the notion of an alienworld alive inside the very borders of home. Through their peculiar way of domesticating and animating the unfamiliar and the unwanted, they secure the home as an ongoing and incomplete process; through their contribution to diversity and the possibility of presences, they contribute to the richness of the home as vibrant and multifaceted singularity.

The home is always a space of many borders, or, rather, it is a living territory whose borders change over time. The multiple borders and boundaries of a single territory might overlap or even be discontinuous, yet as its palimpsestic life unfolds (and as long as it keeps on doing precisely this), there can be no doubt of its meaningful and productive existence.

6 Territorializing Rhythms

Fernand Braudel has a short but telling example of how the knowledge of everyday rhythms might play into the hands of territorial intruders: "Algerian pirates were able to take Gibraltar by surprise in 1540 because they knew all the customs of the place and chose the time of the grape harvest. All the inhabitants were outside the walls, sleeping in their vineyards" (1974, 378). The rhythms of harvesting grapes, just as the rhythms of urban and rural life in general, are territorialized and stabilized in different ways. In agrarian societies these rhythms are predictable insofar as they are based on the cycle of seasons. But just as rhythms play a part in the processes of territorialization, conversely, territories also produce and affect rhythms. Territories are profoundly enmeshed with rhythms: from the animal patrolling its territory and returning recurrently to certain pivotal spots, to the Muzak diffused in the hypermarket designed to set a certain atmosphere and pace for consumption. How can we better specify and articulate such a deep relation between rhythms and territories?

As we noted already in the second chapter, territories evolve when environmental rhythms are made expressive. In this chapter we would like to take this a step further and argue that rhythms, insofar as they are productive repetitions—that is, repetitions that come with embedded differences—are always expressive. In other words, at least from an experiential perspective, all rhythms are to some extent already territorialized; as we start to make sense of our environment, we are already *in the midst of things*, or as Edmund Husserl put it, in *die schon humanisierte Umwelt* of the *Kulturterritorium* (1973, 206).

If rhythms are always territorialized, then rhythmanalysis becomes an essential component for a general territoriology. But this also means that rhythmanalysis, as it has developed over the past decades, cannot stand alone but would rather benefit from becoming part of an integral study of the processes of social formation and territorialization. The important lesson for us is that territories cannot be seen at a glance; they simply do not make sense as merely instantaneous entities, for they are temporal formations. Territories are constituted through rhythms, but concurrently rhythms themselves—as they explicate themselves socially, biologically, or ecologically—cannot but be parts of territorialized endeavors. In addition, following an insight from Gilles Deleuze and Félix Guattari (1980), the life of territories can be said to be not only rhythmic but also *melodic*. From this perspective rhythms do not exhaust the phenomenon of territorialization as a whole. Territories could be seen as refrains of rhythms and melodies joined together. Consequently, lived rhythms are always impregnated with melodies and refrains (cf. also McCormack 2002; Grosz 2008).

The nexus between rhythm and territory lies not only in the coming together of spaces and times but more specifically in the *investments of energy* or the *intensities* that accompany it. For his part Henri Lefebvre acknowledged this fact, writing that "everywhere where there is interaction between a place, a time and an expenditure of energy, there is rhythm" ([1992] 2004, 15). But as we hope to show in the following analysis, rhythmanalysis does not sufficiently clarify the nature of such energetic expenditure. The notions of investment, intensity, and credo are needed as theoretical supplements. What are rhythms an investment in? Ultimately, we submit, rhythms can be regarded as investments in social life as meaning, as measure, and as concerted action. It is, for example, as attempts at synchronization that rhythms have a role to play in social bonding in humans as well as in (other) animals (Launay, Tarr, and Dunbar 2016). The social relation entails the territorialization of social members onto a special stratum characterized by distinctive qualities. Such a stratum, we believe, contains both rhythmic patterns and melodic lines. That is why we need a richer theoretical and analytical framework capable of capturing the specific intensities of the qualitative moments created by rhythms. These singular moments of becoming can be seen as produced by means of more or less salient spaces *and* times as they get caught into a co-constitutive relation—that is, as they become part of territorialization processes.

In the following pages we develop the argument that what we need to attain is neither simply a description of rhythms, nor only an analysis of rhythms. Certainly, these passages are a sine qua non; however, the real goal is to capture the inner life of rhythms as they enter actual territorial formations. Here we again find ourselves in accord with other scholars working with neovitalistic insights, such as Jane Bennett's (2010) critical analysis of vibrant matter, Tim Ingold's (2016) project for a new anthropological vitalism, and Ash Amin's (2015) analysis of the animation of the body-space relationship. Territorial effects and rhythms can never be reduced to human affairs and interactions alone, as other (terrestrial and cosmic, yet social) forces and intensities are entailed. For example, in a specific city, we must consider the ineffable spirit of the city, the *anima urbis* (Wolch 2002) produced by the congregation of animals, crowds, groups, materials, atmospheres, and so forth. As we have argued in the previous two chapters, all sociomaterial involvements potentially imply moments of animation, since personification and actorship often evolve through interaction and not the other way around. Animistic moments are moments of faith, moments of leap when one recognizes the yet-to-be-known forces and figures of an unfolding situation. Consequently, we suggest that the notion of rhythm could be explored not only in terms of the recurrent patterns of the association it defines but also with essential reference to the qualitative singular *intensive situations* to which it corresponds. Our proposal thus consists in an intensification of rhythmanalysis to the point of pushing it beyond itself, to capture the peculiar *eigenstates* created by specific rhythmic steps and melodic lines in social life.

In this chapter we review some notable theorizations of rhythms in the twentieth century, ranging from Émile Durkheim and Marcel Mauss, through Lúcio Alberto Pinheiro dos Santos, Gaston Bachelard, Rudolf Laban, Aby Warburg, Simone Weil and Walter Benjamin, to Henri Lefebvre. This admittedly sketchy attempt of bringing a fragmented field together is important for us, in that it reveals how the tradition of rhythmanalysis

Territorializing Rhythms

is broader than the usual association with the name of Lefebvre alone. We then also point out some insights and some blind spots of Lefebvrian rhythmanalysis, to advance a theoretical discussion that aims to ascertain and clarify the relations between rhythms and synchronizations. The aim of this discussion is to extract a series of analytical points in previous theorizations of rhythm that naturally differ from Lefebvre's. Finally, an elaboration on the notions of intensity, melody, and presence is provided as a key to integrate rhythms and territories.

While one could say that an exhaustive reconstruction of the literature on rhythms would be enough to fill up a book of its own, we emphasize that our treatment of rhythm analytical sources is functional to the laying out of a theoretical space where the notions of life, animation, formation, investment-into-form, and intensity can be brought into a single conversation. Before we go on to this more theoretical analysis of rhythmanalysis and its sources, we would, however, like to begin with another illustration, a mundane example through which some of the stakes of our discussion may emerge. We thus take into consideration the case of walls in cities and then conduct a reconnaissance into the entanglement of qualitative characters and quantitative dimensions that hopefully can help situate some rhythmic peculiarities of territories for the following discussion.

To the Rhythm of Walls

Territories are about boundaries (both in time and space); they are about establishing insides and outsides, and not surprisingly, the one artifact that perhaps most commonly is seen as representing the quintessence of human territoriality in general, and urban territoriality in particular, is the wall. But what is a wall? Most viably, it is a separating device, archetypically made of stones. Although the wall might seem to have mostly spatial effects, its temporal effects are just as important. Territorially speaking, a wall might be a way of dividing not simply people but also different rhythms: urban rhythms from rural rhythms, the rhythms for sleeping from the rhythms of eating, the rhythm of meeting from the rhythm of dispersing. By doing so the wall also "synchorizes" entrance into and exit from certain locations, such as gates or doors.[1] In fact, gates and doors are in themselves but rhythmic walls. The wall can also be a way of delegating the work of territorial patrolling to a material structure or a way to make this same patrolling more continuous, stable, and effective.

Walls and the city have a long, coessentially intertwined history. The urban wall is probably as ancient as the pastoral wall, and cities had walls even before they had streets (Kostof 1992, 26–29). The Italian words *rocca*, *castro*, and *fortezza* and the corresponding English words *stronghold*, *bastion*, and *fortress*, all speak of the coessential relation of the dwelling settlement and the wall (Hirst 1997). In the course of Western history, at least since the late Middle Ages and in Early Modern Europe, the urban wall has constituted perhaps the most representative artifact to define city space—no less representative than the urban gate, itself a rhythmic wall, as we have suggested. The city could then be squarely localized, thanks to the wall that protected it, and it is also through walls that access could be temporally regulated or blocked—for example, during nights, wartimes, plagues, quarantines, and so on. Richard Sennett (1996) has described the urban walls as a technology of immunity, highlighting how institutions such as the lazarettos were located just outside the urban walls to manage the presence of urban outcasts in the city. Philippe Ariès tells us about how the dead were treated in a related way, already during antiquity: "The dead were not to trouble the living or mingle with them. All the same, they were neither banished to some faraway place nor altogether isolated: it was important that one could easily bring them placating offerings or eat and drink close to them. So they were deposited immediately outside the town, at its gates or along the roads leading to it" (1985, 2).

It may here be interesting to compare the location of the dead with that of the little humans in the home that we have examined in chapter 5; the rhythmic play of absence and presence becomes a way to secure the ongoing work of both building (and mediating the relation between) the city of the living and the dead. Analyzing the 1563 treaty titled "On the Fortress City" by Bernard Palissy, Francisco Klauser has suggested that in European history walls have functioned as an integral part of a psychoimmunology

Territorializing Rhythms

of the urban: "The wall, for Palissy, figures as the territorial engagement and mediator of the residents' jointly inhabited life-world" (2010, 327).

During the early modern era, getting inside the city walls could be hard, sometimes impossible. It was not by chance that the Roman army gave a special decoration (*corona muralis*) to the soldier who first climbed the urban wall during the siege of an enemy town. In peaceful times the experience of waiting for the opening of the city gates could be a quite mundane and even a relaxing event as, for instance, described by the traveler William Penn during a visit to Duisburg in 1677:

> Betwixt nine and ten, we reached the walls of Duysburg; but the gates were shut, and there being no houses without the walls, we laid us down together in a field, receiving both natural and spiritual refreshment: blessed be the Lord. About three in the morning we rose, sanctifying God in our hearts that he had kept us that night; and walked till five, often speaking one to another of the great and notable day of the Lord dawning on upon Germany, and of several places of that land that were almost ripe unto harvest. Soon after the clock had struck five, they opened the gates of the city, and we had not long got to our inn. ([1714] 1835, 70–71)

As peaceful as this example might seem, it also shows us how urban gates were acting as a powerful circadian rhythm maker, forcing people coming from and going to the city to synch with its rhythms. The urban wall was an instrument of regular control and validation, where guards at the city gates might take note of the reasons for traveling, the place of origin, and even of the staying address of every traveler entering inside the walls (very much like border police today and post-Covid-19 contact tracing). In Mantua during the sixteenth century, for example, a list of all persons bringing arms inside the walls was daily distributed to all the gates to help the guards keep watch (Maczak 1995, 119). In a way the city walls were thus one of the first tools of policing in the modern sense (Foucault 2004).

From the eighteenth through the twentieth century, the walls of many early modern walled cities were repeatedly torn down and reconstructed in various rounds to be adjusted to the growing urban size. One of the main reasons for this was to accommodate for the new urban rhythms of the industrial society, as well as for the rising bourgeoisie class. The most famous example here is perhaps Vienna: during the late eighteenth century, Emperor Joseph II had already opened the walls to the public, and the defense walls and bastions had quickly become an important destination for recreations, outings, social meetings, and public life among the inhabitants of the city. The administrative and fiscal changes in the wake of the revolution of 1848 made the city walls less important. The lack of housing combined with nationalist aspirations of building public institutions and monuments, inspired by previous projects in London and Paris, finally led Franz Joseph I to tear down the city walls in 1857 (Wulz 1979, 17–42). The Ringstrasse project of Vienna, with its monumental public buildings and large green spaces, exerted a great influence on many European dewalling projects. If Vienna is the most paradigmatic European case of dewalling as an urban development project, the final death of the traditional defensive use of urban walls could perhaps be set to 1870. This was arguably when the last European city wall served an important purpose in battle—that is, when the Aurelian wall of Rome was breached at Porta Pia, just before the Italian unification.

Prolonging the trend of loosening the walled urban perimeter, contemporary urban processes appear to be even more dislocated and scattered on larger suburban territories: in increasingly sprawling urban landscapes, old city gates have been supplanted by shopping malls as new, uncanny city entrances (Kärrholm 2012, 117). Even if the city as a territory seems harder and harder to define as an enclosed and discrete space (Sieverts [1997] 2003), urban territories and walls do, however, still proliferate. In fact, as the city started sprawling into urban regions and found itself no longer surrounded by a single wall capable of demarcating its proper location, an important shift occurred: instead of being embraced by one wall, the city was increasingly fractioned by a number of internal walls. The rationale of these internal walls was, as we know, varied, but one important reason was to allow for different rhythms to coexist within the city, including rhythms of commuting and rhythms of production, reproduction, consumption, and so on.

The spatial separation (desynchorization) of different rhythms could be a way of enabling different activities to coexist within the city (like church-yards, factories, and housing), but it could also be oppressive. Among the first walls for inner urban partition were, for instance, those of the Middle Age Jewish ghetto (Sennett 1996). This partition seems to have worked not just like an urban enclave but more like an urbanized camp (Diken and Laustsen 2006), where especially movement was heavy regulated. The English traveler Fynes Moryson described the ghetto in Venice after a visit in 1594: "The Jews have a place to dwell severally, called Il Ghetto, where each family hath a little house, and all have one court-yard common, so they live as it were in Colledge, or Almes-house; and may not come forth after the gates are locked at night, and in the day they are bound to weare a yellow cap" (1908, 192).

Later, during the course of the nineteenth century, the prototypical inter-nal urban wall also came to be identified with the wall of the disciplinary institution—the prison, the hospital, the school (Foucault 1975). The por-tioning wall was now not just about shelter, visibility, or confinement but also about information and knowledge, and as such it came to play an important part in the production of separate spaces for separate rhythms in the city. Robin Evans, for example, describes the 1836 wall experiments at Millbank Prison in London, where the object was to find the wall that reduced the transmission of information through speaking and shouting rather than noise (1982, 335–38; cf. also Harou-Romain's experiments in the 1840s, reported by Vanderburgh 1994, 327). The tendency to produce spaces of similar rhythms is even stronger in the urban planning of the twentieth century, as different kinds of movements increasingly were separated into different territories.

If territorial and rhythmical control is related to borders and walls, it might involve the tearing down of walls as much as the building of them—that is, rescaling the operations of this control. Territorial (and subsequent rhythmical) rescaling is a well-known strategy used to win an advantage of power and control. In fact, opening gates and demolishing walls has always been part of political struggles and military control. Napoleon, who made several of the conquered European cities tear down their outer defenses (Kostof 1992, 26), went a step further during the invasion of Cairo in 1798, as he tore down a number of interior walls and gates of the city as well. Cairo had a hierarchical system of several territorial levels with local streets and neighbor streets that were locked at night. Napoleon's army tore down the gates to create a continuous public space of flow similar to Paris, from the most public spaces all the way to the front doors of the private houses, thus forcing formerly private or enclosed rhythms of the neighborhood to take place in a more public setting (Habraken 1998, 219; Akbar 1988, 171–72). Napoleon's actions for circulation on Cairo streets was of course famously followed and further improved by Georges-Eugène Haussmann and Napoleon III, as they tore down parts of old Paris for circulation and flow during the mid-nineteenth century. Haussmann's boulevards were then, in turn, countered with a barricade, featured as an iconic "exceptional wall" materialized in the urban landscape to stop the circulation of control; during the Paris Commune in 1871, about six hundred barricades were built on the streets of Paris (Vidler 2011, 109–16). Another example can be seen in the more recent examples of urban warfare in Israel and Palestine, as discussed in chapter 4. The issue of tearing down walls was not so much about producing urban spaces of circulation on the streets as it was through homes, leading the battle inside and through the walls of private houses (Weizman 2007, 185–218; Bleibleh 2015).

As mobilities and rhythms rescale, borders tend to become movable. Consider, for example, the border of the United Kingdom with Europe (well before Brexit), which has been externalized to Calais by the British but would be better seen by the French as located in Kent: in 2016 the then French prime minister Alain Juppé explicitly called for the French-UK border to be moved into Britain (Chrisafis 2016). This fact also alerts us to the multiscalarity or transscalarity of both rhythms and walls, which is essential to comprehend the topology of contemporary politics; for instance, a fence in a certain neighborhood in the city of Belfast can set apart two local communities as well as two national communities and even—when the United Kingdom leaves the EU Customs Union at the end of the post-Brexit transition—two supranational entities (cf. Baliff 2019).

The multiplicity and subdivision of territorial borders becomes clear as new techniques of wall-building evolve (as in the example of R. Evans [1982]). Different partitions set restrictions to what one can hear, smell, and see and where one can go, and these must not always coincide. The senses that interfere in our living bodies are separated; specific percepts become isolated and categorized. Different walls control different aspects and ensure a fine machinery of accountability and measure. Perhaps one could even argue that the development of wall technology has allowed data collecting to replace the use of our perceptive bodies (cf. Serres [1985] 2008). The "stretched door" (Koolhaas, AMO, and Harvard Graduate School 2014, 634) of endless security checks and passport controls at airports is a well-known contemporary example. The separation of different kinds of travelers and goods is often done through technologies specialized in different ways of perceiving, measuring, and sometimes slowing down their moving targets.

Building a wall is usually taken to mean a denial of interaction, expressing anxiety, fear, and even hate toward those who will find themselves on the other side. It can be a way of deflecting certain flows and rhythms, slowing them down or appropriating them for one's own benefit. We should remember, however, that walling is integrally, and has always been, a technology of social interaction and everyday life. In this sense walls are not dumb, deaf, or unilateral; they always entail across-the-wall interactions. Walls of different forms and sizes, such as shop fronts, garden fences, prison walls, neighborhood hedges, planking, and bar counters, are all well-known mediators of social exchanges, enabling and inviting certain interactions while disabling others. Furthermore, if the wall is an instantiation of an "us versus them" dichotomy, wherever the other group or subject is not immediately perceptible or cannot be physically met, it is ipso facto imagined, represented, evoked, or ceaselessly talked about. Even when there is an attempt to forget the other side of the wall, to hide or even erase its rhythmical presence, the absent other is—as psychoanalysis has discovered long ago—an indelible presence, a returning ghost.

Walls are, in short, often the place of a series of intermingling confliction or overlapping territorializations, and as every territory has its rhythms, walls are subsequently also the place of different kinds of rhythmical interactions. This is true even in the case of very strong walls, such as, archetypically, the Berlin Wall. For instance, Neil Ascherson describes how this wall, from the perspective of West Berlin, had been drawn back a little to allow for the east side to better defend itself. There were rumors that these places sometimes were patrolled by the guards of the German Democratic Republic, but since they were almost empty of westerners they also attracted more shady activities. One of these fenced-off pieces of land was the Lenné Triangle, a piece of East Berlin on the West Berlin side of the wall. Ascherson tells us,

> One day in 1987, the Triangle was occupied by a tribe of "alternative" people ("autonomes") in flight from the West Berlin police, who set up a shack and tent city among the bushes, parked their Deux Chevaux against the Wall and invited everyone to come and join them in no-man's-land, the space of freedom between worlds. Visitors poured in, to smoke dope and plan new ways of living or merely to watch autonomes making love in "Biotope." It was too good to last. But when the West Berlin police finally stormed the encampment, East German soldiers suddenly appeared along the top of the Wall and helped the occupiers to escape. (2001, 9)

In this example the attempt by the police to tame the rhythmic occurrence of drug dealing, illegal behavior, and so on was suddenly overruled by a third patrolling part on the other side of the wall. Walls might look like borders between noncommunicating vessels, but in fact they are places of rhythmic interaction. The Lenné Triangle episode somehow redresses the, arguably more famous, opposite movement of defections from East Germany (estimated at around five thousand people), beginning with the *Mauerspringer* (wall jumper) nineteen-year-old soldier, Conrad Schumann, in 1961, just a few days after the wall began to be erected. Less known is the fact that Schumann himself many years later committed suicide at fifty-six, and it is not known to which extent his wall jumping played a role in a subsequent clinical depression. And this is, we argue, in fact what we can expected of territorial boundaries and walls: rhythms might clash, overlap, harmonize, or haunt us, but somehow they interact, one way or the other. These rhythms may strengthen or weaken a territory, but to some extent they are always part of a new territorial formation. As we know, just two years after the event at the Lenné Triangle, the Berlin Wall was about to find itself a totally new role in the city.

Looking, as we have done, at a small panorama of wall histories suggests that the wall is just as much a mediator of different rhythms as one of different territories. From the old urban walls surrounding the city to the security gates at airports, or just the walls between different rooms in a building, wall territories are where rhythms meet and are accentuated, detoured, localized, and faded. But even when rhythms have deterritorializing effects, they are already part of new further processes of territorialization. Even the repetitive sound of a hammer drill against the wall is already on the verge of producing a new territory—some kind of temporary work space for sure and perhaps also a hole or, possibly, a door.

Rhythmanalytical Sources

Rhythmanalysis has ostensibly become an important methodological support in the study of rhythms. Despite the increasing recognition of the importance of rhythms in social and urban studies, rhythmanalysis has, however, not yet become a proper science or a discipline in a specific sense, as its proponents had hoped.[2] Since the slim but important contribution on rhythmanalysis by Lefebvre was published in 1992, shortly after its author's death—and especially since its translation into English in 2004 edited by Stuart Elden—we have seen a wide variety of different empirical applications of rhythmanalysis.[3] This scholarship proves that rhythmanalysis is extremely important and helpful as a sensitizing attitude and a research technique in the social and spatial sciences. It is even safe to grant that rhythmanalysis has become an acknowledged method of inquiry soon to be admitted in methodology textbooks (cf. Lyon 2019).

But simultaneously we believe that the social sciences should now also move *beyond* rhythmanalysis. Clearly, this does not mean throw away the many important insights contained in the rhythmanalytical understanding of social time-spaces. Instead, we suggest, a benefit could come from further developing and integrating such insights into an enlarged science of territories and territorial formations. Today rhythmanalysis is usually associated with the name of Lefebvre; however, Lefebvre comes in late in a long tradition of studies into the nature and power of social rhythms. Since the late nineteenth century, a movement toward the recognition of the importance of rhythms in social existence emerged in a variety of loci and intellectual milieus.[4] Some of the key references in this movement include, for instance, the French school of sociology, with Emile Durkheim and Marcel Mauss; the Portuguese philosopher Lúcio Alberto Pinheiro dos Santos and the reception of his work by the French phenomenologist Gaston Bachelard; the Austro-Hungarian choreographer Rudolf Laban; the German art historian Aby Warburg; the cultural theorist Walter Benjamin; and the French moral philosopher Simone Weil. While these names do not at all form a single school of thought, their elaborations appear to contain, as we hope to show, a number of crucial elements concerning the work of rhythms in social life.

In *The Elementary Forms of Religious Life*, Durkheim (1912) argued that social life functions on the basis of an essentially *dual* rhythm: such is the sequence of *synods* and *dispersals* of a given population through rituals. The synods are moments where the members of a social group meet in ritualistic forms to exist collectively. Durkheim famously believed that, even in the most remote societies (the Australian aboriginals were his case of choice), it is religious assemblies that provide the blueprint for all types of social synodic moments. By establishing the basic dichotomy between the sacred and the profane, religion creates and enforces the cleavage between the collective and the individual, with ritual performances embodying the collective as a kind of God materialized before the individual's eyes. In

Territorializing Rhythms

Durkheim's view social life is thus rhythmic by nature, with social rhythms sitting on, but not coinciding with, cosmic, biological, and psychological rhythms.

An exquisitely heterodox legacy of Durkheimian sociology is the 1939 essay "Theory of the Feast" by Roger Caillois (a chapter from his *Man and the Sacred* [(1939) 1980]). A former student of Mauss, Caillois identifies the feast as that periodic moment of exception that rhythmically reactualizes the original time (*Urzeit*) when society itself is created. At regular intervals social institutions need to be regenerated, purified, and resacralized, by expelling intoxicating elements and accumulated profanations. The rhythmic occurrence of the feast thus acts in a homeopathic way, unleashing the primordial disorder and its unbridled contagious climate, only to seal it in a time-space accurately set apart from the rest of ordinary, "normal" life. The world can be regenerated only by the feast in a *mythic* time-space that stands in opposition to everyday existence (Caillois [1939] 1980, 129–32).

Already Mauss (1947), starting from the general idea that the human being is a rhythmic animal, explored rhythmic social functioning not only in ritual moments (as Durkheim had done) but also in a range of cases such as economic and technological activities (Mauss 1950).[5] Acting with others entails entering a shared rhythm, *synching in* with them, which is something Mauss was interested in observing from the immediate bodily level to the most complex institutional arrangements. What he called "techniques of the body" ([1935] 1973) are tools for acquiring and sustaining a shared rhythm of concerted action with others. When it comes to economic life, the basic formats of exchange are tied to specific rhythmic accomplishments. Most famously, for Mauss the gift—and not the barter—embodies the first type of significant exchange: gift making and receiving and reciprocating gifts are activities crucially sustained by a rhythm. In turn the rhythm of the gift is shaped by the contradictory requirements of morality and competition.[6] For instance, the moral rule that the gift must always be reciprocated establishes an in-between time imbued with waiting and *expectation*. Such a dense time of waiting, filled with the waiting for acceptance and reciprocation, so to speak, *recharges* the rhythm of the exchange itself. Given that the question about *when* is the right time for a gift to be reciprocated remains systematically under-determined, the time of expectation is not a chronological but a chronic time—it is tense and can always degenerate into fight.

Playing (both instruments and more generally), listening to music, and dancing are perhaps some of the activities where rhythm matters most immediately and compellingly at the bodily level. Also these activities are intimately connected among themselves. In his late 1880s tracts against Wagner, for instance, Friedrich Nietzsche protested against Wagnerian music on the ground that the latter inhibits the natural, inborn tendency of the listener toward movement and dance. Wagner represents a perversion in the history of music in that his theatrical approach has engendered "the complete degeneration of rhythmic feeling, chaos in place of rhythm" (Nietzsche 1888, sec. 1, p. 666)—arrhythmic swimming and floating in sound instead of healthy rhythmic walking and dancing. In those same years a similar, intimate association between music and bodily movement was also established by the U.S. child psychologist Thaddeus L. Bolton (1894).[7]

If, in the late nineteenth century, rhythm is saluted as natural, in the 1920s the dancer and aesthete Laban (renowned mainly for his Labanotation, the standard notation system for recording human dancing movements) made the point that rhythm is, in fact, an attainment that requires special training: rhythms must be *produced*. For Laban, there are no a priori preclusions as to what can be *made* rhythmic. Indeed, there is always the possibility of capturing even dissonant events to eurhythmize them.[8] Such is the mission of art and, more specifically, the mission of choreutics understood as *Festkunst*, celebrative art: "The art of celebration is meant to connect to the all-encompassing rhythm in its complete and infinite variability through dance. Essentially, the Festival knows no kakorhythmy" ([1921] 2014). Almost contemporary with Laban—and, like him, a former student from Conservatoire de Musique de Genève—Émile Jaques-Dalcroze developed the pedagogical tool of eurythmics. He taught that rhythm is not an external measure to be followed passively but rather something to be felt and experienced through one's own body. To become eurhythmic,

Territorializing Rhythms

he contended, one needs to move until one feels the rhythm from within rather than just reproduce something imprinted from the outside (1921, esp. sec. 4).

In the following decades a direct confrontation with modern industrial temporality was undertaken by Weil. Reflecting on her work experience at the assembly line in the French Alsthom factory during the years 1934–35, Weil ([1942] 1991) elaborated a distinction between *rhythm* and *cadence*: the assembly line, she contends, is defined by an endless repetition of movements, a mechanical cadence that never amounts to a veritable rhythm. What the mechanical cadence of factory work lacks is a privileged moment of suspension, which Weil describes as the "flash of consciousness." A real rhythm affords smoothness and ease in gesture, which, on the contrary, simple cadence denies. The two appear irreconcilable as traditional craftsmanship, on the one hand, and modern industrial mass production, on the other. For Weil rhythms are vital, and cadences deadly. We may notice, in particular, that the fluidity of the rhythmical gesture is created precisely by the possibility of pausing—that is, perhaps paradoxically, by a moment of discontinuity. Weil also observes that those who proceed comfortably in their rhythm may look slow, even though, in fact, they advance in a quite expedite way; instead, workers in a factory appear to constantly hasten themselves in a "miserable precipitation that spoils them of any grace and dignity." In sum, for Weil a rhythm contains more than the clockwork time of industrial production as well as, we may add, of modern organized life. It is the luxury of the pause, the alternation of action and thinking—and especially, the control over such alternation—that makes rhythms superior to sheer cadences. Weil's reflection importantly highlights that the energy invested in the production of oscillating phenomena has a specific coloration of its own, accounting for the distinction between the diverging experiences of cadences and rhythms.

Ranging from large public events to minute bodily gestures, the notion of rhythm thus seems to be pivotal in Western modern theorization. Some major cultural theorists from the 1920s and 1930s confirm this fact. In 1929 Warburg completed the introduction to his otherwise unfinished Mnemosyne Project, aimed at producing a visual atlas of "pathetic forms" in art history and beyond. His analysis opens with a view of culture at large as a rhythmic—not to say, bipolar—enterprise. Specifically, in Warburg's view the fundamental oscillation in human culture occurs through a series of "swings" that alternatively establish and eliminate a conscious distance between human subjects and the world in which they live.[9] A similar, universal intuition seems to have paved Pinheiro dos Santos's lost treaty *A ritmanalise* (1931). The Portuguese philosopher's speculation on rhythm is known only through Bachelard ([1936] 1950), who summarizes these ideas in *La dialectique de la durée*. In dos Santos rhythm develops into a whole metaphysics: he poses a theory of vibration that is not without similarities with Henri Bergson's philosophy and resonates with his classmate Leonardo Coimbra's (1958) "creationist rhythmontology." In turn all these authors might have been influenced—perhaps unknowingly—by Gabriel Tarde's (1890) theory of *universal repetition*. A Leibniz-inspired monadology underpins Tarde's vision, where harmony is appreciated as an instantiation of rhythmic resonance.[10]

In Pinheiro dos Santos rhythmanalysis was first conceived as a *therapeutic discipline* aimed at improving living rhythms; avoiding disrhythmias, arrhythmias, and cacorhythmias; and enhancing an active rhythmic production on the part of the individual. His attempt thus somehow also resonates with Laban's. Their aim was not just that of setting up a research technique; rather, creating a valuable tool for transforming subjective situations was the actual stake. In this sense Bachelard ([1936] 1950) parallels, and opposes, rhythmanalysis to psychoanalysis: whereas the latter offers a gloomy view of the immutable power of the unconscious, the former corresponds to a theory that believes in, and in turn strengthens, the human capacity of transformation and renewal.[11] Dos Santos's rhythmanalysis is therefore not about *rhythm* in the singular and the abstract but about *rhythms* in the plural and the concrete.

Bachelard was the only prominent European philosopher to endorse Dos Santos, yet he did so enthusiastically. Following Dos Santos (and, with him, Coimbra) Bachelard recognizes that rhythm is the fundamental temporal notion and "real basis" of temporal effectiveness ([1936] 1950, secs. 8–9). Bachelard draws largely on Bergsonian ontology, but he contradicts it on a crucial point—namely the issue of *continuity*. Indeed, for Bachelard, the notion of temporal duration—as well as, more generally, the notion of time—cannot be explained in abstraction from the dialectic tensions that compose it. Duration is rhythmic, made of discontinuities between moments of effort and moments of rest, where time features as, alternatively, a *resource* (affordance) and an *obstacle* (wall).[12] Because life is a discontinuous succession of events, human rhythm cannot but be an active effort at rhythmizing that which mixes active and passive components.

In urban planning and architecture, modernist theorists developed an interest in incorporating rhythms in planning and design. The Russian German Israeli architect Alexander Klein, for instance, investigated what has been called "Frictionless Housing for Functional Living" during the late 1920s. Klein developed a graphic method for the mapping of everyday choreographies and presented dwellings that could afford predictable and desynchorized rhythms of movement (Lueder 2017). Le Corbusier ([1924] 1966) famously constructed the spatial necessities of city planning on the basis of the everyday shift between work time and spare time (*heure du travail* and *heure du repos*). This reads as an interesting elaboration on the Durkheimian dichotomy between the individual and the collective and on the ensuing rhythms of gathering and dispersing the population. The well-planned city envisaged by Le Corbusier was one with steady, predictable rhythms. The modernist vision of society and the city (that then dominated the 1950s and 1960s, stretching until the 1970s) can in turn be seen as different from the following more fluid approach to rhythms endorsed by theorists writing in the so-called post-Fordist wave, imbued with an ideology known as postmodernism in the arts as well as the social sciences. In the postmodernist transition rhythms have become less univocal and more fragmented (Lynch 1972). The current interest by urban planners and human geographers in a range of phenomena known, for instance, as splintering, temporary, and event-oriented urbanism (Graham and Marvin 2001) do, however, reveal the continued interest toward the underlying social phenomena capable of shaping and sustaining rhythms that get transcribed into spatial formations at the urban scale (see, e.g., Secchi 2005).

Lefebvre's take on rhythms can at least to some extent be seen as part of his critique against the abstract spaces and temporalities of the modern society and its urban condition. In the period from the 1960s through the 1980s, synthesizing this Bergson–Dos Santos–Bachelard lineage and the Marxist perspective, as well as drawing influences from the situationists, Lefebvre highlighted that rhythms are not merely natural and social occurrences but also means of class domination. Lefebvre brought up the subject of rhythms in volume 2 of *Critique de la vie quotidienne* (1961), then extensively discussed rhythmanalysis in *The Production of Space* ([1974] 1991) and later devoted several texts to the subject during the 1980s (Lefebvre [1981] 2005; Lefebvre and Régulier 1985, 1986), later collected as *Éléments de rythmanalyse: Introduction à la connaissance des rythmes* (Lefebvre 1992).[13] As hinted at earlier, Lefebvre's rediscovery of rhythmanalysis in the 1970s and 1980s brought a lot of different themes together but also tended to obscure the many sources that, before him, had already investigated the topic.

In fact, other contemporary French thinkers were interested in the rhythms of everyday life. For example, during the 1970s the writer Georges Perec and the semiologist Roland Barthes pointed toward a rhythmanalysis more firmly based in the study of everyday mundane behavior, and they were both less caught up in dichotomies than Lefebvre in his work. Perec had made his own literary rhythmanalysis (although never named it as such) through brief and repeated observation studies conducted in the early 1970s, working, as Michael Sheringham (2006, 266) notes, with the problem of how to represent rhythms through difference. For example, in Perec's observation of recurrent busses in *Tentative d'épuisement d'un lieu parisien* (1974), he makes small variations in his notation; first he writes "un 63 passe" then just "un 63" and then, inverting the order, "passe un 63." In his 1977 course at the Collège de France, Barthes cast a specific interest in rhythms through the concept of *idiorrythmie* (Barthes 2002; Sheringham

Territorializing Rhythms

2006, 201–6). The idea of idiorrhythm comes from monastic life and was originally used to describe the life of the monks on Mount Athos that parted from regulated monastic community. These monks lived as hermits and joined the other monks in the monasteries only during certain festivities. Barthes uses the concept in a more general sense to discuss "the way the subject engages with the social and cultural code" (Sheringham 2006, 202) on his or her own premises.

Barthes's interest thus went toward understanding how the individual could interact with a community without being controlled or subdued by it. Idiorrhythmics has to do with how individuals in their relation to others might follow their own path, yet always act through the moods, affects, and desires that intersect their life. In a sense it lays close to Lefebvre's later theory in that it seeks to capture conflicting rhythms and resistance to temporal homogenization—but there is also a difference. Dolidon explains, "To put oneself in an idiorrythmic state presupposes that one lives at a different pace from the rest of society *within* society" (2010, 313). This state of rhythmic difference, presupposing some kind of negotiation, implies a more heterotopic approach than the one advocated by Lefebvre; the different rhythms mirror one another in different ways, but there is no pregiven moral or natural right inscribed in any of them. The idea of idiorrhythm allows different rhythms to be both within and outside one another simultaneously. Rather than basing a discussion in dichotomies—that is, focusing on dominating or dominated rhythm—we need to look at rhythms of different paces and saliences, or gradients of interdependent or at least coexisting (synchronous and synchorous) territorializations (Kärrholm 2017).

These theoretical discussions (and perhaps especially in the case of Lefebvre) are related to a modern history of urban development, which cannot be developed here (but see, for example, Smith and Hetherington 2013). While the authors discussed so far may seem to not have much in common, we in fact believe that a number of analytical insights can be extracted from their interweaving preoccupations. Indeed, they showed not simply a general sensitivity toward rhythms but contributed to work out a bundle of analytical points—namely, (1) society has a rhythmical constitution; (2) rhythms are not clockwork productions but envelop a degree of nonlinear interaction; (3) rhythms become the support of meaning as well as basic regulatory devices; and (4) a given rhythmic configuration provides a portrait of a specific society. In particular, the insight that rhythms do not simply intersect space and time but crucially interweave energy and meaning is the *fil rouge* that runs through this literature, to which we may simply add: society is meaning; meaning is intensity. Rhythms thus represent ways to cope and articulate intensity in social encounters. Once put in this context, the Lefebvrian synthesis becomes more understandable, albeit less original. A critical reconstruction of Lefebvre's project, which we attempt in the next section, paves the way for a discussion that interprets rhythms as one component among many in the life of territories.

Territorializing Rhythmanalysis

Even though Lefebvre, as stated earlier, was not very keen on recognizing his sources of inspiration, there are several merits in his recapitulation and reactualization of rhythmanalysis.[14] The following key analytical points might not have been invented by Lefebvre, but they are made particularly clear in his work. First, whereas Bergson had emphasized temporal continuity (duration) and Bachelard opposed evental discontinuity (dialectics), Lefebvre highlighted that the two aspects must coexist. Indeed, a rhythm introduces both a qualitative difference between *moments* (discontinuity) as well as, simultaneously, a single *movement* that leads through the moments and connects them (continuity).[15] In other words, the first insight is that rhythm itself is a special struggle between continuity and discontinuity.

Second, rhythm is contradistinguished not only by *returns* but, more pointedly, by *accents*. The notion of *stress*—ranging from linguistics, through psychology, to everyday language—hints at the existence of qualitatively distinct (stressed) moments, which we may also call *salient* moments. Rhythm thus presupposes the existence of qualitative differences between temporal moments—in Bergson's parlance, these are differences of nature that cannot be reduced to differences of degrees. Both the vitalist and the phenomenological perspectives teach that, for instance, acceleration and deceleration are not simply symmetric events; on the contrary, they possess and convey different and irreplaceable *meanings* in terms of lived experience. Yet the distinction between strong and weak times also makes sense from a structuralist perspective: so, in Durkheim and Caillois, a distinction is advanced between the dense, heightened time of the synod (the rite or public event) and the sparse time of mundane private life (for instance, leisure activities, family business, etc.).

Third, the duality of *calculative* and *emotional* dimensions—the rational-legalistic and the intimate-passionate sides—is identified by Lefebvre in these terms: "Rhythm appears as regulated time, governed by rational laws, but in contact with what is least rational in human being: the lived, the carnal, the body." As seen earlier with Mauss, the body is an important source and receptacle of rhythms. In fact, Lefebvre suggests that the body is "the paradigm of rhythmological study" ([1992] 2004, 68). Following classical French anthropology, Lefebvre discusses how the extended rhythms of the body in the use of tools such as the hammer but also gestures and mimicry (given that, with Mauss, the body represents the first technical tool of humanity), produce well-characterized spaces. Also in consonance with the studies of microsocial interaction (from Simmel to Goffman), Lefebvre comes quite close to describe the process we call "rhythmic ter-ritorialization": "through the mediation of rhythms . . . an animated space comes into being which is an extension of the space of bodies" ([1974] 1991, 207).[16] The body is both a rhythm machine and a producer of space, capable of expressing and sharing as well as concealing and withdrawing meaning.

At this point, however, a number of questions still remain unanswered: on the one hand, which specific spatial effects do these rhythms and ges-tures generate? And on the other, which other dimensions do these spaces draw on that in turn intersect and affect rhythms? Here is where the Lefe-bvrian approach reveals its limitation. While rich in interesting examples and suggestions, Lefebvre often ends up in discussions reduced to stark oppositions that at times are just naive. This is especially true about his last book, *Rhythmanalysis*, which reads as a veritable catalog of contradictions and oppositions (see in particular Lefebvre [1992] 2004, 68). Ultimately, Lefebvre's understanding of rhythmanalysis remains too dialectic, too dualistic. This is especially unsatisfactory by his own standards, given his long-term advocacy of trialectics and the introduction of a "third body" capable of brining indeterminacy into a system. In particular, Lefebvre's repeatedly discussed opposition of *temps cyclique* versus *temps linéaire* (already introduced in Lefebvre 1961), while intuitive and at first sight appealing, turns out to be misleading. This dichotomy is in fact a reiteration of a nostalgic and, at bottom, moralistic idea about modern time regarded as mechanic and unhealthy, as opposed to the ancient time seen as organic and curative. The opposition of qualitative and quantitative, or cyclical and linear, rhythms indulges a Manichean vision of good versus bad (something that also lurks in Weil but is more subtly elaborated). It is not hard to claim that we need a more rounded understanding of rhythms capable of remaining open and sensitive to rhythmic phenomena and the role they play, without trying to define their nature—whether they are endogenous or external, good or bad—outside of the situations in which they are enacted.

In a similar way Lefebvre's characterization of eurhythmia and arrhythmia appears as a transcription of classic notions of utopia and dystopia that is not particularly helpful. In fact, we must acknowledge that there is no *fundamentum in re* for this distinction: the prefixes *eu-* and *dys-* or *a-* are always correlative to a judgment, to an evaluative point of view. Therefore, similar distinctions cannot be grounded in pseudouniversal binaries such as nature/culture and so on, as Lefebvre does; instead, what amounts to a good or bad rhythm must be gauged in the light of a political stance and a cultural context.

Finally, Lefebvre's approach to rhythmanalysis is imbued in a phenomenological background, as his insistence on lived temporality confirms. Here we are far from disputing the importance of phenomenology for social theory; but as we have argued elsewhere, phenomenology—understood as the analysis of the absolute local here-and-now—must be complemented by ecology—that is, the analysis of relative global elsewhere-at-other-times (Brighenti 2008). That is why, as detailed in the next section, to advance toward a more complete understanding of the processes at stake, rhythms must encounter territories, the latter being complex creations that are as much phenomenal (imbued with meaning) as they are ecological (generated by operative relations).

Synchronization and Presence

"Operative relations" is another expression to indicate affections. Indeed, affection proves pivotal for a territoriological understanding of rhythmic productions and transformations. The immediately affective dimension of rhythm has been widely recognized: what is rhythm if not an *attempt at synchronizing* affects (action + reaction—that is, interaction)? The role (and different scales) of synchronizing movements was early on acknowledged in time geography (Buttimer 1976; Carlstein 1978), but the animations and affects of synchronizations have been less studied. In fact, through its affective component a rhythm often tends to induce other rhythms: the beat of the drum or the rhythm of a swing often brings out a mimicking bodily movement; other people's gestures can be mimicked and even predicted and synchronized with as part of social bonding (Launay, Tarr, and Dunbar 2016, 782). Retail has known and exploited this tendency of mimicry—through, for example, Muzak, escalators, and revolving doors, setting a rhythm to keep up the pace of the shopper—for decades if not more (Kärrholm 2009). Affect affords synchronization through mimesis. Some studies suggest that rhythms without a specific sender might have an agency and can improve behaviors as a kind of socializing by proxy (Launay 2015). Synchronous behaviors such as music, dance, sports, and exercise might be developed to enable more time-efficient ways of bonding with larger groups than, for example, through interindividual grooming (Launay, Tarr, and Dunbar 2016). Affective synchronization is thus—much like objects, as viewed by Shirley Strum and Bruno Latour (1991)—something that makes our societies stick together, something that helps us structure large patterns of order.

We suggest that rhythm can be best tackled as part of the process of territorialization. It is, of course, well known that rhythms tend to extend from bodies and into social space and that rhythms are constituents of everyday interactions (Mels 2004, 6; Edensor 2010). There is also a growing literature on the role and specificities of *urban* rhythms (Crang 2001, 2007; Smith and Hetherington 2013; Mareggi 2013; Mulíček, Osman, and Seidenglanz 2015). But even while the relation between rhythms and territories has been recognized (for example, Deleuze and Guattari 1980; Brown and Capdevila 1999; McCormack 2002), rhythms in general still tend to be treated as unrelated to the processes of territorialization on which they rely and through which they find their form. Here is where we think that rhythms cannot do without territories, just as territories cannot do without rhythms. Rhythm is a functional component of a territory, in that it enables the synchronization of associates within a synchoric (co-spatial) situation. But rhythms themselves cannot account for the synchorization essential to enable consociates to interact. A rhythm gives an *imprint* to a territory but does not resolve it. Territories are experiments with social life and social encounters; they contain both a stabilizing dimension (supported by rhythms) and an expressive dimension (a radically empirical measure-setting attempt that escapes rhythm). Rhythms are always-already part of a territorialized body or formation—they have *intensity* as well as *presence*. So rhythms are always-already entangled in processes of territorialization and are thus also always-already territorialized. Rhythms have, as we have suggested, a kind of life of their own; correspondingly, to live or to come to life (to animate) is also a process of formation, an investment in a living and to some extent continuous body. We are thus never talking about an abstract, disassociated rhythm per se but rather about heartbeats, drum rolls, tides, cigarette breaks, and so on—all these rhythms are embodied and territorialized, and as such they always echo into other kinds of territorial production.

Following Deleuze and Guattari (1980), territorializations are not only rhythmic but also melodic; they generate whole landscapes. Melodies mingle with rhythms to create the intensity and singularity of a particular

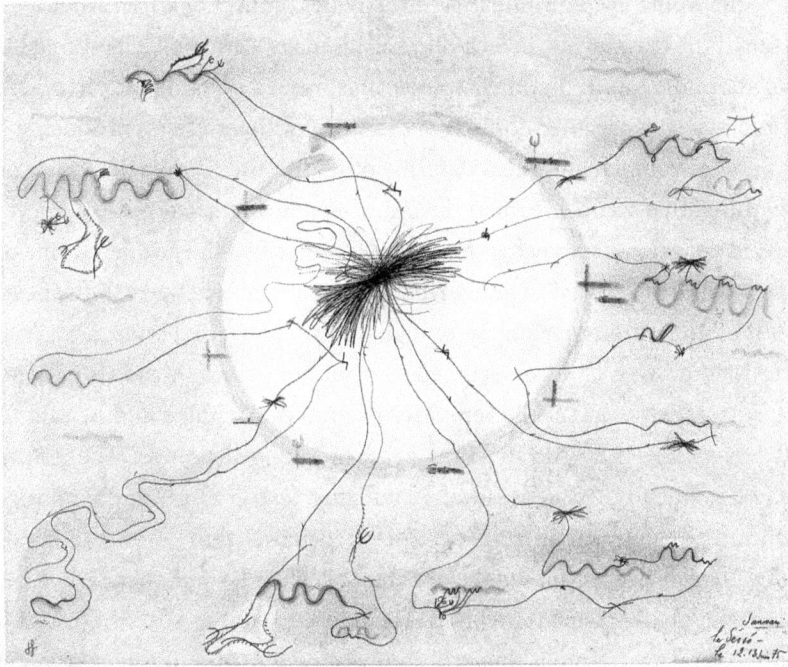

12. Wander lines of Janmari in Le Serret, June 12–13, 1975. Map traced by Jean Lin from Fernand Deligny's network. Reprinted from F. Deligny, *Cartes et lignes d'erre: Traces du réseau de, 1969–1979* (2013). © L'Arachnéen, www.editions-arachneen.fr.

territorial presence so that meaning can be perceived and put to fruition. For instance, children who play compose their own melody of movement and sound; interacting children will likewise compose plural—harmonic or disharmonic—lines. Certainly, these lines also possess rhythm, but the rhythms of play are always counterpointed by melodic elements that express their unique presence. In this sense Deleuze and Guattari speak of refrains, which they also conceptualize as "blocs of becoming" (1980, 300). A refrain, it appears, is as much rhythmic as it is melodic. In their theorization of territorial "lines of flight," Deleuze and Guattari were influenced by the French educator Fernand Deligny (2013), who had described as *lignes d'erre* (wander lines) the trajectories traced by the autistic children he was taking care of in the early 1960s in the Cevennes region of central France (see fig. 12).

Some would even dispute that the activities of these children amounted to anything like playing; in fact, drawing his maps, Fernand Deligny and his collaborators found that their wanderings formed certain patterns where some key spots seemed to be more important than others, producing a kind of refrain. Deligny also describe other instances when activities, or rhythms, that at first seemed devoid of meaning turned out to carry a melody of sorts. Deligny has, for example, described the problem some of these children showed in going from one moment or activity to the next, such as going from peeling an orange to eating it ([1981] 2008, 212; 2015, 222). Here some children seemed to lose themselves in the singularity of each activity so that the repetitive rhythm of peeling could be said to deterritorialize the associated time-space of "eating an orange." The gesture is not fulfilled but kept as if before a hiatus, lost in a seemingly nonsignificant rhythm. But an activity is never just a rhythm: "If the acting of scrupulously peeling an orange remains suspended—and, then, a gesture, we might say that what is involved is an offering without a 'to whom'" (216; 2015, 225). The rhythm is thus still an investment in life—it is part of *a* life; it is alive. In the writings of Deligny, we see how action seemingly devoid of intention and signification, without the thought-out project, also has its melodies. Actions such as drifting and searching, Deligny tells us, can be seen as belonging to the same order; they both involve investments and intensities (31; 2015, 52). The rhythms of certain gestures might look empty to us; they might at first seem like detours without any discernible patterns or nonsensical and stuck in endless repetition, but even so they have melodic counterpoints pregnant with a refrain.

Similarly, Bruno Bettelheim, working at the Orthogenic School for Disturbed Children at the University of Chicago in the immediate aftermath of World War II, noticed that emotionally disturbed children tended not to play in official playing spaces but rather privileged in-between spaces like stairways (1950, 116–18). By doing so they were undermining established territorial associations. In other words, playing children can also derhythmize the allotted playing spaces by introducing their own specific melodic counterpoints. By establishing playful activities out of place, they de/reterritorialize both the staircase and the playground. Again, what from the perspective of the rhythmanalysist might seem as the adding or breaking of a rhythm, might in fact be a new emergent ecology of play, full of new territorial associations.

The difference between rhythm and melody that we would like to assert here can perhaps be explained in parallel with the distinction between *affectio* and *affectus* in Baruch Spinoza (Deleuze 1981, 66–67): whereas *affectio* (affection) is the synchronic geometric image that encapsulates the situation of bodies as they encounter and are affected by other external bodies, *affectus* (affect) refers to the ongoing sentimental variations and transitions that in a living duration correspond to a higher or lower capacity to act in a body. In other words, affects are feelings formed by the geometry of affections. Similarly, the image of rhythms is made transitive by the emergence of melodies. In sum it seems as if the generation and regeneration of territorial production is as melodic as it is rhythmic: the territory is born again; it can seemingly become the same, over and over again, while also changing and ever increasing its own complexity.

Rhythms are not found in pure states. Instead, they come to exist only in landscapes of ecological relations, as soon as those relations come to be territorialized. In fact, it is only through an ecological perspective, where different operational relations across different times and space are at play, that the territory-rhythm complex can be fully understood. The formation of a specific territorial duration demands some kind of temporal desingularization—that is, when the territory at one moment becomes increasingly similar or replaceable with itself at another moment. The order that makes a present territory share an identity with that of its past is rhythmical, even *chronological*. But this difference does not evolve in accordance with chronological measures; rather, it brings with it recurrent *chronic* ruptures with processes of resingularization in its wake. This way the territory also becomes a veritable *individual*, a unique moment in time and space, different from other similar territorial sorts but also different from itself as it was before. Similarity and difference are co-produced simultaneously. Besides being rhythmic, the territory—understood as a synchorous production—enfolds its elements in melodic ways that might transform or change its existing rhythms into new ones. In sum rhythms are never neutral or devoid of melody. The seeming neutrality of the rhythm is an effect of the process of abstraction and temporal desingularization, where one moment becomes associable with another. This production of rhythm is, however, always part of a process of singularization that entails the presence of an intensity (if nothing else, in the intensity of a now different from a then), whereby an investment of energy is discernible.

Beyond Rhythmanalysis

As should be clear now, going beyond rhythmanalysis, as we have suggested earlier, does not mean discarding it but rather prolonging it into a more rounded theoretical and research endeavor. In this chapter we aim to make rhythms encounter territories to theorize how rhythmic production interweaves with territorialization processes at large in all its dimensions. Reviewing some crucial theorizations of rhythm since the late nineteenth century, and more intensively during the 1920s and 1930s, and looking at the continuation of this tradition since the 1970s, we have observed how rhythms have been studied as a vital part in the very forming of society, as well as of its different fields, such as religion, urbanism, dancing, pedagogy, and so on. We see that rhythms are co-producers of complex and vibrant landscapes of activity through their peculiar character of being absent and present at the same time—in other words, through their transformative potential. Bridging distances in time and space, rhythms afford and produce connections and patterns, but they are born with melodic lines and counterpoints, and it is through encounters with these that they become intensive and turn into actual living creatures. One condition for this animation of rhythms, we have contended, is to move beyond dichotomies such as linear/cyclic, mechanic/organic, continuous/discontinuous, and qualitative/quantitative that have burdened Lefebvre's rhythmanalytical project.

In our view a territoriological continuation of rhythmanalysis seems more promising since it enables a study of rhythms together with melodies and refrains—that is, it allows for a study of rhythms by means of the spatiotemporal processes and contexts through which rhythms come alive and take on meanings. A territoriological perspective points toward the study of the de/territorialization and de/singularization of territorial sorts as well as the spatiotemporal expression of properties in the form of affections and operative relations that enable territorial formation to carry and convey social meaning. Rhythms are never encountered as abstract entities but are always produced in complex processes of territorialization, and it would thus also make sense to advance the study of rhythms through in-depth investigations of spatiotemporal intensities and presences instead of paralyzing dichotomies. Rhythms are an inherent part of living intensities, social interactions, and formations of meaning.

In conclusion, retrieving a vitalistic take on rhythms, melodies, and territories seems to invite us to complement rhythmanalysis with territoriology. In particular we argue for an approach that is grounded in phenomenology yet also stretches beyond it, to capture the rhythmic, melodic, presential, and intensive dimensions of living territories. When dealing with rhythms, the notion of presences and absences, and the operational relations of intensities, dormant associations and investments in meaning need to be addressed in a more ecological way. Rhythms depend on, and simultaneously are a constituent part of, living and continuously shifting territorial landscapes.

7   Affording Play

The playground can be regarded as a specific urban type, or rather as a territorial sort, which acts as an inciter of play and playful activities. These activities, however, are known to take place both inside and outside of the playground itself. We thus follow a cue from the previous chapter to investigate how a specific type of territory—such as the playground—might act as a kind of rhythm machine, territorializing rhythms both within and outside its own perimeters. Moreover, we discuss how the playground and its territorialized rhythms might function as an incubator for new urban *affordances*. The notion of affordance refers to the way in which certain perceptions, evaluations, and actions are made available (afforded) by the environment to a perceiving subject and an acting body (Gibson 1979). From this perspective one territorial formation particularly relevant in relation to the playground is what we call the urban interstice (Brighenti 2013b). As an interstice, the playground belongs to those minor presences in the urban landscape simultaneously correlated to a complexity of overlapping and concurring functions. Social rhythms, we suggest, examined as an instance of urban interstice, should not be considered as utterly opposed to the unpredictability of imagination and play (which we call "melodies") and their capacity to imprint the city.

Historically speaking, the playground represents a building type that has emerged as a locator, provider, and attractor of children's playing activities. Certainly, the playground seems to substantiate Roger Caillois's (1967) claim that play is a type of activity bounded and "carefully sealed off" from the rest of life.[1] But in practice play must still encounter its play space. While the confinement of play and games may be largely unquestioned for adults, children actually play as they live and as they breathe and are only slowly taught by parents and caregivers to separate the domain and the spaces of playing activities from the other more "serious" domains.

The playground as we know it was primarily an invention of the nineteenth century, linked to the accelerated territorialization of society in the aftermath of the Industrial Revolution (Sack 1986; Markus 1993). This building type has been the object of severe critiques by leading progressive authors such as Jane Jacobs (1961) and Colin Ward (1978), who argued that children should be granted the freedom to play unrestrained in the streets rather than being confined in dedicated spaces. Similarly, a Foucaultian approach suggests to interpret the playground in terms of a disciplinary device (Foucault 1975; Franzén 1982). Contrary to these critical approaches, however, the playground could alternatively also be seen as an invention that increases interaction and opens up new uses of the everyday urban environment well beyond the sandpit and the swing. Taking both perspectives into account, we argue that, while the playground certainly contains a disciplinary dimension, it also allows for the production of new perceptual, spatial, and social affordances in the city. If a territory comes into being together with the environment in which it sits, then the playground might of course play a disciplining role both within and outside its own perimeters, but it might also have enabling and transformative effects.

To explore the ambivalence of the playground, the first questions that interest us here are how kids' play is contained and how playing kids are "guided" into given play spaces. At the same time we are also interested in how the playground exceeds the sheer function of play and becomes a receptacle for further reservoirs of social interaction and additional forms of urban coexistence. Consequently, we also ask another question: which are the perceptual and social affordances granted by the playground to urban dwellers? The last two are, in fact, twin questions, concerning, respectively, how the playground has affected the possibility of children to take part in the everyday life of the city, and how in turn the possibility of play has affected the urban landscapes outside of the playground itself. Exploring these twin questions, we highlight that the playground is not something fully controlled but rather a device that, once introduced, takes on a life of its own.

The kind of minor archipelago in the city formed by playgrounds could also be described as a territorial sort, in other words, a type of territory publicly associated with an activity and sometimes with a specific category of users, capable of persisting even in the wake of changing actors and forms (Kärrholm 2004, 2007). Understood as an urban interstice and a territorial sort, the playground appears as a changing yet somehow stable-enough entity that affects the ecology of urban everyday life. Playgrounds seek to enact the synchorization of children's play with specific times and places, through multiple synchronizations: the synchronization of proper behavior and specific moral values, the synchronization of bodies and bodily techniques, and, eventually, the synchronization of the whole city as a network where children can identify their own apposite territories. From this point of view, the playground appears as an interesting social-spatial innovation, a territorial rhythmical machine that in terms of synchronization is quite outstanding.

Besides being a synchronizer, the playground is also a veritable mine of perceptual and interactional affordances. In line with affordance theory (Gibson 1979; Heft 2001), one can argue that the playground does not just afford play but is in itself a vehicle for the implantation of play and the perception, creation, and use of new urban affordances. To see something *as a playground* is an act of association that suddenly permits new social formations and affordances to emerge—a veritable process of "territorial conversion."[2] Playful activities might in these cases also have important transformative qualities (Katz 2004).

Genealogy of the Playground

Despite its humble appearance among the many architectural and urban types of our cities, the playground has increasingly gained identity as a territorial sort during the course of its history. The idea of establishing places for play is, of course, old. In Sweden, for example, the establishment of specific places for play was advocated already in the school regulations of 1611 (Larsson, Norlin, and Rönnlund 2017, 35). The idea of the modern and more thoroughly designed playground is, however, often said to be introduced during the early nineteenth century in Germany to teach children how to play "in the right way," whereas the first proper public playground is believed to have been built in Manchester in 1848 (Norlin 1999, 287–90).[3] Of course, children playing in the street can turn every place into a virtual playground: from this point of view, the main purpose assigned to the playground as an architectural formation was precisely to *territorialize* (localize) and *synchronize* (regulate) children's playing activities. In other words, these infrastructures were conceived mainly as spaces to manage the scale and rhythm of playing together.

In the United States, inspired by the German examples, the playground was introduced during the late nineteenth century, especially to instill U.S. middle-class values in lower-class and immigrant children (Chudacoff 2007, 73). Quite soon the U.S. playground also became a territory for middle-class kids, especially as a vehicle of personal development (Spano 1991), shifting the focus from controlling bodies in space to implicitly inviting children to exert control on their own body and develop their identity—including, for instance, gender identity. Elisabeth Gagen (1998, 2000) has, for example, showed how the development of supervised playgrounds in the United States during the early twentieth century also came with gender norms. Gagen tells us, "Playgrounds provided a perfect opportunity to lure children into the open and to supervise their leisure time in a controlled, visible space" (2000, 602), and specific gendered play cultures soon evolved through this supervision. Studying playground management in Cambridge, Massachusetts, Gagen also reconstructs the gendered dimension of playgrounds: for boys, play was about team building and loyalty, even preparation for war, whereas for girls the notion of domestic work and handicraft were more important. If playgrounds were designed as places of visibility, restrictions around *how* to be visible soon became a pivotal issue for girls.

The Nordic European example seems to have focused on physical activity and control, but perhaps somewhat less on a narrowly defined acquisition of social roles. In Copenhagen the first playground was built in 1870 (Rasmussen 1969, 208). The question of playgrounds was raised in Stockholm in 1894, and the first twelve instances were built around 1902, most of them quite plainly designed as simple sand heaps. In 1963 there were 102 playgrounds in Stockholm, and several of them had also hired supervision personnel (1998, 46–49). Although the raison d'être of playgrounds had to do with both empowering (enabling physical and social activity and development) and control (territorializing and socializing play), the kids' *will to play* was often seen as the basic force and rationale to justify the playgrounds' existence. The Swedish architect Holger Blom put it this way: "It is pointless to get a park in order without first satisfying the children's need of playgrounds. The children's need to play will have its course. If they lack their living space [*livsrum*] they will spread like the locusts of Egypt, swarm the more delicate arrangements, and damage them" (1948, 536; our translation).

The underlying logic was one of confinement: every park needs a playground because children need to play, and this play should be both synchronized and territorialized in the direction of separation; simultaneously, though, all play should be supervised and the playground should be visually accessible by adults (Norlin 1999, 301). But this is not the only rationale invested in playgrounds. An interesting legacy insists, for instance, of the kids' self-training in manual skills. After inspiration from the book *Parkpolitik*, written by the Danish garden architect Carl Theodor Sørensen in 1931, the first *skrammel-legeplads*, junk playground or adventure playground, opened in Emdrup in 1943. There kids could build and assemble objects, employing loose parts like ropes, bricks, and wood and using real tools such as hammers and nails. Junkyards were supposedly freer and potentially more creative, despite the presence of supervision staff. In Sweden the first junk playground (in Swedish: *bygglek*) opened in 1948, and the concept still exists today.

In England, also inspired by Sørensen's junk playground, the "adventure playground" was introduced during the 1940s and prospered during the 1960s and 1970s. The adventure playground became important as a way to enable a freer and explorative kind of play, which, however, was continuously supervised and assessed by adults (Ward 1961; Rasmusson 1998, 53–57; Kozlovsky 2016). In the United States there are only a few early examples of these types of playgrounds, like the Yard in Minneapolis; most were established during the 1970s and 1980s (Chudacoff 2007, 187).

Playgrounds as Rhythm Machines

The public playground as an architectural and urban object seems to have had a golden age in the immediate aftermath of World War II. For example, Le Corbusier crowned his *Unités d'habitation* (1946–52) with a playground on the roof (Lefaivre 2007, 47). One of the most famous cases of playground building is, however, the postwar playgrounds of Amsterdam.[4] We use the Amsterdam case to describe how the playground came to be integrated in the urban fabric. These playgrounds synchorized and synchronized the rhythms of play, but they also formed a series of interstices overlapping with other urban activities. In a sense they became what can be seen as a connected set of *rhythm machines* echoing across the urban landscape.

As a result of war bombing, the city of Amsterdam abounded in vacant lots where, as of 1947, playgrounds started to be built in the interstices of the urban fabric. About 700 of these were planned and designed by the modernist architects Aldo van Eyck, Cornelis van Eesteren, and Jacoba Mulder (see fig. 13). The rise was also quantitatively impressive: the number of playgrounds in the city increased from fewer than 30 in 1947 to more than 1,000 in 1968 (to compare with the 102 in Stockholm in 1963), adding up to an average of about 50 new playgrounds every year (Lefaivre 2002, 2007, 44; Magnusson 2016, 164–67).

Amsterdam was a dense and crowded city, where calls to organize suitable places for children's play were repeatedly launched by citizens. During the 1940s and 1950s, the complaint about the lack of dedicated places for children represented a leitmotif in the open letters sent to the city administration. Some letters begged for organized sandpits, as the children anyhow used the pavement for playing with sand or removed paving bricks to dig and find the sand below. One writer complained about how football players kept breaking windows and wondered if play equipment could be installed to keep the footballers out (E. Schmitz 2002). The playground became a means of territorializing the playing children. In Amsterdam

13. Sand play in one of Aldo van Eyck's few remaining playgrounds, Frederik Henrik-plantsoen, in 2013. Photo by and courtesy of Jesper Magnusson.

the playgrounds were part of the territorial strategies of the Department of Public Works, the city developers, and the involved architects, down to quite a minute level: the head of city development, Cornelis van Eesteren, could even be found discussing in letters to citizens details about the design and dimensions of a specific sandpit in a given neighborhood (E. Schmitz 2002, 59).

Although the supporters of playgrounds were greater in number than their antagonists, as more and more playgrounds were built, complaints did not lack (E. Schmitz 2002). An analysis of complaint letters sent from citizens to the municipality is quite revealing of the many stakes surrounding the playgrounds. Several people argued that, after a hectic day at work, they were only looking for peace but were instead welcomed by loud noises from kids. Parents complained about the hygiene of the sandpits. There was also a personal protest against the planning of a new playground, based on the concern that the kids on the climbing frames would be able to peep into a private home. One letter suggested that the

Affording Play

overcrowded playgrounds badly needed trash cans "to prevent the streets near these sites from being made untidy by all kinds of sweet wrappers" (E. Schmitz 2002, 64). Another letter complained about the regular problem of blowing sand from the sandpits. In short, playing together generated both opportunities and conflicts. Sometimes criticism was not directed so much toward activities or objects ending up in the wrong places (sand, animal excrements, balls, etc.) but toward age groups as a whole, as reflected in a letter arguing against the building of a playground on a planted site: "We adults would also like to see a piece of greenery in the city. Many adults do not go outside even one day a year, and then the view of the garden is delightful" (E. Schmitz 2002, 62).

What were the more general effects of the playgrounds on the city? The new playgrounds brought about a new synchronization at an urban scale: many of them stood on bombed sites where, for example, homes of deported Jews had been. As Liane Lefaivre notes, "Filling them with life, in the face of these facts, was a redeeming, therapeutic act, a way of weaving together once again the fabric of the devastated city. The intention was to thwart what Huizinga in his chapter 'Play and War' had called the 'agonal' by overcoming it through play" (2002, 45).

A territorial strategy was envisaged that synchronized and distributed public play, enabling the children's identification with the city and with an appropriation of city space within but also beyond the local neighborhood: "As the number of playgrounds increased, they came to form a network—spread through the fabric of the city was a network of places that children could identify as their own territory, places where they were recognised as members of the city from one neighbourhood to another" (Strauven 2002, 81).

To synchronize with other children within a local block or a small neighborhood is one thing, but during the years of youth it becomes crucial to synchronize with other youths and even adults, to rehearse one's behavior in public space (Jacobs 1961; Lofland 1998). Research has highlighted that children and youths appropriate first local places, such as backyards, then their neighborhood, and, as they become teenagers, also a number

14. Teenagers playing with the swings at a rebuilt Aldo van Eyck playground, Jonas Daniël Meyerplein, in 2013. Photo by and courtesy of Jesper Magnusson.

of selected central locations of the city (Lieberg 1992). These successive appropriations concern not only spaces but also times (Gwiazdzinski 2013). The network of the Amsterdam playgrounds opened up for quite varied spatiotemporal appropriations, for both younger and older children (see fig. 14). By doing so the playgrounds afforded the synchronization of children from different parts of the city as well as of different cohorts of age.

The Amsterdam case thus provides us with an interesting picture of how the playground allowed children to take part in the city space in a more sustained and structured way and probably lowered the threshold for children to be able to access urban space, establishing interstices in the urban fabric where they could move in more uncontested ways. This fact, in turn, refutes the narrow idea of the playground as an encaging figure of discipline. Sure, the playground might privilege specific forms of play at the expense of others, but the playgrounds also took on a series of roles other than just disciplining children and giving them a fixed space. These roles have to do with territorial productions that unfold in a larger

Affording Play

territory well beyond the relation between the child and the playground. Notably, the temporary, interstitial playgrounds in Amsterdam were a matter of in-between timing: they were "actions in space occurring where and when needed" (Lefaivre 2002, 45). They tactically echoed the rhythm of World War II bombings and represented counterpoints to the rhythm of postwar urban development. As new postwar urban plans were being laid out and holes from bombs filled, the small temporary playgrounds tended to disappear, one after another. The paradox was that, while they had a therapeutic function in the immediate aftermath of the armed conflict, they also caused the war atmosphere to stay. Hence, in connection with urban development and densification, there was a certain pressure to supersede the interstitial playgrounds.

The synchronization of children's play in Amsterdam was part of a longer Dutch tradition—discernible already in the *Kinderspielen* paintings by Brueghel and others (Lefaivre 2007, 42)—of implementing a certain culture of play imbued with republican values (2002, 40). The visibility of children on the streets and their mingling with the rest of the population played a part in the rhythmic production and presence of a specific kind of Dutch citizenship.[5] Additionally, the formation and design of the Amsterdam playgrounds are associated with the theories of Aldo van Eyck and Team X, in opposition to CIAM (Congrès Internationaux d'Architecture Moderne) and their ideas of hierarchical design with centers and subcenters. Van Eyck deliberately approached interstitial spaces with a bottom-up strategy mixed with a "dirty real aesthetics" (Lefaivre 2002, 28–30), working with simple materials and nonfigurative playground objects—for instance, leaving the rough firewalls around the playgrounds unpainted in a more brutalist manner (Lichtenstein and Schregenberger 1993).

In this sense the playgrounds became part of an alternative way of organizing space as well as part of a reflexive modernistic critique in architecture. Most important, in Amsterdam as elsewhere, playgrounds made visible and salient a series of everyday life rhythms that were not always easily reconcilable: for instance, for local children, playing together after school and before or after dinner was part of a weekday rhythm, whereas for adults tired after work, the noise from the playground constituted a rhythmic reminder of stress and an unfulfilled need of silence.[6]

In short, we can see how the Amsterdam playgrounds acted as rhythm machines, both attracting, producing, and exporting different rhythms across the city. Before we go on to describe how playground rhythms get liberated from the playground and exported to other places, we say something about the decades and trends that followed the construction of these (and other) urban playgrounds. As mentioned earlier, in the 1960s and 1970s the critique of modernist planning led to taking a position against functional zoning. Famously, Jacobs (1961) and followers regarded playgrounds negatively as separated, monofunctional spaces. In fact, during the late 1970s the focus on children supervision and designed playgrounds decreased, and play was increasingly considered as an activity that should be possible on areas other than playgrounds (Rasmusson 1998, 50). One well-known example here is Ward, who, already in 1961, criticized the more traditional playgrounds in a quite harsh way:

> The need to provide children's playgrounds as such is a result of high-density urban living and fast-moving traffic. The authoritarian solution to this need is to provide an area of tarmac and some pieces of expensive ironmongery in the form of swings, see-saws and roundabouts, which provide them a certain amount of fun (though because of their inflexibility children soon tire of them), but which call for no imaginative or constructive effort on the child's part and cannot be incorporated in any self-chosen activity. Swings and roundabouts can only be used in one way, they cater for no fantasies, for no developing skills, for no emulation of adult activities, they call for no mental effort and very little physical effort. (193)

Later, in his *The Child in the City* (1978), Ward took a deeper interest in how children appropriate, play, and produce meaning in the city—or one could perhaps also say cope with the city—at places and in ways that probably never were intended by planners or adults (1978; cf. Cloke and Jones 2005).

One could thus argue that the notion of a playground could be said to either have weakened or, conversely, to have expanded to the point of

Affording Play

designating a general approach to urban space. As it usually happens, what has been lost in intensity has been gained in extension and vice versa. To put it differently, besides being a specific building type to be implemented locally, the playground as territorial sorting is capable of giving a special "coloration" to the whole city: the city itself can be turned into a playground by a series of practices including, for instance, new urban sport and urban art (Annunziata and Mattiucci 2013). Similarly, all sorts of expressive and spatially expansive urban sports, such as parkour and skateboarding, use urban space in a playground-like way (Borden 2001; Nilsson 2010). The possibilities of play in public space has thus not only been "liberated from children" and connected to people of all ages (Woodyer 2012) but has also become an increasingly important aspect of new public spaces and their design (Stevens 2007).

Concerning formal playgrounds, a different historical trend than dispersion can be recorded: from the 1990s onward European cities often saw fewer, but larger and in many cases themed, playgrounds, usually planned in the peripheries rather than in city centers (Strauven 2002, 82). These playgrounds sometimes became attractions and destinations for kids from all over the city and beyond. Although movements across various urban districts might be positive in itself in terms of social mixing, the new playgrounds may also be increasingly synchronized to weekends, being used only when the children can be accompanied there (in most cases, driven) by their parents, thus creating new patterns of dependence.

Interestingly, the synchronization of play relies on and in turn actualizes different spatial formations. What we have tried to show is that an array of historical, societal, cultural, and aesthetical rhythms manifest themselves through the playground and have an impact far beyond it, in the larger urban realm. Strategies, appropriations, associations, and tactics evoke their own specific set of rhythms and synchronizations. In terms of appropriations and tactics, playgrounds can be used and claimed by different groups, including children and parents but also youth in nighttime hangouts, as well as other urban animals such as cats, raccoons, and so on. Playgrounds may also elicit manifold territorial associations: more than just play, they can be associated, for example, with noise and disturbance, and dirt and danger, as well as excitement, freedom, and even patriotism (as in the Amsterdam case). In short, this building type can turn into a platform for multiple urban territorializations.

Play and the Function of Affordances

As we have seen, the playground is a territory designed to provide affordances for various types of play to unfold, as well as to facilitate or foster certain bodily activities. Starting with sandpits but developing with special tools such as swings, slides, balancing beams, roundabouts, and later even "construction sites" for children, playgrounds became a crucial instrument in the synchronizing and disciplining of bodily techniques but also an environment of new and different kinds of affordances. Although most playgrounds were dedicated to smaller children, the development of junkyard playgrounds was meant for older children and early adolescents. Different kinds and dimensions of climbing frames, arches, globes, funnels, and so on also made some playgrounds attractive to teenagers (Roode 2002). Over time a rich paraphernalia of playing equipment was developed, where special tools such as play tables for baking sand cakes (as part of playing with the sand) or stepping stones (as part of games like, "Let's not touch the ground") synchronized different kinds of play within the playground area or even between different playgrounds.

The playground has thus developed and tried different means to induce play, but the question remains as to whether it can successfully reclaim all urban play for itself. The playground works through material and bodily activations and associations, both to reproduce well-known plays and games and to produce—by trial and error—an arena for the exploration of possibilities and impossibilities, which is then slowly allowed to stabilize into bodily skills and knowledge of local affordances. This mechanism involves "territorial radiation" (Kärrholm 2013). Radiation is a type of territorial stabilization that unfolds through a persistent use of a specific territory where certain mechanisms or states seem to be sustained over time (it does not break, it keeps its shape, etc.), slowly producing a feeling of trust and reliance related to absences rather than presences. Through play a multitude of different possibilities unfold and so does the idea of something more stable; the unexpected (variation) is always produced together with the expected (repetition). The protected space of the playground, in particular, allows for multiple trials and rehearsals protracted in time. This can be contrasted with playing on the street, where children's play unfolds in terms of territorial tactics and appropriations, essentially operating on someone else's ground for short periods and thus often working in a more discontinuous manner. Although this kind of playing for sure also entails an investigation into affordances, and it could perhaps be said that it allows for a wider spectrum of different spatial investigations, the continuous investment and investigation into bodily skills and into the manipulation of specific affordances might be less intense.

Of particular interest to us is how the playground may offer affordances for the production of bodily motion and movement. In the classic *The Mental Growth of the Preschool Child* (1925), the U.S. pediatrician Arnold Gesell insisted on the centrality of motor development for junior mental growth; similarly, in the early 1900s Maria Montessori (1952) developed the view that children's desire for motility should be encouraged by all means and supported (not imposed on) by the provision of adequate spaces. Zooming in onto actual play occasions may tell us more about how design elements can be activated by users. For instance, in an ethnography of seven- to nine-year-old children playing in schools in Odense (Denmark), Helle Skovbjerg Karoff (2015, 114–16) has individuated four basic spatial patterns of play practices, which she has called *sliding* (repetition of actions according to simple patterns), *shifting* (rapid changes in speed, direction, and height), *displaying* (being onstage for the benefit of others) and *exceeding* ("the crazier the play, the better"). These patterns also correspond to four emotional states: devotion (feeling of being in flow), intensity (butterflies in the stomach), tension (awareness of showing oneself to others), and euphoria (unrestrained silliness).

For her part Ellen Beate Hansen Sandseter (2010) has also examined ethnographically how risky play and well-being are strictly correlated. In her view the way children explore and experience height (climbing, jumping), speed (bicycle, swings), and other bodily risks, including handling sharp tools and having struggles with peers, is a fundamental provision in play spaces to enable healthy development. Taken together these considerations remind us of that universal human attitude toward play that Caillois (1967) once called *ilinx*, or giddiness. The quest for verticality in climbing, clinging, and jumping, as well as the desire for speed in swinging, sliding, pushing, and shifting are all elements of *ilinx* in play. Caillois's thesis is that play always involves a tension between this dimension of *paidia* (turbulence, improvisation, exuberance: the spontaneous manifestation of the play instinct) and another dimension, that of *ludus* (arbitrary conventions and rules to be addressed through patience, aim, and skill: the pleasure of measuring oneself with a difficulty that has been created ad hoc). In a sense the swing and the sandpit stand as artifacts that embody the two ideal types of *paidia* and *ludus*—the first connected to the immersive experience of gravity and falling, the second with the possibility of carefully giving way to new shapes.

So play does not simply entail spinning out of control, although such drive is certainly present; rather, one seems to explore a marginal region where the rules are always on the verge of being decoded and reassembled. It is a territory on the making, whereby play spaces mean for children, adolescents, and even adults the possibility of moving in a fringe area of control. The debate about whether play is inherently instrumental or noninstrumental (Woodyer 2012) does then not make much sense—play is intrinsically explorative and evolving, and the question of instrumentality can appear only later. Explorations of space are also and inherently explorations of social encounters and intercourses where children learn to take the measure of the other—such is the peculiarity of territories as constructs that articulate actual spaces and active imaginations. The point for us is to then observe how these requirements get transformed and activated in given spatial and architectural contexts. For instance, Tezuka Architects' Fuji Kindergarten in Tokyo, completed in 2007, is designed to accommodate five hundred children aged two to six. The architecture is inspired by Montessori's educational ideas: an oval one-story building (a roof height of only 2.1 meters) with classes and sections without walls for most of the year, allowing children to move about freely in the whole school. The circular roof-playground is the main play space and is accessible at all time through ramps. No special play equipment is installed there; rather, it is the architecture itself that affords play elements, including, for instance, a few trees that cut through the roof and the wooden frames of the roof windows.

While Tezuka's kindergarten and its playground are separated from the surrounding urban space, what is interesting is their use of the round space, which allows children to run smoothly and continuously—and with a view on the city—without experiencing hard boundaries of confinement. Also notable is the Montessori-inspired organization, whereby children are at all time allowed to roam freely across different spaces and activities. It is up to them, in other words, to territorialize on either the playground or the class. Tezuka's leading idea is that rhythms can be allowed to emerge from the children themselves, while at the same time the architecture can be designed to provide strong affordances for producing such synchronization of play.[7] In a sense Tezuka's Tokyo playground can be seen as an example of a certain playground ideal: the closed or even hidden treasure world always affording new kinds of playing experiences.

From a territoriological point of view, the notion of affordance may be helpful to capture the relation between space and society in a nondeterministic way. As classically defined by James J. Gibson (1966), drawing from Gestalt theory, affordances are perceptual meanings—perceptions understood not as the stimulation of receptors but as a system of active, sensual, and embodied perceptions. Affordances are simultaneously *relational* (they depend on the relation between the subject and its environment), *individual* (they are related to an individual living being), and *environmental* ("an affordance points both ways, to the environment and to the observer" [1979, 129]). This might at first seem odd, as things are usually located in either the mind or the world (Heft 2001, 125–29). But if an affordance is first of all a relation (a kind of "pure experience" in William James's parlance or an "actual occasion" in Alfred Whitehead's), the subjective and the objective aspects of this relation can be produced only as distinct yet always-associated entities. In other words, the affording and afforded elements are co-produced. Contrary to some of his later advocates, Gibson himself was not a dualist and avoided crude distinctions, for example, between cognitive and physical affordances (Hartson 2003) or between real and perceived affordances (Norman 1999). In fact, for Gibson (and we concur) we are never in front of a purely physical or cognitive world but rather *in the midst* of a number of overlapping and crisscrossing sociomaterial territories (see also Kopljar 2016, 42–47).

The world is already territorialized in so many ways, and we do not start from scratch; rather, we *adjust* and *alter* ourselves as well as the environment and its properties (Heft 2001, 133). When I perceive a branch as affording me to climb it, it is a direct and singular relation, not one filtered or mediated through structures. This does not exclude training or exploration but maintains that certain traits or characteristics in the environment immediately resonate with me and in me (see also Ingold 2000): there is a match between me in a *territorializing* or *territorialized* role as a climber and the environment in a *territorializing* or *territorialized* role as a specific kind of climbscape (cf. Brighenti and Kärrholm 2018a). With Baruch Spinoza we could say that we enter the world of affordances only when we pass from the first type of knowledge (knowledge of extensive bodies) to the second type (knowledge of constitutive relations). When something, such as a tree, affords climbing, it is of course not some kind of ideal "pure climbing" but a climbing highly specific and contingent to the situation, perhaps associable to other instances of climbing, yet born in relation to the unique situation where I, for example, might be looking for something to do while waiting for my friend to arrive (and perhaps a spot from where I can see her as she arrives). In this way one can talk of a production of an affordance in me *and* in the environment simultaneously, when certain roles match. The territorialized roles of me as a climber in the state of waiting for someone and the tree as a climbing tree and a place full of vantage points simultaneously activate certain subjective and objective features of the situation. Strictly speaking, there is no distinction between *recognizing* and *creating* an affordance. We perceive an affordance and might thus find a good place for climbing, but we do not draw on earlier experiences as on some neutral self, nor do we simply apply a previously acquired conceptual knowledge to the case at hand. What happens is that I *become* a climber on the lookout; I embody a certain territorial role as the environment turns into a potential terrain and a territory for my actions.

Through our engagement with the world we live in, affordances are thus produced, manipulated, and utilized: the environment and the subject take form and evolve different roles together (Ingold 2000, 166–68). To perceive and use affordances is, for Gibson, also intimately related to evolution: it is an important way through which species survive and develop (Heft 2001, 146). We constantly develop ways of exploiting new affordances, and we adapt to suboptimal affordances while striving for better ones. The practical use of the playground may be premised on sticking to existing rules and expectations, as we let the playground discipline us for the good and for the bad and it pushes us to cultivate certain skills at the expense of others. But we might also manipulate the playground to make it become something else—a sandpit might become a fort, a hangout place for drug addicts, a litterbox for cats, and so on. Perhaps even more interesting, by becoming a playground-kid, we can manipulate the whole city.

The playground as a territorial sort comes with territorial roles and couplings that allow us to utilize even nonplayground environments as veritable playgrounds.[8] The *ludus* examined by Caillois, the will to measure ourselves against the conventions and rules of different games, is already in place; its rhythms echo in our bodies and help us produce new associations, new rhythms, and new melodies in unexpected places. This is what we mean by territorial conversion: a type of territorial production that not only adds to the territorial complexity of a specific place but also manipulates one or several existing territorial productions *of that same place*. As an empty concrete pond is appropriated by skaters, it might also lose some its former associations; it might stop being popularly known as "the empty pond" and take on a new name. In a similar way just as parts of the city become some kind of playground, the playground can become part of the city in its entirety; a playground might become a node in an intricate network of different everyday life places or even the central node of a more complex play involving places collected from all over the neighborhood.

Swing sets, slides, climbers, jungle gyms, roundabouts, teeterboards, spring riders, playhouses and little castles, sandpits, pipes, and other equipment commonly installed in playgrounds could be said to function as *attractors* in a mathematical sense, where children (and others) who do not yet know one another will "spontaneously" congregate. To be more precise, such an outcome is the effect of the affordances children are able to envisage in the equipment. Again the work of affordances is inherently relational. Relations are territories at many levels: so territorial associations and sorts are connected to territorial strategies, which is confirmed in traditional building-type theory (Pevsner 1976; Markus 1993), where certain buildings are planned and designed to produce certain associations but also to accommodate certain affordances and—to borrow Roger Barker's concept—*behavior settings* (Heft 2001, 253–56). Territorial strategies are in no way mastering the associations or affordances they rely on. On the contrary, the perception and production of affordances might be the trigger of new unforeseen associations: the moment when a specific rhythm can be given a new melody *as a gift*, when the department store can become the ideal setting for a hide-and-seek game by two nine-year-olds, or when an equestrian statue on a square can become a climbing route for teenagers. These examples of territorial conversion might draw on earlier investments into climbing and playing, made at or around the local playground. To learn the different particularities and affordances of a territorial sort, such as the public playground, helps us to grow different territorial roles, which in turn might produce new ways of understanding, stabilizing, and transforming other public spaces.

Multiplying Affordances in the City

As we have seen, the historical logic of the playground pivoted around the function of segregating and controlling children's and early adolescents'

Affording Play

bodily practices both in space and in terms of interaction patterns. In this sense the playground has represented a chapter in the history of how social rhythms come to be territorialized. But the agency of children and users is never anodyne—for instance, toys provide affordances for playing, but to work they have to be *animated*. It is children who confer such animation to the toys they use (as we have recalled in the first chapter, children are indeed nearly perfect animists). Here is why the production of affordances is never deterministic: an affordance cannot be designed.

The synchronization of playing can be seen as the formation of intense moments of territorial production, and the continuation of produced territories is rhythmical and has consequences beyond its narrow local borders—it becomes entangled in larger landscapes and ecologies. Territories are rhythmical no less than rhythms are territorial; in other words, rhythms are always-already part of a territorialized body or form and have *intensity* as well as *presence*. So rhythms are always-already taken into processes of territorialization and are thus also always-already territorialized. But rhythms also have a kind of *life of their own*, and to live or to come to life is also a process of formation, an investment in a living, continuous body. Rhythms, as recalled previously, are not abstract mathematical entities but rather about heartbeats, drum rolls, tides, and cigarette breaks. Rhythms are embodied and territorialized, and as such they always echo and resonate in different kinds of territorial production.

What we learn at the playground does not stay at the playground and vice versa. The playground draws on the presence of heterogeneous urban rhythms that act on its territorialization, but in turn it plays its own roles in the territorialization of ampler urban rhythms, both within and beyond its local boundaries. We propose to understand the relation between the playground and the affordances in a similar way: the playground is a stage for the production and transformation of affordances, but these are always related to other experiences and affordances in the city. Playgrounds were born as part of the experience of the public city. As public places, playgrounds are inevitably *spaces of irritation* (Brighenti and Pavoni 2017) and a not-always-smooth coexistence: consider, for instance, teenagers leaving cigarette butts where small kids will play the next day, unnerving the latter's parents; unknown childrenless adults being looked on with suspicion just because of their presence in the surrounding regions; and, more generally, the usual problems ensuing from some users' reluctance or unwillingness to share supposedly shareable common equipment. The playground might come with certain expected territorial rules (and roles), but it is also a place where territorial roles (and rules) are crafted, and thus it cannot help but be a stage for frictions and negotiations.

One of the important questions of this chapter has been to investigate how a territory might reach outside itself and beyond its closest surroundings. Here we argue that affordances sit at the nexus of the rhythms and associations that emanate from any territorial production. Territorialized rhythms and associations enable us to discover, or rather produce, new affordances at unexpected places. Playgrounds (also in the wider sense of the word) are territories of experiment; they are places in which we might increase our bodily repertoire and produce new meanings. As they allow for new associations and affordances, they also tend to increase the fluidity of certain territories and territorial roles. In conclusion we might thus suggest that the playground's major shortcoming (its alleged disciplination effect) in fact provides scope for its potential in territorial conversions beyond its local boundaries. The significance of the urban playground may indeed reside in its potential as an incubator for the production and transformation of perceptual, spatial, and social affordances.

Conclusion

In this book we have approximated the study of territories through a series of investigations centered around the sort of theoretical and practical questions this specific instance of life raises. Such questions include, for instance, "How does a territory come into existence?"; "What temporality can a territory produce?"; "How do territories sustain rhythms of concerted action?"; and, "Which sort of encounters does a certain territory encourage?" Examining specific cases—as we have done with John Soane's house-museum, the Amsterdam playgrounds, and others—we realize that territories have inescapably plural constitutions. This fact, however, does not hamper the development and refinement of theoretical work in territoriology. In fact, we believe that, in the development of this science, cases and theory can fruitfully co-construct each other. Theorizing territories cannot but be an attempt to tackle the vagaries and vicissitudes of their life, together with their unforeseen combinations.

Certainly, at this point the reader might also legitimately wonder why we have picked precisely these cases rather than some of the many possible others. In making our selection we deployed a number of strategies but also conceded to lightning inspirations: sometimes we started with a territorial phenomenon that, for a number of reasons, caught our curiosity—like the house deities presiding and contradistinguishing specific home territories. A priori there is a sense of how these minor domestic cults are intertwined with issues of maintaining visibility, practicing law, accepting others, making ritual gifts, and managing the space of coexistence. A whole ecology of the home seems to be entailed—but the specific connections and their meanings needed to be unearthed and highlighted. At other times it was a more theoretical puzzle that drove us to investigate, for instance, the process of form taking as it unfolds across different domains, ranging from brick-and-mortar walls to an array of human assemblies. The theory of form—as renewed through Gestalt psychology, Gilbert Simondon's energetics, and René Thom's salience and pregnance schema—promised an important backup for the science of territories, and it was at this level that a theoretical advancement seemed to be called forth.

As said, we have proposed territoriology as a platform where empirical investigation and theory making can inform each other, but the conceptual scaffold of territoriology also needs to be renewed before its program—which seems to have fallen out of fashion since the 1960s and 1970s—can be reproposed today. When we say that territoriology presents itself as a general theory, we refer to a theory that takes the wide range of phenomena seriously, without letting disciplinary borders predefine what is and what is not to be part of the subject matter. In other words, we believe that the potential for territory making can be treated as a single cross-disciplinary phenomenon. A science of territories will inevitably set up its tent on spots other sciences have already practiced—including ecology, geography, anthropology, sociology, law, politology, psychology, ethology, and so on. Seen as social formations and spatiotemporal (or rhythmic-melodic) intensities, territories are always produced through the relations between actors that are constitutionally distinct and different and who are nonetheless capable of entering unique compositions. It is the lens of such uniqueness that is central to territoriology. It raises questions of stabilization, resistance, and change. At the same time, the actors, and even the type of actors that can be included in a territory, are hardly ever predefined. This is also why territoriology needs to be specific as much as it seeks to be general. If territorialization can be related to phenomena ranging from singing birds to nation-states, it is only by attending the specifics of the empirical materials and the contingent formations involved in the manifold territorializations that we can learn how certain aspects may remain relevant across disparate environments, dimensions, and scales. Territoriology is a slowly growing field of associations and comparisons between different concrete cases and their theoretical discussion.

Perhaps more than anything else, territoriology represents for us a research practice and a research attitude. In this sense, rather than summarizing and signposting the discussion presented in the former chapters, we would like to conclude this book with a few thoughts about the implications of imagining territoriology as one such practice. In short, we ask: What can it mean to "practice territoriology"? We hope that further future explorative paths can be opened up precisely where we end our current exploration.

First, territoriology is a theoretical stance that does not strictly correspond to a set of fixed methods or techniques. The specific empirical studies could be quantitative or qualitative; they could be wide and speculative, or narrow and deep, in scope and cases (in all science the reasons why we end up studying one phenomenon rather then another are as natural and clear as they ultimately remain mysterious and ineffable). As long as there is ambition to tackle territorial issues in an encompassing way, beyond the empirical cases at hand, we can talk of a territoriological ambition. At the same time we do not suggest that the intradisciplinary theories of territory—such as the ones developed, for instance, within political geography, anthropology, or ethology—should be discarded and replaced. Rather, we propose a version of territoriology that can be appreciated as a strategy of abstraction capable of engaging cases of study while reenacting case-based reality in novel ways, including a crucial shift through different levels of abstraction. There are several ways to extend and develop the enterprise presented in this book—certainly, for instance, one could be to establish stronger connections with the most updated findings coming from a variety of special disciplines (ecology, biology, architecture, anthropology, politology, etc.), further relating these different levels of abstractions to one another. In recent decades the recurrent critiques against universalism have led to a view of theory as always situated and drawn from specific locations, articulated in specific languages and within "finite provinces of meaning," as Alfred Schütz (1962, 341) once put it. But this does not necessarily mean that findings cannot be discussed at different levels or that all passage across different levels of abstraction is necessarily barred.

Learning depends on abstraction as well as on the ability to recognize the differences and similarities between one object or moment and another or others. What is sometimes forgotten is that there can be a dialogue between different ways and levels of abstraction—here is precisely where we suggest that current research on territories and territoriality could benefit from the development of a broader territoriological perspective.

Second, although we have stated that territoriology allows for a wide variety of methods and techniques, the crafting of these special techniques is, of course, of importance. As declared at the outset, we strive above all to avoid the conflation of territoriology with some kind of fluffy postmodernist talk. We believe that, so much as theory must be free, critical, and open, no less must empirical analysis be careful and even positivist. Certainly, in this book we have been more focused on theory than methods, but a discussion of different ways of territorial investigation is an important task on the agenda. In the preceding discussion we have given more space to the need of ensuring the openness of theoretical elaboration through a necessary yet "homeopathic" degree of chaos and anarchy. That methodological preoccupations receded in the background was inevitable in this context. The chapter where we have more directly engaged methodological questions is probably the chapter on rhythmanalysis, where we have sought to show how rhythmanalysis, precisely because it has failed to become a proper science or a discipline in a specific sense, can be fruitfully integrated into a territoriological framework. More generally, the leading working question for us becomes how we can develop specific "territoriographies"—that is, sets of methods and techniques that give justice to the full scope and the multidimensionality of territorial phenomena. An important task is to mix traditional and experimental methods but also to address new empirical fields beyond the paradigmatic territorial cases of animal ethology, gang turfs, shopping-mall customers, and politics among the nations. There are a lot of territorial phenomena that seem to be understudied, and the development of more adequate methodology might help us discover and tackle territorial problems in unforeseen locations. To just mention some possibilities, it could be intriguing to bring into territoriological research methods and techniques coming from visual studies, sensory ethnography, art criticism, science and technology studies, data visualization, digital and collaborative mapping, and so on. We have hosted some of these perspectives in more empirical collections of essays, such as our recent book on urban walls (Brighenti and Kärrholm 2018b).

Third, we have hinted various times at a possible renewal of territoriology beyond its classical sources in ethology and social psychology. The theoretical choices we have made in this book are, admittedly, to some extent idiosyncratic. We have consciously made them in view of contributing to a reformulation of territoriology in a less naive key. We hope to have made it sufficiently clear by now that, in our view, territoriology should not be a narrowly determinist, one-dimensional science. On the contrary, its zero degree lies in the recognition that, in each given locale, there exists a virtual multiplicity of phenomenologically experienced ongoing and interacting territorializations—just as across different locales different territorializations overlap in ecological relational ensembles, without necessarily ever becoming aligned with one another. Territorial productions have often been discussed in the singular, as a kind of one-front war between two opposed forces. In fact, processes of territorialization undo installed dichotomies by making them proliferate, creating additional and even irregular fractional dimensions (at $n.x$ dimensions). As in the opening example of this book, the Roman Colosseum, we are dealing with complex landscapes of overlapping, dormant, conflicting, or co-constituted territorializations as they exist at different scales and different temporal compasses. A challenge for future empirical territoriographies is, in this sense, to describe and analyze the complex relations that territorial environments entertain with their ecology—in other words, their *Umwelt*.

An additional move in the rearticulation of territoriology pursued in the course of this book has consisted in giving attention to the dimension of life and the vitality of territories. We have started by outlining the concept of territory in relation to the basic actions of living (environments), feeling (atmospheres), and making (networks). This in turn has enabled us to see how certain moments of animation act like sparks of life in territorial formations, contributing to the special coloration of each territory as well as to the precipitation of events and the becoming of territorial composites. In this respect one is reminded of Georg Simmel's ([1918] 2010) characterization of life as self-transcendence. In parallel with Simmel, territories could likewise be said to be simultaneously *more-territories* and *more-than-territories*. Territories establish gravitations, including a growing number of elements in their composition: in this sense they vegetate and grow (more-territory); by doing so, however, they also subject their constituent parts to new compositions endowed with novel nature (more-than-territory). This is why, as we have contended, the most interesting aspect of vitalism does not lie in claiming to advance a full-fledged theory of life but in persisting (according to Aby Warburg's notion of *Nachleben*) as a kind of undercurrent vis-à-vis all other theories. The vitalism that has interested us is that special invitation to look slantwise, underneath measurable phenomena, or phenomena measured only according to standardized metrics, scouting for neglected manifestations and potencies. Eschewing from a straightforward organicist or holistic notion of territory, we have rather drawn from a compositional view inspired by the philosophy of Gilles Deleuze and his take on Baruch Spinoza. A territory is an encounter in a Deleuzian sense, in the measure in which participating in a territorialization not simply connects but also affects the actors that participate in it—affection being the experience of the rearticulation of one's own constitutive relations.

Planned or unplanned as they may be, territories exhibit a vitality—an *exigency* of vitality—that speaks not only and not so much about their degree of organization as much as of their capacity to express singular conditions: so, for instance, as recalled by Deleuze, an old cat may be looking for a territory where to die; someone might have had to spend a whole night out in the suburban territory waiting for the city gates to be opened; or someone else might be taken in the dream of transforming one's home into a museum or even a mausoleum, where he and his kin would live and be buried. Having ourselves drawn from a certain philosophical tradition, however, we absolutely do not rule out the possibility that different tracks of territoriology might be developed following other philosophical traditions and other insights associated with those traditions. No strict observance of a system of thought or a doctrine is particularly commended—here one can be reminded of Friedrich Nietzsche's pun that having a system is a lack of integrity. A certain theoretical eclecticism may prove fruitful to advance territorial studies; at the same time, as we have also insisted on, this should not lead to an everything goes–styled, sloppy theorizing. Rather, the experimental and processual intuition of territories and territory making, which we have outlined in this book, issues a double invitation: to take territories seriously and to take them joyfully.

Notes

Introduction

1. The spelling of *territorology* is accepted, and we ourselves have used it in the past. But the standard way for the creation of scientific neologisms is to combine a root and a suffix. In our case the Latin word *territorium* contains the root *territori-*, to which should then be added the usual suffix *-logy*, meaning "the science of."

1. For a Science of Territories

1. In the original Middle-Age Latin, the phrase is "quamdiu stabit Colyseus, stabit et Roma; cum cadet Colyseus, cadet et Roma; cum cadet Roma, cadet et mundus."

2. Arguably, the "classic" season of territoriology spanned the 1930s through the 1960s and produced some well-recognizable, albeit somehow simplistic, definitions, such as Hediger's one: "A territory is a measurable piece of the surface of the earth and often the individual territories of the members or groups of the same species touch one another like the pieces of a mosaic. A territory has to be acquired or conquered and more or less permanently defended, mainly against members of the same species" (1969, 531).

3. "The term origin [*Ursprung*]"—Benjamin famously claimed—"is not intended to describe the process by which the existent came into being, but rather to describe that which emerges from the process of becoming and disappearance. Origin is an eddy in the stream of becoming [*im Fluß des Werdens*], and in its current it swallows the material involved in the process of genesis [*Entstehung*]" ([1928] 1974, 226; 1998, 45).

4. We do not seek to provide a comprehensive bibliography here. We would like to simply single out some of the works that for us are most representative and that, while classics, can still be inspirational for research and theoretical development.

5. Deligny for his part writes, "If the spider has been looking [for the wall corner], we can also say that the corner was waiting" ([1981] 2008, 11; 2015, 33).

6. In a recent collection, for instance, Normandin and Wolfe have diagnosed a "growing level of interest in vitalistic and organismic themes," especially in intellectual regions "lying at the boundaries or liminal spaces of what counts as 'science'" (2013, 1).

7. Late in his life, Deleuze famously claimed, "All I have written was meant to be vitalistic, or at least I hope so [Tout ce que j'ai écrit était vitaliste, du moins je l'espère]"

(1990, 196). We consider that a similar vitalistic invitation is issued by Whitehead through his notions of "relatedness" and "objective immortality," "whereby"—as Whitehead puts it—"what is divested of its own living immediacy becomes a real component in other living immediacies of becoming" ([1929] 1978, xiii–xiv).

8. Simmel has suggested that from a Kantian perspective the idea of individual law does not make any sense, insofar as, for Kant, "whatever commands the individual must be something beyond the individual" ([1918] 2010, 105–6). There is, in fact, a type of Ought (*Sollen*) that "does not stand over against life, but is instead a mode of its entire fulfillment" (*ein Modus seines gesamten Vollzuges*) (105). The Ought is thus an "original phenomenon" (*Urphänomen*) of life. Such Simmelian *Sollen*—grounded in the individual but not merely subjective—corresponds to what we pursue in terms of vitalistic sensitivity.

9. In his brilliant monograph on Uexküll, Brentari has documented how, during the Nazi period, Uexküll's Institut für Umweltforschung, working under its founder's vitalist, ecological, and anti-Darwinian perspective, remained marginalized and underfinanced, while the lion's share of national research funds was directed toward genetics and mutations studies (2015, 34–43).

2. Environments, Atmospheres

1. Philippopoulos-Mihalopoulos, elaborating on Deleuze and Guattari, suggests that the milieu is not so much a "center" as much as a middle and, simultaneously, a medium: "just as the leaves of grass move with the wind, the space in the middle consist[s] of the *encounter* between the grass and the wind" (2015, 83). Incidentally, one can recall the poet Edouard Glissant's characterization of Deleuze as a *penseur de la source et du prés* (thinker of the source and the grass) and of Guattari as a *penseur des villes* (thinker of cities)—an apt reminder that every theorizing has its own milieu. For his part describing their co-writing, Deleuze (2003, 218) compares himself to a hill and Guattari to the sea.

2. For a detailed historical and theoretical reconstruction of Uexküll's theory, we refer to Brentari (2015).

3. Interestingly, for this crucial point Deleuze uses the Simondonian notion of transduction and also refers to Uexküll's idea of the *Umwelt* as music, which we have evoked earlier. Transduction is, arguably, one of the most original and difficult notions in Simondon's work. While an exhaustive discussion is not possible here, let us simply recall Simondon's initial definition: "By transduction we mean a physical, biological, mental or social operation by which an activity diffuses from neighbor to neighbor within a given domain, and where diffusion is based on the progressive structuration of the domain: each region of the constituted structure serves as constitutive principle for the next region, so that a modification diffuses progressively along with the structuring operation" ([1964–89] 2013, 32). In short, transduction could be

described as that "moving limit" in a structuring and phase-transition movement that progresses from neighbor to neighbor. In turn, it may be possible that both Deleuze and Simondon were influenced by Whitehead. Indeed, Whitehead can be said to have elaborated a "participationist" ontology, where everything is implicated with everything else: "There is no possibility of a detached, self-contained local existence. The environment enters into the nature of each thing" (1934, 18).

4. The idea that networks are opposed to and incompatible with territories is a trope that can be found, for instance, in Lévy (1994), Castells (1996), W. J. Mitchell (1995), and, more recently, Jessop, Brenner and Jones (2008).

5. An influential work in this direction is *Splintering Urbanism* by Graham and Marvin (2001).

6. Law and Mol draw on Wittgenstein's concept of family resemblance but suggest a possible difference from Wittgenstein's concept in stating that it "may or may not be possible to separate a fluid into its components" (1994, 660).

7. A third—inspired by Law's notion of fire topology (Law and Mol 2001)—is, for example, discussed in Kärrholm (2008), and a fourth is discussed in Kärrholm (2013).

3. Multitemporality

1. We draw the association of Kronos and Cronus from Kerényi ([1951] 1980).

2. Here are the original words: "C'est un temps extrêmement agité. C'est le temps des générations qui s'affrontent, qui se renversent. C'est un temps sauvage. C'est vraiment un temps sauvage, je veux dire déchaîné, un temps non domestiqué. . . . Je dirais presque, ce qui appartient au mythe c'est un temps sauvage et non domestiqué. C'est à dire, un temps comme abîme, d'où sortent les générations successives, et dans lequel elles combattent—un temps terrible, un temps de la terreur, un temps qui est un sans fond, une espèce de sans fond de la terreur et de la lutte des dieux."

3. In Benjamin's phrasing, "Thinking involves not only the flow of thoughts, but their arrest as well. Where thinking suddenly stops in a configuration pregnant with tensions, it gives that configuration a shock, by which it crystallizes into a monad" ([1940] 1968, 262–63).

4. In parenthesis the authoritative violence that maintains the law described by Benjamin ([1921] 1999) is strikingly similar to Schmitt's (1942) reinterpretation of the Christian eschatological notion of *katéchon*.

5. But simultaneously, the presence of such an uncanny piece of furniture as a sarcophagus in a home curiously recalls Benjamin's analysis of the nineteenth-century bourgeois interior as a "case" that is adhering perfectly to the person of the homeowner—an adherence and an intimate mirroring that Benjamin describes in terms of "addiction to dwelling": "The nineteenth century, like no other century, was addicted to dwelling. It conceived the residence as a receptacle for the person, and

it encased him with all his appurtenances so deeply in the dwelling's interior that one might be reminded of the inside of a compass case, where the instrument with all its accessories lies embedded in deep, usually violet folds of velvet. What didn't the nineteenth century invent some sort of casing for!" ([1927–40] 1999, 220–21).

6. The house-museum is thus also a story of male domination at the outset of a male-dominated, bourgeois century, with all its typical obsessions later to be recounted by psychoanalysis. We have to keep this in mind, especially in the light of the feminist critique of the paternalistic ontology of the West. Indeed, female temporality would offer a completely different way of interweaving the aeonic, the chronic, and the chronological register.

4. Morphogenesis and Animistic Moments

1. More broadly, the notion of investment in form must be placed in the context of Thom's (1983) case for a "living mathematics" that stands in opposition to merely formalistic approaches.

2. The notion of singularity is also extensively employed in philosophy by both Simondon ([1964–89] 2013) and Deleuze (1969). As we try to show throughout this book, it ranks as a key notion for the study of territories.

3. Of course, it is just the case to recall that Western social science has been afflicted by a veritable distrust for becoming. For Durkheim and Mauss (1903), for instance, the type of metamorphic thought that characterizes "archaic" populations, as well as the popular classes in the West, represented an instance of "absolute mental confusion." The rehabilitation of becoming is, by contrast, at the core of Deleuze's philosophy, who in turn drew from Whitehead's notion of "process."

4. Simmel describes this process in terms of "damming." Each individual is akin to a dam that "contains" the flow of life: "Although the stream of life flows through—or more accurately, as—these individuals, it nevertheless dams up in each of them and becomes a sharply outlined form" ([1918] 2010, 9).

5. The cover of this book is, inter alia, out attempt to pay homage to Simondon's inspiring discussion of brick making.

6. One can notice how Deleuze will be influenced by this idea. Only apparently should Deleuze be regarded as an enemy of morphogenesis or even of formal analysis. Certainly, he famously contended that, for a Spinozist, "the important thing is to understand life, each living individuality, not as a form, or a development of form, but as a complex relation between differential velocities, between deceleration and acceleration of particles" ([1981] 1988, 123). But, we suggest, Simondon's ([1964–89] 2013) disciplines of *allagmatics* and human energetics provide precisely the missing link between morphology and territoriology from a dynamic (metastable, or vitalistic) perspective.

7. Simondon suggests a deep connection between pregnance and animation, through the notion of "informational tension": "The pregnance of a form is not its stability as understood by the thermodynamics of stable states and of convergent transformation series, but rather its capacity to traverse, animate and structure a varied domain, and even increasingly varied and heterogeneous domains. . . . The tension of information is the property that a scheme has to structure a whole domain, to propagate through it, ordering it" ([1964–89] 2013, 550; our translation). This vision of the structuring movement is clearly quite different from the structuralist, or even genetic-structuralist, one, insofar as it also accounts for animation. Accordingly, we regard it as more interesting for us.

8. This point is tackled extensively by Combes (2012) in her beautiful monograph on Simondon.

9. Massumi recalls two crucial philosophical formulas by, respectively, Deleuze and Whitehead: "The whole is not of the parts, but alongside them and in addition to them," and, "The many become one, and are augmented by one" (2009, 40). Taken together these two formulas indicate the complex relation between parts and whole in the perspective of becoming.

10. Webster and Goodwin in this respect argue, "The key to this unexpected uniformity of emergent order in complex systems appears to lie in the way they are organized rather than their composition. Their properties of spontaneous bifurcation from spatially uniform to non-uniform patterns that characterize excitable media, combined with principles of symmetry breaking that follow constraints arising from the dynamic and geometric symmetries of the system, result in symmetry-breaking cascades" (1996, 232).

11. For an extended description of this architectural process, see Srivastava (2009, 210–20). The Kahn-brick encounter can also be remarkably illuminated by Simondon's critique of hylomorphism. For Simondon form and matter never encounter as such. Instead, it is the actual dynamism of the operation of molding that brings into co-presence a given material and a given form through a work of reciprocal adaptation. Both the mold and the material to be molded go through an accurate preparation aimed at enabling their coexistence within a "common operation" ([1964–89] 2013, 43). In other words, the animistic moment of brick molding lies in the fact that "it is as *forces* that matter and form are put into reciprocal presence" (44).

12. In an interesting attempt to engage Deleuze and Guattari, and Levinas, Black has written that the face "represents the paradox of imagining that the Other experiences an inner life like one's own while simultaneously only being able to interact with the Other as a sealed exteriority, which implacably hides the truth of this posited interior life from us" (2011, 20).

5. Domesticity and Animation

1. To our knowledge there is no comprehensive study of this phenomenon in current anthropology. Our assessment, however, might be mistaken, and we seek for interlocutors who might correct us on this point.
2. A similar visibility issue is raised by the Arabic *jinn*, or genies, usually treacherous demons whose name is related to the verb "to hide" or "to conceal." *Jinn* are a recurrent presence in the Quran's surah.
3. A Japanese friend informs us that the third point raised by Gerow (2010)—namely, the ideogram of temporariness—might be spurious. It is nonetheless conceptually stimulating.
4. All these words clearly derive from a deformation of the term *monk*. These "little monks" also carry an association with unbaptized dead babies.
5. Gunnar Landtman (1878–1940) was an early Finnish social anthropologist who, among other things, did fieldwork in Papua New Guinea from 1910 to 1912. Interestingly, Landtman points to similarities between the Scandinavian tomte and the mythical creature *etengena*, who lives in trees nearby plantations and whom people of the Kiwai Island in Papua New Guinea made sacrifices to. A father might at some point also take his young son and introduce him to the *etengena* (1922, 43–44).
6. An interesting parallel can be found in the "little hunchback," a figure of German folklore and children's tales that Benjamin describes as someone who steals, eats others' food, and induces clumsiness: "Whoever is looked at by this little man pays no attention. Either to himself or to the little man" (2002, 385).
7. In Canetti's ([1960] 1984) elaboration, the prototypical "double crowd" is the one formed by the living and the dead, or by the creatures and the spirits.
8. An example is the legend collected by Serao (1881), where one clearly detects how a modern popular tale can be sewed onto a much older underlying anthropological stratum.
9. On the formative and deforming powers of dust, see in particular Stoppani (2007a, 2007b).

6. Territorializing Rhythms

1. The reader is invited to be aware of the difference between *synchronization* (a contemporality, timing different events with one another) and *synchorization* (a conspatiality, localizing different events or activities in the same space).
2. See, for example, Lefebvre: "Rhythmanalysis, a new science that is in the process of being constituted" ([1981] 2005, 130).
3. See, for example, McCormack (2002, 2014), Highmore (2005), Cronin (2006), Edensor and Holloway (2008), J. Middleton (2009), Edensor (2010, 2012), Prior (2011), Lin (2012), Simpson (2012), Schwanen et al. (2012), Smith and Hetherington

(2013), Wunderlich (2013), Goh (2014), Yeo and Heng (2014), Mulíček, Osman, and Seidenglanz (2015), Paiva (2016), Reid-Musson (2017), and Prieto de la Fuente (2018).

4. Our reconstruction of the sources of rhythmanalysis is necessarily selective. For an extensive review, see, for example, McCormack (2002, 476–77) and Mels (2004).

5. Indeed, Caillois took Mauss's classes from 1933 to 1939. In turn Mauss was Durkheim's nephew. Caillois directly references both in his work.

6. Far from being a merely pacified interaction, the gift always borders with war, so veritable "gift races" are found among various populations (most famously, the potlatch of the northwestern American Chinook people).

7. For example, Bolton claimed, "So strong is this impulse in all classes of people that no one is able to listen to music in which the rhythm is strong and clear without making some kind of muscular movements" (1894, 163).

8. Laban expressed it like this: "The boundary between eurhythmy and kakorhythmy is, however, fluid. A subtly tuned organ of perception knows how to detect the rule, the order, the structure of the complexity—in short, the existence of harmonic flow even in the most apparently complicated kakorhythmy" ([1921] 2014, 76).

9. In Warburg's words, "The establishment of a conscious distance [*Bewusstes Distanzschaffen*] between the self and the external world may be described as the basic act of human civilization; and if such in-between space [*Zwischenraum*] becomes the substrate of artistic creation, then the prerequisites are met by which the awareness of such a distance can become a permanent social function which, through the rhythm [*Rhythmus*] of swinging into [*Einschwingen*] matter and swinging out [*Ausschwingen*] toward Sophrosyne, signifies the cycle between pictorial and symbolic cosmology, whose adequacy or failure as an orienting spiritual instrument thus signifies the fate of human culture at large" ([1929] 2010, 629; our translation).

10. In the 1910s Leonardo Coimbra was formulating a new monadology, while Pinheiro dos Santos was taking Bergson's classes in Paris, where he met Bachelard (Cunha 2008). In turn Bergson had taken Tarde's post at the Collège de France and was well acquainted with the latter's work.

11. Decades later Lefebvre will also follow a similar therapeutic perspective of rhythmanalysis. Echoing Bachelard, in one of his own very first mentions of the concept (in *The Production of Space*), Lefebvre suggests that "rhythm analysis might eventually even displace psychoanalysis, as being more concrete, more effective and closer to a pedagogy of appropriation (the appropriation of the body, as of spatial practice)" ([1974] 1991, 205).

12. On this point Bachelard also crucially refers to the psychology of Pierre Janet.

13. So rhythmanalysis is actually not first introduced as a concept in the third volume of *Critique de la vie quotidienne*, as Sheringham (2006, 160) seems to claim.

14. Fraser has also documented a consistent attitude in Lefebvre to obscure his sources, especially never mentioning Bergson as a major source: Lefebvre, comments Fraser, "continues to work with Bergsonism without calling it by that name" (2008, 342).

15. More precisely, Bachelard ([1936] 1950, 76) characterizes rhythm as simultaneously "structure" and "construction," which might be a sophisticated way to include both unity and variation. A similar notion of unity with multiplicity is also already present in Canetti's ([1960] 1984) conceptualization of crowds, specifically where Canetti describes the crowd as a wavelike event that is unique and multiple at the same time. Also the Durkheimian sociologist George Gurvitch (1963, 53) had remarked that rhythms entail a constant search for balance between temporal continuity and discontinuity.

16. The idea that social interaction animates space was clearly first elaborated by Simmel in his major *Sociology* book ([1908] 2009, sec. 9).

7. Affording Play

1. In Cailliois's words, "Play is an occupation that is essentially severed, carefully isolated from the rest of existence, and generally performed within precise temporal and spatial boundaries. There is a space of play: the case, the hopscotch, the chessboard, the checkerboard, the stadium, the racetrack, the 'lice,' the ring, the scene, the arena, and so on. Nothing that happens outside of this ideal boundary matters to the game" (Caillois 1967, 37; our translation).

2. As Certeau once suggested of memory, the association to a territorial sort "produces in a place that does not belong to it" (1986, 86).

3. Friedrich Fröbel's introduction of the German kindergarten, from the 1830s and onward, was an important part of this trend.

4. For a somewhat parallel story of the playgrounds in the postwar United Kingdom, see Kozlovsky (2016).

5. For another discussion on the relation between rhythms and nationalism, in this case Irishness, see Edensor and Holloway (2008).

6. Since the rhythm of a specific game may evolve over days, the need might be felt each time to remind one another of the rules and rewrite them.

7. Details for our description of Fuji Kindergarten are taken from Block (2017).

8. Kopljar discusses a similar phenomenon with her concept-carried affordances (2016, 230–31).

References

Agnew, J. 1994. "The Territorial Trap: The Geographical Assumptions of International Relations Theory." *Review of International Political Economy* 1 (1): 53–80.

Agnew, J., and S. Corbridge. 1995. *Mastering Space: Hegemony, Territory and International Political Economy*. London: Routledge.

Akbar, J. 1988. *Crisis in the Built Environment: The Case of the Muslim City*. Singapore: Concept Media.

Alder, K. 2002. *The Measure of All Things*. New York: Free Press.

Alliès, P. 1980. *L'Invention du territoire*. Grenoble, France: Presses Universitaires de Grenoble.

Altman, I. 1975. *The Environment and Social Behavior*. New York: Brooks-Cole.

Altum, B. 1868. *Der Vogel und sein Leben*. Münster: Niemann.

Amin, A. 2015. "Animated Space." *Public Culture* 27 (2): 239–58.

Anderson, B. 1983. *Imagined Communities*. London: Verso.

———. 2009. "Affective Atmospheres." *Emotion, Space and Society* 2 (2): 77–81.

Anderson, M. 1996. *Frontiers: Territory and State Formation in the Modern World*. Cambridge: Polity.

Annunziata, S., and C. Mattiucci, eds. 2013. *La città in gioco/Playing the City*. Special issue, *Lo Squaderno* 27. www.losquaderno.professionaldreamers.net/?cat=160.

Archer, M. S. 1995. *Realist Social Theory: The Morphogenetic Approach*. Cambridge: Cambridge University Press.

———. 2013. "Morphogenic Society: Self-Government and Self-Organization as Misleading Metaphors." In *Social Morphogenesis*, edited by M. S. Archer, 145–64. New York: Springer.

Ardrey, R. 1966. *The Territorial Imperative: A Personal Inquiry into the Animal Origins of Property and Nations*. New York: Atheneum.

Arendt, H. 1958. *The Human Condition*. Chicago: University of Chicago Press.

Ariès, P. 1985. *Images of Man and Death*. Cambridge MA: Harvard University Press.

Árnason, A., S. B. Hafsteinsson, and T. Grétarsdóttir. 2007. "Acceleration Nation: An Investigation into the Violence of Speed and the Uses of Accidents in Iceland." *Culture, Theory and Critique* 48 (2): 199–217.

Ascherson, N. 2001. "Reflections on International Space." *London Review of Books* 23 (10): 7–11.

Bachelard, G. (1936) 1950. *La dialectique de la durée*. Paris: Puf.

———. 1957. *La poétique de l'espace*. Paris: Puf.

Baliff, F. 2019. "Dismantling Belfast Peace Walls: New Material Arrangements for Improving Community Relations." In Brighenti and Kärrholm 2018b, 35–58.

Barad, K. 2007. *Meeting the Universe Halfway: Quantum Physics and the Entanglement of Matter and Meaning*. Durham: Duke University Press.

Barthes, R. 1980. *Camera Lucida*. Paris: Gallimard.

———. 2002. *Comment vivre ensemble: Cours et séminaires au Collège de France, 1976–1977*. Paris: Seuil/Imec.

Bataille, G. 1967. *La part maudite*. Paris: Minuit.

Baudrillard, J. 1994. "The System of Collecting." In Elsner and Cardinal 1994, 7–24.

Bell, D. 2007. "The Hospitable City: Social Relations in Commercial Spaces." *Progress in Human Geography* 31 (1): 7–22.

Benjamin, W. (1921) 1999. "Zur Kritik der Gewalt." In *Gesammelte Schriften*, edited by R. Tiedemann and H. Schweppenhäuser, 179–204. Vol. 2. Pt. 1. Frankfurt am Maim: Suhrkamp.

———. (1927–40) 1999. *The Arcades Project*. Cambridge MA: Harvard University Press.

———. (1928) 1974. *Ursprung des deutschen Trauerspiels*. In *Gesammelte Schriften*, edited by R. Tiedemann and H. Schweppenhäuser, 203–430. Vol. 1. Pt. 1. Frankfurt am Main: Suhrkamp.

———. (1940) 1968. "Theses on the Philosophy of History." In *Illuminations*, edited by H. Arendt, 253–64. New York: Schocken Books.

———. 1998. *The Origin of the German Tragic Drama*. London: Verso.

———. 2002. *Selected Writings*. Vol. 3, *1935–1938*. Cambridge MA: Belknap.

Bennett, J. 2010. *Vibrant Matter: A Political Ecology of Things*. Durham: Duke University Press.

Bergson, H. 1889. *Essai sur les données immédiates de la conscience*. Paris: Alcan.

Besky, S., and J. Padwe. 2016. "Placing Plants in Territory." *Environment and Society* 7 (1): 9–28.

Bettelheim, B. 1950. *Love Is Not Enough: The Treatment of Emotionally Disturbed Children*. Glencoe IL: Free Press.

Biehler, D. D. 2013. *Pests in the City: Flies, Bedbugs, Cockroaches, and Rats*. Seattle: University of Washington Press.

Biehl-Missal, B., and M. Saren. 2012. "Atmospheres of Seduction: A Critique of Aesthetic Marketing Practices." *Journal of Macromarketing* 32 (2): 168–80.

Bird-David, N. 1999. "Animism Revisited, Personhood, Environment, and Relational Epistemology." Supplement, *Current Anthropology* 40:67–79.

Black, D. 2011. "What Is a Face?" *Body and Society* 17 (4): 1–25.

Bleibleh, S. 2015. "Walking through Walls: The Invisible War." *Space and Culture* 18 (2): 156–70.

Block, I. 2017. "Tokyo Kindergarten by Tezuka Architects Lets Children Run Free on the Roof." *Dezeen*, October 2, 2017. www.dezeen.com/2017/10/02/fuji-kindergarten-tokyo -tezuka-architects-oval-roof-deck-playground/.

Blom, H. 1948. "Den offentliga parken." In *Trädgårdskonst: Den moderna trädgårdens och parkens form*, edited by G. Paulsson, S. Hermelin, W. Bauer, and H. Blom, 535–47. Stockholm: Natur och Kultur.

Blomley, N. 1994. *Law, Space and the Geographies of Power*. New York: Guildford.

Blomley, N., D. Delaney, and R. Ford, eds. 2001. *The Legal Geographies Reader*. Oxford: Blackwell.

Boccagni, P., and A. M. Brighenti. 2015. "Immigrants and Home in the Making: Thresholds of Domesticity, Commonality and Publicness." *Journal of Housing and the Built Environment* 32 (1): 1–10.

Böhme, G. 1993. "Atmosphere as the Fundamental Concept of a New Aesthetics." *Thesis Eleven* 36 (1): 113–26.

Bolton, T. L. 1894. "Rhythm." *American Journal of Psychology* 6 (2): 145–238.

Bonnes, M., and G. Secchiaroli. 1995. *Environmental Psychology: A Psycho-social Introduction*. London: Sage.

Borch, C. 2014. *Architectural Atmospheres: On the Experience and Politics of Architecture*. Basel, Switzerland: Birkhäuser.

Borden, I. 2001. *Skateboarding, Space and the City: Architecture and the Body*. London: Berg.

Boullier, D. 2010. *La ville-événement: Foules et publics urbains*. Paris: Puf.

Bourdieu, P. 1972. *Esquisse d'une théorie de la pratique: Précédé de Trois études d'ethnologie kabyle*. Geneva: Droz.

Bowker, G., and S. L. Star. 1999. *Sorting Things Out: Classification and Its Consequences*. Cambridge MA: MIT Press.

Braudel, F. 1974. *Capitalism and Material Life, 1400–1800*. London: Fontana.

Brentari, C. 2015. *Jakob von Uexküll: The Discovery of the Umwelt between Biosemiotics and Theoretical Biology*. Dordrecht: Springer.

Brighenti, A. M. 2006a. "Did We Really Get Rid of Commands? Thoughts on a Theme by Elias Canetti." *Law and Critique* 17 (1): 47–71.

———. 2006b. "Dogville, or The Dirty Birth of Law." *Thesis Eleven* 87 (1): 96–111.

———. 2006c. "On Territory as Relationship and Law as Territory." *Canadian Journal of Law and Society/Revue Canadienne Droit et Société* 21 (2): 65–86.

———. 2007. "Visibility: A Category for the Social Sciences." *Current Sociology* 55 (3): 323–42.

———. 2008. "Visual, Visible, Ethnographic." *Etnografia e Ricerca Qualitativa* 1 (1): 91–113.

———. 2009a. "Pour une térritoriologie du droit." In *Géographie du droit: Épistémologies, développements et perspectives*, edited by P. Forest, 239–60. Québec: Presses de l'Université de Laval.

———. 2009b. *Territori migranti: Spazio e controllo della mobilità globale.* Verona: Ombre Corte.

———, ed. 2009c. *The Wall and the City.* Trento: Professionaldreamers.

———. 2010a. "Lines, Barred Lines: Movement, Territory and the Law." *International Journal of Law in Context* 6 (3): 217–27.

———. 2010b. "On Territorology: Towards a General Science of Territory." *Theory, Culture and Society* 27 (1): 1–21.

———. 2010c. *The Publicness of Public Space: On the Public Domain.* Monographic issue, *Quaderni del dipartimento di sociologia e ricerca sociale* 49. University of Trento. https://core.ac.uk/download/pdf/11830069.pdf.

———. 2010d. "Tarde, Canetti, and Deleuze on Crowds and Packs." *Journal of Classical Sociology* 10 (3): 291–314.

———. 2010e. *Visibility in Social Theory and Social Research.* Basingstoke UK: Palgrave Macmillan.

———. 2012. "New Media and Urban Motilities: A Territorologic Point of View." *Urban Studies* 49 (2): 399–414.

———. 2013a. "Teoria dei territori." *Scienza e Politica* 25 (48): 175–83.

———, ed. 2013b. *Urban Interstices: The Aesthetics and the Politics of the In-Between.* Farnham UK: Ashgate.

———. 2014a. *The Ambiguous Multiplicities: Materials, Episteme and Politics of Some Cluttered Social Formations.* Basingstoke UK: Palgrave Macmillan.

———. 2014b. "Mobilizing Territories, Territorializing Mobilities." *Sociologica* 8 (1): 1–24.

———. 2015. "Graffiti, Street Art and the Divergent Synthesis of Place Valorisation in Contemporary Urbanism." In *Handbook of Graffiti and Street Art*, edited by J. I. Ross, 158–67. New York: Routledge.

———. 2016a. "Expressive Measures. An Ecology of the Public Domain." In *Graffiti and Street Art: Reading, Writing and Representing the City*, edited by K. Avramidis and M. Tsilimpounidi, 119–34. London: Routledge.

———. 2016b. "Onore, sacro, intensità: Per una sociologia del timotico." *La Società degli Individui* 19 (2): 43–55.

———. 2016c. "The Public and the Common: Some Approximations to Their Contemporary Articulation." *Critical Inquiry* 42 (2): 306–28.

———. 2017. "The Visible: Element of the Social." *Frontiers in Sociology*, November 6, 2017. www.frontiersin.org/articles/10.3389/fsoc.2017.00017/full.

———. 2018. "The Vegetative City." *Culture, Theory and Critique* 59 (3): 251–31.

Brighenti, A. M., and M. Kärrholm. 2018a. "Atmospheres of Retail and the Asceticism of Civilized Consumption." *Geographica Helvetica* 73 (3): 203–13.

——, eds. 2018b. *Urban Walls: Political and Cultural Meanings of Vertical Structures and Surfaces.* London: Routledge.

——. 2019. "Three Presents: On the Multi-temporality of Territorial Production and the Gift from John Soane," *Time and Society* 28 (1): 375–98.

Brighenti, A. M., and C. Mattiucci. 2008. "Editing Urban Environments: Territories, Prolongations, Visibilities." In *Mediacity: Situations, Practices, and Encounters*, edited by F. Eckhart, 81–104. Berlin: Frank und Timme/Bauhaus-Universität.

——. 2012. "Visualising the Riverbank." *City: Analysis of Urban Trends, Culture, Theory, Policy, Action* 16 (1–2): 221–34.

Brighenti, A. M., and A. Pavoni. 2017. "City of Unpleasant Feelings: Stress, Comfort and Animosity in Urban Life." *Social and Cultural Geography* 20 (2): 137–56.

Brown, B. 1987. "Territoriality." In *Handbook of Environmental Psychology*, edited by D. Stokol and I. Altman, 505–31. New York: Wiley.

Brown, S., and R. Capdevila, 1999. "Perpetuum Mobile: Substance, Force and the Sociology of Translation." In Law and Hassard 1999, 26–50.

Buttimer, A. 1976. "Grasping the Dynamism of Lifeworld." *Annals of the Association of American Geographers* 66 (2): 277–92.

Caillois, R. (1939) 1980. *L'homme et le sacré.* Paris: Gallimard.

——. 1967. *Les jeux et les hommes: Le masque et la vertige.* Paris: Gallimard.

Canetti, E. (1960) 1984. *Crowds and Power.* New York: Farrar, Straus and Giroux.

——. 1975. *Das Gewissen der Worte.* Munich: Hanser.

Caneva, G., A. Pacini, L. C. Grapow, and S. Ceschin. 2003. "The Colosseum's Use and State of Abandonment as Analysed through Its Flora." *International Biodeterioration and Biodegradation* 51 (3): 211–19.

Canguilhem, G. (1952) 1965. *La connaissance de la vie.* Paris: Vrin.

——. 1966. *Le normal et le pathologique.* Paris: Puf.

Caniggia, G., and G. L. Maffei. 2001. *Architectural Composition and Building Typology: Interpreting Basic Building.* Florence: Alinea Editrice.

Carlstein, T. 1978. "Innovation, Time Allocation and Time-Space Packing." In *Human Activity and Time Geography*, edited by T. Carlstein, D. Parkes, and N. Thrift, 146–61. London: Arnold.

Casey, E. 1997. *The Fate of Place: A Philosophical History.* Berkeley: University of California Press.

Castells, M. 1996. *The Information Age: Economy, Society and Culture.* Vol. 1, *The Rise of the Network Society.* Oxford: Blackwell.

Certeau, M. de. 1986. *The Practice of Everyday Life.* Los Angeles: University of California Press.

Cheetham, F., M. McEachern, and G. Warnaby. 2018. "A Kaleidoscopic View of the Territorialized Consumption of Place." *Marketing Theory* 18 (4): 473–92.

Chrisafis, A. 2016. "Alain Juppé Calls for UK Border to Move from Calais to Kent." *Guardian*, October 20, 2016.

Chudacoff, H. P. 2007. *Children at Play: An American History*. New York: New York University Press.

Citroni, S., and M. Kärrholm. 2017. "Neighbourhood Events and the Visibilisation of Everyday Life: The Cases of Turro (Milan) and Norra Fäladen (Lund)." *European Urban and Regional Studies* 26 (1): 50–64.

Cloke, P., and O. Jones. 2005. "'Unclaimed Territory': Childhood and Disordered Space(s)." *Social and Cultural Geography* 6 (3): 311–33.

Coimbra, L. 1958. *O Criacionismo: Síntese filosófica; Obras completas*. Vol. 2. Porto: Tavares Martins.

Combes, M. 2012. *Gilbert Simondon and the Philosophy of the Transindividual*. Cambridge MA: MIT Press.

Conzen, M. R. 2004. *Thinking about Urban Form: Papers on Urban Morphology, 1932–1998*. Oxford: Lang.

Coole, D., and S. Frost. 2010. *New Materialisms: Ontology, Agency and Politics*. Durham: Duke University Press.

Counihan, C. 1999. *The Anthropology of Food and Body: Gender, Meaning, and Power*. London: Routledge.

Crang, M. 2001. "Rhythms of the City." In *Timespace*, edited by J. May and N. Thrift, 187–207. London: Routledge.

———. 2007. "Speed=Distance/Time: Chronotopographies of Action." In *24/7: Time and Temporality in the Network Society*, edited by R. Hassan and R. Purser, 62–88. Stanford: Stanford University Press.

Crawford, M. 1992. "The World in a Shopping Mall." In *Variations on a Theme Park*, edited by M. Sorokin, 3–30. New York: Hill and Wang.

Cronin, A. M. 2006. "Advertising and the Metabolism of the City: Urban Space, Commodity Rhythms." *Environment and Planning D: Society and Space* 24 (4): 615–32.

Cunha, R. S. 2008. "A filosofia do ritmo portuguesa: Da monadologia rítmica de Leonardo Coimbra a Lúcio Pinheiro dos Santos e a ritmanálise." *Philosophica* 31:161–91.

Darley, G. 1999. "Soane: The Man and His Circle." In Richardson and Stevens 1999, 16–25.

Deakin, R. 1855. *Flora of the Colosseum, or Illustrations and Descriptions of Four Hundred and Twenty Plants Growing Spontaneously upon the Ruins of the Colosseum of Rome*. London: Groombridge and Sons.

Degen, M. M., and G. Rose. 2012. "The Sensory Experiencing of Urban Design: The Role of Walking and Perceptual Memory." *Urban Studies* 49 (15): 3271–87.

de la Cadena, M. 2015. *Earth Beings: Ecologies of Practice across Andean Worlds*. Durham: Duke University Press.

De Laet, M., and A. Mol. 2000. "The Zimbabwe Bush Pump: Mechanics of a Fluid Technology." *Social Studies of Science* 30 (2): 225–63.

Delaney, D. 1998. *Race, Place, and the Law, 1836–1948*. Austin: University of Texas Press.

——. 2005. *Territory: A Short Introduction*. Malden MA: Blackwell.

Delaplace, G., and R. Empson. 2007. "The Little Human and the Daughter-in-Law: Invisibles as Seen through the Eyes of Different Kinds of People." *Inner Asia* 9 (2): 197–214.

Deleuze, G. 1969. *Logique du sens*. Paris: Minuit. English ed. *The Logic of Sense*. New York: Columbia University Press, 1990.

——. 1981. *Spinoza: Philosophie pratique*. Paris: Minuit. English ed. *Spinoza: Practical Philosophy*. San Francisco: City Lights, 1988.

——. 1984. "Cinema: Vérité et temps; La voix de Gilles Deleuze en ligne." February 7, 1984. www2.univ-paris8.fr/deleuze/article.php3?id_article=328.

——. 1990. *Pourparlers, 1972–1990*. Paris: Minuit.

——. 2001. *Pure Immanence, Essays on a Life*. New York: Zone Books.

——. 2003. *Deux régimes de fous: Textes et entretiens, 1975–1995*. Paris: Minuit.

Deleuze, G., and P. Guattari. 1980. *Mille plateaux: Capitalisme et schizophrénie 2*. Paris: Minuit. English ed. *A Thousand Plateaus*. Minneapolis: University of Minnesota Press, 1987.

Deligny, F. (1981) 2008. *L'Arachnéen et autres textes*. Paris: L'Arachnéen.

——. 2013. *Cartes et lignes d'erre: Traces du réseau de, 1969–1979*. Paris: l'Arachnéen.

——. 2015. *The Arachnean and Other Texts*. Minneapolis: University of Minnesota Press.

De Quincey, T. (1847) 1897. "Protestantism." In *Collected Writings of Thomas De Quincey: Speculative and Theological Essays*, edited by D. Masson, 8:244–309. London: A and C Block.

Diken, B., and C. B. Laustsen. 2006. "The Camp." *Geografiska Annaler: Series B, Human Geography* 88 (4): 443–52.

Dolidon, A. 2010. "Barthesian Idiorrythmic Forms of Micro-resistance in the Work of Jocelyne François." *Forum for Modern Language Studies* 46 (3): 310–20.

Dorey, H. 1999. "12–14 Lincoln's Inn Fields." In Richardson and Stevens 1999, 150–73.

——. 2015. "Crude Hints: An Introduction." In Soane 2015, 1–16.

Douglas, M. 1991. "The Idea of a Home: A Kind of Space." *Social Research* 58 (1): 287–307.

Dovey, K. 1985. "Home and Homelessness." In *Home Environments*, edited by I. Altman and C. Werner, 33–64. New York: Fordham University Press.

——. 2010. *Becoming Places: Urbanism/Architecture/Identity/Power*. London: Routledge.

Dupuy, G. (1991) 2008. *Urban Networks–Network Urbanism*. Amsterdam: Techne.

Durkheim, E. 1912. *Les formes élémentaires de la vie religieuse*. Paris: Puf.

Durkheim, E., and M. Mauss. 1903. "De quelques formes primitives de classification. Contribution à l'étude des représentations collectives." *L'Année Sociologique* 6:1–72.

Dyson-Hudson, R., and E. A. Smith. 1978. "Human Territoriality: An Ecological Reassessment." *American Anthropologist* 80 (1): 21–41.

Edensor, T. 2010. "Walking in Rhythms: Place, Regulation, Style and the Flow of Experience." *Visual Studies* 25 (1): 69–79.

——, ed. 2012. *Geographies of Rhythm: Nature, Place, Mobilities and Bodies.* Farnham UK: Ashgate.

Edensor, T., and J. Holloway. 2008. "Rhythmanalysing the Coach Tour: The Ring of Kerry, Ireland." *Transactions of the Institute of British Geographers* 33 (4): 483–501.

Edney, J. 1974. "Human Territoriality." *Psychological Bulletin* 81:959–75.

Ehrensvärd, U. 1979. *Den svenska tomten.* Stockholm: Svenska Turistföreningen.

Eibl-Eibesfeldt, I. 1970. *Ethology: The Biology of Behavior.* New York: Holt, Rinehart and Winston.

Einstein, A. 1949. *The World as I See It.* New York: Philosophical Library.

Elden, S. 2005. "Missing the Point: Globalization, Deterritorialization and the Space of the World." *Transactions of the Institute of British Geographers*, n.s., 8:8–19.

——. 2007. "Government, Calculation, Territory." *Environment and Planning D: Society and Space* 25 (3): 562–80.

——. 2013. *The Birth of Territory.* Chicago: University of Chicago Press.

Elsner, J. 1994. "A Collector's Model of Desire: The House and Museum of Sir John Soane." In Elsner and Cardinal 1994, 155–76.

Elsner, J., and R. Cardinal, eds. 1994. *The Cultures of Collecting.* London: Reaktion Books.

Ericksen, E. G. 1980. *The Territorial Experience: Human Ecology as Symbolic Interaction.* Austin: University of Texas Press.

Eriksson, J. 2010. *Monstret och människan: Paré, Deleuze och teratologiska traditioner i fransk filosofi, från renässanshumanism till posthumanism.* Lund, Sweden: Lund University.

Escobar, M. P. 2014. "The Power of (Dis)Placement: Pigeons and Urban Regeneration in Trafalgar Square." *Cultural Geographies* 21 (3): 363–87.

Etkin, W. 1967. *Social Behavior from Fish to Man.* Chicago: University of Chicago Press.

Evans, E. P. 1906. *The Criminal Prosecution and Capital Punishment of Animals.* London: Heinemann.

Evans, R. 1982. *The Fabrication of Virtue: English Prison Architecture, 1750–1840.* Cambridge: Cambridge University Press.

Feinberg, S. G. 1984. "The Genesis of Sir John Soane's Museum Idea: 1801–1810." *Journal of the Society of Architectural Historians* 43 (3): 225–37.

Ficino, M. (1469) 1987. *El libro dell'amore.* Edited by Sandra Niccoli. Florence: Olschki.

Ford, R. T. 1999. "Law's Territory: A History of Jurisdiction." *Michigan Law Review* 97 (4): 843–930.

Forty, A. 1986. *Objects of Desire: Design and Society since 1750.* London: Thames and Hudson.

——. 2000. *Words and Buildings: A Vocabulary of Modern Architecture.* London: Thames and Hudson.

Foucault, M. 1975. *Surveiller et punir: Naissance de la prison.* Paris: Gallimard.

References

———. (1978) 2004. *Sécurité, territoire, population: Cours au Collège de France*. Paris: Seuil/Gallimard.

Franzén, M. 1982. "Gatans disciplinering." *Häften för Kritiska Studier* 15 (5): 3–25.

Frascari, M. 1990. *Monsters of Architecture: Anthropomorphism in Architectural Theory*. Lanham MD: Rowman and Littlefield.

Fraser, B. 2008. "Toward a Philosophy of the Urban: Henri Lefebvre's Uncomfortable Application of Bergsonism." *Environment and Planning D: Society and Space* 26 (2): 338–58.

Frazer, J. G. (1906–15) 1959. *The New Golden Bough: A New Abridgment of the Classic Work*. New York: New American Library.

Freud, S. 1913. *Totem und Tabu*. Vienna: Heller.

———. 1919. *Das Unheimliche* [The uncanny]. In *The Standard Edition of the Complete Psychological Works of Sigmund Freud*, edited by A. Strachey, 17:217–56. London: Hogarth.

Furján, H. 2004. "Scenes from a Museum." *Grey Room* 17:64–81.

———. 2009. "Exhibitionism: John Soane's 'Model House.'" In *Intimate Metropolis: Urban Subjects in the Modern City*, edited by V. Di Palma, D. Periton, and M. Lahtouri, 90–109. London: Routledge.

———. 2011. *Glorious Visions: John Soane's Spectacular Theater*. London: Routledge.

Gagen, E. 1998. "Playing the Part: Performing Gender in America's Playgrounds." In *Children's Geographies: Playing, Living, Learning*, edited by S. Holloway and G. Valentine, 223–39. New York: Routledge.

———. 2000. "An Example to Us All: Child Development and Identity Construction in Early 20th-Century Playgrounds." *Environment and Planning A* 32 (4): 599–616.

Gandhi, A. 2012. "Catch Me If You Can: Monkey Capture in Delhi." *Ethnography* 13 (1): 43–56.

Gandy, M. 2017. "Urban Atmospheres." *Cultural Geographies* 24 (3): 353–74.

Gehl, J., and L. Gemzöe, L. 1996. *Public Space, Public Life*. Copenhagen: Arkitektens and Kunstakademiets Forlag.

Geoffroy Saint-Hilaire, E. 1818. *Philosophie anatomique*. Paris: Baillière.

———, 1830. *Principes de philosophie zoologique*. Paris: Pichon et Didier.

Gerow, A. 2010. "The Borrower Arrietty/Karigurashi no Arietti." *Tangemania*, July 17, 2010. www.aarongerow.com/news/the-borrower-arrietty-karig.html.

Gesell, A. 1925. *The Mental Growth of the Preschool Child*. London: Macmillan.

Gibbon, E. 1896–1900. *The Decline and Fall of the Roman Empire*. Edited by J. B. Bury. 7 vols. London: Methuen.

Gibson, J. J. 1966. *The Senses Considered as Perceptual Systems*. Boston: Houghton Mifflin.

———. 1979. *The Ecological Approach to Visual Perception*. Boston: Houghton Mifflin.

Goethe, W. v. (1790) 1983. *Versuch die Metamorphose der Pflanzen zu erklären* [The metamorphosis of plants]. In *Scientific Studies*, edited by D. Miller, 76–97. New York: Suhrkamp.

———. (1817). *Italienische reise: Band 2*. Stuttgart: Cotta. www.gutenberg.org/ebooks/2405.

Goffman, E. 1971. *Relations in Public: Microstudies of the Public Order*. New York: Basic Books.

Goh, D. P. S. 2014. "Walking the Global City: The Politics of Rhythm and Memory in Singapore." *Space and Culture* 17 (1): 16–28.

Gottman, J. 1973. *The Significance of Territory*. Charlottesville: University Press of Virginia.

Graham, S., and S. Marvin. 2001. *Splintering Urbanism, Networked Infrastructures, Technological Mobilities and the Urban Condition*. London: Routledge.

Greco, M. 2005. "On the Vitality of Vitalism." *Theory, Culture and Society* 22 (1): 15–27.

Grosz, E. 2001. *Architecture from the Outside: Essays on Virtual and Real Space*. Cambridge MA: MIT Press.

———. 2008. *Chaos, Territory, Art: Deleuze and the Framing of the Earth*. New York: Columbia University Press.

Gruber, P. 2011. *Biomimetics in Architecture: Architecture of Life and Buildings*. Vienna: Springer.

Gurvitch, G. 1963. *La vocation actuelle de la sociologie*. Paris: Presses Universitaires de France.

Gwiazdzinski, G. 2013. "Teenagers in the Contemporary City: Hypermodern Times, Spaces and Practices." In Henckel et al. 2013, 61–74.

Habraken, N. J. 1998. *The Structure of the Ordinary: Form and Control in the Built Environment*. Cambridge MA: MIT Press.

Häkli, J. 1994. *Territoriality and the Rise of the Modern State*. Helsinki: Geographical Society of Finland.

Hall, E. 1959. *The Silent Language*. Garden City NY: Doubleday.

Halvorsen, S. 2018. "Decolonising Territory: Dialogues with Latin American Knowledges and Grassroots Strategies." *Progress in Human Geography* 43 (5): 790–814.

Hartson, R. 2003. "Cognitive, Physical, Sensory, and Functional Affordances in Interaction Design." *Behaviour and Information Technology* 22 (5): 315–38.

Healey, P. 1997. *Collaborative Planning: Shaping Places in Fragmented Societies*. Vancouver: University of British Columbia Press.

Healy, S. 2014. "Atmospheres of Consumption: Shopping as Involuntary Vulnerability." *Emotion, Space and Society* 10:35–43.

Hediger, H. P. 1961. "The Evolution of Territorial Behaviour." In *The Social Life of Early Man*, edited by S. L. Washburn, 17–33. London: Methuen.

———. 1969. "Biological Glimpses of Some Aspects of Human Sociology." *Social Research* 36 (4): 530–41.

Heft, H. 2001. *Ecological Psychology in Context: James Gibson, Roger Barker and the Legacy of William James's Radical Empiricism*. New York: Psychology Press.

Heidegger, M. (1951) 1971. *Building, Dwelling, Thinking*. New York: Harper Colophon Books.

Henckel, D., S. Thomaier, B. Könecke, R. Zedda, and S. Stabilini, eds. 2013. *Space-Time Design of the Public City*. Dordrecht: Springer.

Herbert, S. 1996. "The Normative Ordering of Police Territoriality: Making and Marking Space with the Los Angeles Police Department." *Annals of the Association of American Geographers* 86 (3): 567–82.

Highmore, B. 2005. *Cityscapes: Cultural Readings in the Material and Symbolic City*. Basingstoke UK: Palgrave Macmillan.

Hillier, B. 1996. *Space Is the Machine: A Configurational Theory of Architecture*. Cambridge: Cambridge University Press.

Hillier, B., and J. Hanson, 1984. *The Social Logic of Space*. Cambridge: Cambridge University Press.

Hirst, P. 1997. "The Defence of Places: Fortifications as Architecture." *AA Files* 33 (pt. 1): 13–26; 34 (pt. 2): 6–17.

Holder, J., and C. Harrison, eds. 2003. *Law and Geography*. Oxford: Oxford University Press.

Holmberg, T. 2015. *Urban Animals, Crowding in Zoocities*. London: Routledge.

Howard, H. E. 1920. *Territory in Bird Life*. London: J. Murray.

Hugo, V. (1829). *Le dernier jour d'un condamné*. Paris: Gosselin. www.gutenberg.org/ebooks/6838.

Husserl, E. 1973. *Zur Phänomenologie der Intersubjektivität: Texte aus dem Nachlass*. Part 3, *1929–1935: Husserliana, Edmund Husserl Gesammelte Werke*, edited by I. Kern. Vol. 15. The Hague: Nijhoff.

Hyltén-Cavallius, G. O. 1863. *Wärend och Wirdarne: Ett försök i Svensk Ethnologi*. Stockholm: Norstedt.

Ingold, T. 1986. *The Appropriation of Nature: Essays on Human Ecology and Social Relations*. Manchester: Manchester University Press.

———. 2000. *The Perception of the Environment: Essays on Livelihood, Dwelling and Skill*. London: Psychology Press.

———. 2007. *Lines: A Brief History*. London: Routledge.

———. 2011. *Being Alive: Essays on Movement, Knowledge and Description*. London: Routledge.

———. 2016. *The Life of Lines*. New York: Routledge.

Jacobs, J. 1961. *The Life and Death of Great American Cities*. New York: Random House.

Jacobson, D. 1997. "New Frontiers: Territory, Social Spaces, and the State." *Sociological Forum* 12 (1): 121–33.

Janet, P. 1889. *L'automatisme psychologique*. Paris: Alcan.

———. 1929. *L'évolution psychologique de la personnalité*. Paris: Chahine.

Jaques-Dalcroze, E. 1921. *Rhythm, Music and Education*. New York: Putnam's Sons.

Jennison, G. 1937. *Animals for Show and Pleasure in Ancient Rome*. Manchester: Manchester University Press.

Jerolmack, C. 2013. *The Global Pigeon*. Chicago: University of Chicago Press.

Jesi, F. (1969) 2000. *Spartakus: Simbologia della rivolta*. Turin, Italy: Bollati Boringhieri.

Jessop, B., N. Brenner, and M. Jones. 2008. "Theorizing Sociospatial Relations." *Environment and Planning D: Society and Space* 26 (3): 389–401.

Julmi, C. 2016. "The Concept of Atmosphere in Management and Organization Studies." *Organizational Aesthetics* 6 (1): 4–30.

Jung, C. G. 1940. *The Psychology of the Child Archetype: Collected Works*. Vol. 9. Princeton NJ: Princeton University Press.

——. 1956. *Symbols of Transformation*. Princeton NJ: Princeton University Press.

Kahn, N. 2003. *My Architect: A Son's Journey*. Documentary film. www.myarchitectfilm.com/.

Karoff, H. S. 2015. "Reconceptualising Children's Play: Exploring the Connections between Spaces, Practices and Emotional Moods." In *Children's Spatialities: Embodiment, Emotion and Agency*, edited by A. Hackett, L. Procter, and J. Seymour, 112–27. Basingstoke UK: Palgrave.

Kärrholm, M. 2004. *Arkitekturens territorialitet: Till en diskussion om territoriell makt och gestaltning i stadens offentliga rum*. Lund, Sweden: Lund University.

——. 2005. "Territorial Complexity in Public Spaces: A Study of Territorial Production at Three Squares in Lund." *Nordic Journal of Architectural Research* 18 (1): 99–114.

——. 2007. "The Materiality of Territorial Production: A Conceptual Discussion of Territoriality, Materiality, and the Everyday Life of Public Space." *Space and Culture* 10 (4): 437–53.

——. 2008. "The Territorialisation of a Pedestrian Precinct in Malmö: Materialities in the Commercialisation of Public Space." *Urban Studies* 45 (9): 1903–24.

——. 2009. "To the Rhythm of Shopping: On Synchronisation in Urban Landscapes of Consumption." *Social and Cultural Geography* 10 (4): 421–40.

——. 2012. *Retailising Space, Architecture, Retail and the Territorialisation of Public Space*. Ashgate Studies in Architecture Series. Farnham UK: Ashgate.

——. 2013. "Building Type Production and Everyday Life: Rethinking Building Types through Actor-Network Theory and Object-Oriented Philosophy." *Environment and Planning D: Society and Space* 31 (6): 1109–24.

——. 2015. "The Main Square Revisited, a Comparison of Daily Usage of Stortorget Malmö, between 1978 and 2013." In *Urban Squares, Spatio-temporal Studies of Design and Everyday Life in the Öresund Region*, edited by M. Kärrholm. Lund, Sweden: Nordic Academic Press.

——. 2016. "The Animistic Moment: Clarice Lispector, Louis Kahn and the Reassembling of Materialities." *Lo Squaderno* 39:71–77.

——. 2017. "The Temporality of Territorial Production: The Case of Stortorget, Malmö." *Social and Cultural Geography* 18 (5): 683–705.

Kärrholm, M., and J. Wirdelöv. 2019. "The Neighbourhood in Pieces: The Fragmentation of Local Public Space in a Swedish Housing Area." *International Journal of Urban and Regional Research* 43 (5): 870–87.

Katz, C. 2004. *Growing up Global: Economic Restructuring and Children's Everyday Lives.* Minneapolis: University of Minnesota Press.

Kazig, R., D. Masson, and R. Thomas 2017. "Atmospheres and Mobility: An Introduction." *Mobile Culture Studies* 3:7–20.

Kerényi, C. (1951) 1980. *The Gods of the Greeks.* London: Thames and Hudson.

Keswani, K. 2017. "The Practice of Tree Worship and the Territorial Production of Urban Space in the Indian Neighbourhood." *Journal of Urban Design* 22 (3): 370–87.

Klauser, F. R. 2010. "Splintering Spheres of Security: Peter Sloterdijk and the Contemporary Fortress City." *Environment and Planning D* 28 (2): 326–40.

Klingmann, A. 2007. *Brandscapes, Architecture in the Experience Economy.* Cambridge MA: MIT Press.

Knox, T. 2009. *Sir John Soane's Museum, London.* London: Merrell.

Koch, R., and A. Latham. 2013. "On the Hard Work of Domesticating a Public Space." *Urban Studies* 50 (1): 6–21.

Koolhaas, R., AMO, and Harvard Graduate School of Design. 2014. *Wall.* Venice: Marsilio.

Kopljar, S. 2016. *How to Think about a Place Not Yet.* Lund, Sweden: Lund University.

Korosec-Serfaty, P. 1984. "The Home from Attic to Cellar." *Journal of Environmental Psychology* 4 (4): 303–21.

Kostof, S. 1992. *The City Assembled: The Elements of Urban Form through History.* London: Thames and Hudson.

Kotler, P. 1973. "Atmospherics as a Marketing Tool." *Journal of Retailing* 49 (4): 48–64.

Kozlovsky, R. 2016. *The Architectures of Childhood: Children, Modern Architecture and Reconstruction in Postwar England.* London: Routledge.

Kracauer, S. 1978. *Schriften Bd. 1: Soziologie als Wissenschaft; Der Detektiv-Roman: Die Angestellten.* Frankfurt am Main: Suhrkamp.

Krebs, J. R. 1977. "The Significance of Song Repertoires: The Beau Geste Hypothesis." *Animal Behaviour* 25 (2): 475–78.

Laban, R. (1921) 2014. "Eurhythmy and Kakorhythmy in Art and Education." *Body and Society* 20 (3–4): 75–78.

Landtman, G. 1922. "Hustomtens förvantskap och härstamning." In *Folkloristiska och etnografiska studier III*, edited by K. R. V. Wikman, 1–48. Helsinki: Svenska Litteratursällskapet i Finland.

Larsson, A., B. Norlin, and M. Rönnlund. 2017. *Den svenska skolgårdens historia.* Lund, Sweden: Nordic Academy Press.

Latimer, J., and R. Munro 2009. "Keeping and Dwelling: Relational Extension, the Idea of Home, and Otherness." *Space and Culture* 12 (3): 317–31.

Latour, B. 1999a. "On Recalling ANT." In Law and Hassard 1999, 15–25.

———. 1999b. *Pandora's Hope: Essays on the Reality of Science Studies*. Cambridge MA: Harvard University Press.

———. 2005. *Reassembling the Social: An Introduction to Actor-Network-Theory*. Oxford: Oxford University Press.

———. 2010. *On the Modern Cult of the Factish Gods*. Durham: Duke University Press.

Launay, J. 2015. "Musical Sounds, Motor Resonance, and Detectable Agency." *Empirical Musicology Review* 10 (1): 30–40.

Launay, J., B. Tarr, and R. Dunbar. 2016. "Synchrony as an Adaptive Mechanism for Large-Scale Human Social Bonding." *Ethology* 122 (10): 779–89.

Law, J. 2002. "Objects and Spaces." *Theory, Culture and Society* 19 (5–6): 91–105.

Law, J., and J. Hassard, eds. 1999. *Actor Network Theory and After*. Oxford: Blackwell.

Law, J., and A. Mol. 1994. "Regions, Networks and Fluids: Anemia and Social Topology." *Social Studies of Science* 24 (4): 641–71.

———. 2001. "Situating Technoscience: An Inquiry into Spatialities." *Environment and Planning D: Society and Space* 19 (5): 609–21.

Le Corbusier. (1924) 1966. *Urbanisme*. Paris: Vincent, Fréal.

Lefaivre, L. 2002. "Space, Place and Play, or The Interstitial/Cybernetic/Polycentred Urban Model Underlying Aldo van Eyck's Quasi-Unknown but, Nevertheless, Myriad Postwar Amsterdam Playgrounds." In Lefaivre and de Roode 2002, 16–57.

———. 2007. *Ground-Up City: Play as a Design Tool*. Rotterdam: 010.

Lefaivre, L., and I. de Roode, eds. 2002. *Aldo van Eyck: The Playgrounds and the City*. Rotterdam: Netherlands Architecture Institute/Stedelijk.

Lefebvre, H. 1961. *Critique de la vie quotidienne*. Vol. 2, *Fondements d'une sociologie de la quotidienneté*. Paris: l'Arche.

———. (1974) 1991. *The Production of Space*. Oxford: Blackwell.

———. (1981) 2005. *Critique of Everyday Life*. Vol. 3. London: Verso.

———. 1992. *Éléments de rythmanalyse: Introduction à la connaissance des rythme*. Paris: Syllepse.

———. (1992) 2004. *Rhythmanalysis*. Edited by Stuart Elden. London: Continuum.

Lefebvre, H., and C. Régulier. 1985. "Le projet rythmanalytique." *Communications* 41:191–99.

———. 1986. "Essai de rythmanalyse des villes méditerranéennes." *Peuples Méditerranéens* 37:5–16.

Levi, C. (1945) 2013. *Cristo si è fermato a Eboli*. Turin, Italy: Einaudi.

Lévy, J. 1994. *L'Espace légitime: Sur la dimension géographique de la fonction politique*. Paris: Presses de la Fondation Nationale des Sciences Politiques.

Ley, D., and R. Cybriwsky. 1974. "Urban Graffiti as Territorial Markers." *Annals of the Association of American Geographers* 64 (4): 491–505.

Lichtenstein, C., and T. Schregenberger, eds. 1993. *As Found: The Discovery of the Ordinary*. Baden, Switzerland: Müller.

Lieberg, M. 1992. *Att ta staden i besittning: Om ungas rum och rörelser i offentlig miljö*. Lund, Sweden: Lund University.

Lin, W. 2012. "Wasting Time? The Differentiation of Travel Time in Urban Transport." *Environment and Planning A* 44 (10): 2477–92.

Lofland, L. 1998. *The Public Realm: Exploring the City's Quintessential Social Territory*. New York: De Gruyter.

Lorenz, K. Z. 1966. *On Aggression*. New York: Harcourt, Brace and World.

———. 1981. *The Foundations of Ethology*. New York: Springer.

Lueder, C. 2017. "Evaluator, Choreographer, Ideologue, Catalyst: The Disparate Reception Histories of Alexander Klein's Graphical Method." *Journal of the Society of Architectural Historians* 76 (1): 82–106.

Lyman, S. M., and M. B. Scott. 1967. "Territoriality: A Neglected Sociological Dimension." *Social Problems* 15 (2): 236–49.

Lynch, K. 1972. *What Time Is This Place?* Cambridge MA: MIT Press.

Lyon, D. 2019. *What Is Rhythmanalysis?* London: Bloomsbury.

Macdonald, R. A. 2002. *Lessons of Everyday Law*. Montreal, Quebec: McGill-Queen's University Press.

Maczak, A. 1995. *Travel in Early Modern Europe*. Cambridge: Polity.

Magnus, O. 1555. *Historia de gentibus septentrionalibus, earumque diversis statibus, conditionibus, moribus, ritibus, superstitionibus*. Rome: Apud Johannem Mariam de Viottis Parmensem.

Magnusson, J. 2016. *Clustering Architectures: The Role of Materialities for Emerging Collectives in the Public Domain*. Lund: Lund University.

Maier, C. S. 2016. *Once within Borders: Territories of Power, Wealth, and Belonging since 1500*. Cambridge MA: Belknap Press of Harvard University Press.

Maier, E. 1975. "Torah as Movable Territory." *Annals of the Association of American Geographers* 65 (1): 18–23.

Malmberg, T. 1980. *Human Territoriality: Survey of Behavioural Territories in Man with Preliminary Analysis and Discussion of Meaning*. The Hague: Mouton.

Mandich, G., and V. Cuzzocrea. 2016. "'Domesticating' the City: Family Practices in Public Space." *Space and Culture* 19 (3): 224–36.

Manfredini, M., and A. D. Ta. 2017. "The Production of Pluralistic Spatialities: The Persistence of Counter-Space Territories in the Streets of Hanoi, Vietnam." In *La città creativa*, edited by R. Galdini and A. Marata, 373–81. Rome: Consiglio Nazionale Architetti Pianificatori Paesaggisti e Conservatori.

Marc, F. 1915. "Die hundert Aphorismen: Das zweite Gesicht." *Zeno*. www.zeno.org/Kunst/M/Marc,+Franz/Schriften/Aus+der+Kriegszeit/35.+Die+100+Aphorismen.

Marcus, S. 1999. *Apartment Stories: City and Home in Nineteenth-Century Paris and London*. Berkeley: University of California Press.

Mareggi, M. 2013. "Urban Rhythms in the Contemporary City." In Henckel et al. 2013, 3–20.

Markus, T. A. 1993. *Buildings and Power: Freedom and Control in the Origin of Modern Building Types*. London: Routledge.

Massey, D. 2005. *For Space*. London: Sage.

Massumi, B. 2009. "'Technical Mentality' Revisited: Brian Massumi on Gilbert Simondon." *Parrhesia* 7:36–45.

Mauss, M. (1924) 1950. *Essai sur le don*. In *Sociologie et anthropologie*. Paris: Puf.

———. (1935) 1973. "Techniques of the Body." *Economy and Society* 2 (1): 70–88.

———. 1947. *Manuel d'ethnographie*. Paris: Payot.

McCormack, D. P. 2002. "A Paper with an Interest in Rhythm." *Geoforum* 33 (4): 469–85.

———. 2014. *Refrains for Moving Bodies: Experience and Experiment in Affective Spaces*. Durham: Duke University Press.

McLuhan, M. 1964. *Understanding Media: The Extensions of Man*. New York: McGraw-Hill.

Mels, T. 2004. "Lineages of a Geography of Rhythms." In *Reanimating Places: A Geography of Rhythms*, edited by T. Mels, 3–44. Aldershot UK: Ashgate.

Merleau-Ponty, M. 1945. *Phénoménologie de la perception*. Paris: Gallimard.

———. 1964. *Le visible et l'invisible*. Paris: Gallimard.

———. 1995. *La nature: Cours du Collège de France*. Paris: Seuil.

Merriman, P. 2012. "Human Geography without Time-Space." *Transactions of the Institute of British Geographers* 37 (1): 13–27

Middleton, J. 2009. "Stepping in Time: Walking, Time, and Space in the City." *Environment and Planning A* 41 (8): 1943–61.

Middleton, R. 1999. "Soane's Spaces and the Matter of Fragmentation." In Richardson and Stevens 1999, 26–37.

Mitchell, W. J. 1995. *City of Bits: Space, Place, and the Infobahn*. Cambridge MA: MIT Press.

Mitchell, W. J. T. 2005. *What Do Pictures Want? The Lives and Loves of Images*. Chicago: University of Chicago Press.

Mol, A. 2010. "Actor-Network Theory: Sensitive Terms and Enduring Tensions." Special issue, *Kölner Zeitschrift für Soziologie und Sozialpsychologie* 50:253–69.

Monheim, R. 2003. "The Role of Pedestrian Precincts in Adapting City Centres to New Lifestyles." In *Sustainable Transport: Planning for Walking and Cycling in Urban Environments*, edited by R. Tolley, 326–38. Cambridge: Woodhead.

Montessori, M. 1952. *La mente del bambino*. Milan: Garzanti.

Moryson, F. 1908. *An Itinerary Containing His Ten Yeeres Travell: Through the Twelve Dominions of Germany, Bohmerland, Sweitzerland, Netherland, Denmarke, Poland, Italy, Turky, France, England, Scotland and Ireland*. 4 vols. Glasgow: MacLehose and Sons.

Mulíček, O., R. Osman, and D. Seidenglanz. 2015. "Urban Rhythms: A Chronotopic Approach to Urban Timespace." *Time and Society* 24 (3): 304–25.

Murphy, A. B. 1990. "Historical Justifications for Territorial Claims." *Annals of the Association of American Geographers* 80 (4): 531–48.

Newman, O. 1973. *Defensible Space: Crime Prevention through Urban Design.* New York: Macmillan.

Nietzsche, F. 1888. *Der Fall Wagner, ein Musikanten-Problem.* Leipzig, Germany: Neumann.

———. 1889. *Götzen-Dämmerung oder Wie man mit dem Hammer philosophiert.* Leipzig, Germany: Neumann. English ed. *Twilight of the Idols.* In *The Anti-Christ, Ecce Homo, Twilight of the Idols, and Other Writings,* edited by A. Ridley and J. Norman. Cambridge: Cambridge University Press, 2005.

Nilsson, E. 2010. *Arkitekturens kroppslighet/Staden som terräng.* Lund: Lund University.

Norlin, C. 1999. *Till Stadsbornas nytta och förlustelse: Den offentliga parken i Sverige under 1800-talet.* Stockholm: Byggförlaget.

Norman, D. A. 1999. "Affordance, Conventions, and Design." *Interactions* 6 (3): 38–43.

Normandin, S., and C. T. Wolfe, eds. 2013. *Vitalism and the Scientific Image in Post-Enlightenment Life Science, 1800–2010.* Berlin: Springer.

O'Neal, E., C. Caldwell, and G. G. Gallup. 1977. "Territorial Invasion and Aggression in Young Children." *Environmental Psychology and Nonverbal Behavior* 2 (1): 14–25.

Paasi, A. 1996. *Territories, Boundaries and Consciousness: The Changing Geographies of the Finnish-Russian Border.* London: Wiley.

Paiva, D. 2016. "Collapsed Rhythms: The Impact of Urban Change in the Everyday Life of Elders." *Space and Culture* 19 (4): 345–60.

Papapetros, S. 2005. "Malicious Houses: Animation, Animism, Animosity in German Architecture and Film: From Mies to Murnau." *Grey Room* 20:6–37.

Peirce, C. S. 1931. *Collected Papers.* Cambridge: Harvard University Press.

Penn, W. (1714) 1835. *William Penn's Journal of His Travels in Holland and Germany in 1677.* London: Darton and Harvey.

Penrose, J. 2002. "Nations, States and Homelands: Territory and Territoriality in Nationalist Thought." *Nations and Nationalism* 8 (3): 277–97.

Perec, G. 1974. *Espèces d'espaces.* Paris: Galilée.

Pevsner, N. 1976. *A History of Building Types.* London: Thames and Hudson.

Philippopoulos-Mihalopoulos, A. 2015. "Milieu, Territory, Atmosphere: New Spaces of Knowledge." In *Knowledge-Creating Milieus: Firms, Cities and Territories,* edited by A. Philippopoulos-Mihalopoulos and A. Cusinato, 79–95. New York: Springer.

Pløger, J. 2010. "Presence-Experiences: The Eventalisation of Urban Space." *Environment and Planning D: Society and Space* 28 (5): 848–66.

Portmann, A. 1990. *Essays in Philosophical Zoology: The Living Form and the Seeing Eye.* Lewiston NY: Mellen.

Prieto de la Fuente, P. 2018. *Rhythm Architecture: On Sequential Aspects of Materialities in Urban Space.* Lund: Lund University.

Prior, N. 2011. "Speed, Rhythm, and Time-Space: Museums and Cities." *Space and Culture* 14 (2): 197–213.

Raffestin, C. 1980. *Pour une géographie du pouvoir*. Paris: Librairies Techniques.

Rasmussen, S. E. 1969. *København: Et bysamfunds særpræg og udvikling gennem tiderne*. Copenhagen: Gad.

Rasmusson, B. 1998. *Stadsbarndom: Om barns vardag i en modern förort*. Lund: Lund University.

Reid-Musson, E. 2017. "Intersectional Rhythmanalysis: Power, Rhythm, and Everyday Life." *Progress in Human Geography* 42 (6): 881–97.

Richardson, M. 1999. "Soane's Legacy." In Richardson and Stevens 1999, 48–61.

Richardson, M., and M. Stevens, eds. 1999. *John Soane, Architect*. London: Royal Academy of Arts.

Roode, I. de. 2002. "The Play Objects: More Durable Than Snow." In Lefaivre and de Roode 2002, 84–101.

Roos, P. D. 1968. "Jurisdiction: An Ecological Concept." *Human Relations* 21:75–84.

Runkel, S. 2016. "Zur Genealogie des Atmosphären-Begriffs: Eine kritische Würdigung der Ansätze von Hermann Schmitz und Gernot Böhme." In *Atmosphären des Populären II: Perspektiven, Projekte, Protokolle, Performances, Personen, Posen*, edited by U. Wünsch, 20–39. Berlin: Uni-Edition.

Ruskin, J. (1849) 1880. *The Seven Lamps of Architecture*. London: Waverley.

Russell, E. S. 1945. *The Directiveness of Organic Activity*. Cambridge: Cambridge University Press.

Rybczynski, W. 1986. *Home*. New York: Viking.

Sack, R. D. 1986. *Human Territoriality: Its Theory and History*. Cambridge: Cambridge University Press.

Sandseter, E. B. H. 2010. *Scaryfunny: A Qualitative Study of Risky Play among Preschool Children*. Trondheim: Norwegian University of Science and Technology.

Sassen, S. 2006. *Territory, Authority, Rights: From Medieval to Global Assemblages*. Princeton NJ: Princeton University Press.

Schmitt, C. 1922. *Politische Theologie: Vier Kapitel zur Lehre von der Souveränität*. Munich: Duncker und Humblot. English ed. *Political Theology*. Edited by George Schwab. Cambridge MA: MIT Press, 1986.

———. 1932. *Der Begriff des Politischen*. Munich: Duncker und Humblot. English ed. *The Concept of the Political*. Chicago: University of Chicago Press, 2007.

———. 1942. *Land und Meer*. Leipzig: Reclam.

Schmitz, E. 2002. "'Let Our Children Have a Playground: They Need It Very Badly!' Letters to the Department of Public Works, 1947–1958." In Lefaivre and de Roode 2002, 59–65.

Schmitz, H. 2016. "Atmospheric Spaces." *Ambiances* 2:1–12.

Schön, E. 2006. *Vår svenske tomte*. Stockholm: Hjalmarson och Högberg.

Schütz, A. 1962. *The Problem of Social Reality*. The Hague: Nijhoff.

Schwanen, T., I. van Aalst, J. Brands, and T. Timan. 2012. "Rhythms of the Night: Spatiotemporal Inequalities in the Nighttime Economy." *Environment and Planning A* 44 (9): 2064–85.

Secchi, B. 2005. *La città del ventesimo secolo.* Rome: Bari; Laterza.

Sennett, R. 1996. *Flesh and Stone: The Body and the City in Western Civilization.* New York: Norton.

Serao, M. 1881. *Leggende napoletane.* Milan: Ottino.

Serres, M. 1980. *Le parasite.* Paris: Grasset.

———. (1985) 2008. *The Five Senses: A Philosophy of Mingled Bodies.* London: Continuum.

———. 1995. *The Natural Contract.* Ann Arbor: University of Michigan Press.

———. 2011. *Malfeasance: Appropriation through Pollution?* Stanford: Stanford University Press.

Sheringham, M. 2006. *Everyday Life: Theories and Practices from Surrealism to the Present.* Oxford: Oxford University Press.

Sieverts, T. (1997) 2003. *Cities without Cities: An Interpretation of the Zwischenstadt.* London: Spon.

Simmel, G. (1908) 2009. *Sociology: Inquiries into the Construction of Social Forms.* 2 vols. Leiden: Brill.

———. 1913. *Goethe.* Leipzig, Germany: Klinkhardt.

———. (1913) 2007. "The Philosophy of Landscape." Translated by J. Bleicher. *Theory, Culture and Society* 24 (7–8): 20–29.

———. (1918) 2010. *The View of Life: Four Metaphysical Essays.* Translated by J. A. Y. Andrews and D. N. Levine. Chicago: University of Chicago Press.

Simondon, G. (1964–89) 2013. *L'individuation à la lumière des notions de formes et d'information.* Paris: Millon.

Simpson, P. 2012. "Apprehending Everyday Rhythms: Rhythmanalysis, Time-Lapse Photography, and the Space-Times of Street Performance." *Cultural Geographies* 19 (4): 423–45.

Sloterdijk, P. 2005. "Atmospheric Politics." In *Making Things Public: Atmospheres of Democracy,* edited by B. Latour and P. Weibel, 944–51. Cambridge MA: MIT Press/Karlsruhe, Germany: Zentrum für Kunst und Medien.

———. 2011. *Bubbles: Spheres.* Vol. 1, *Microspherology.* Translated by W. Hoban. Los Angeles: Semiotext(e).

———. 2014. *Globes: Spheres.* Vol. 2, *Macrospherology.* Translated by W. Hoban. Los Angeles: Semiotext(e).

———. 2016. *Foams: Spheres.* Vol. 3, *Plural Spherology.* Translated by W. Hoban. Los Angeles: Semiotext(e).

Smith, R. J., and K. Hetherington, eds. 2013. *Urban Rhythms: Mobilities, Space and Interaction in the Contemporary City.* Chichester UK: Wiley.

Soane, J. 2015. *Crude Hints towards an History of My House in Lincoln's Inn Fields*. Oxford: Archaeopress.

Soja, E. W. 1971. *The Political Organization of Space*. Washington DC: Association of American Geographers.

———.1989. *Postmodern Geographies: The Reassertion of Space in Critical Social Theory*. London: Verso.

Sommer, R. 1959. "Studies in Personal Space." *Sociometry* 22 (3): 247–60.

———. 1967. "Sociofugal Space." *American Journal of Sociology* 72 (6): 654–60.

———. 1969. *Personal Space: The Behavioral Basis of Design*. Englewood Cliffs NJ: Prentice Hall.

Spano, R. G. 1991. "The Social Transformation of Children's Play and Organized Activities, 1880–1990: A Socio-historical Study." PhD diss., City University of New York.

Speck, F. G. 1915. "The Family Hunting Band as the Basis of Algonkian Social Organization." *American Anthropologist* 17 (2): 289–305.

Srivastava, A. 2009. "Encountering Materials in Architectural Production: The Case of Kahn and a Brick at IIM." Landscape Architecture and Urban Design, School of Architecture, University of Adelaide, Australia.

Steadman, P. 1983. *Architectural Morphology: An Introduction to the Geometry of Building Plans*. London: Pion.

Steinbock, A. J. 1995. *Home and Beyond: Generative Phenomenology after Husserl*. Evanston IL: Northwestern University Press.

Stengers, I. 2011. "Reclaiming Animism." In *Animism: Modernity through the Looking Glass*, edited by A. Franke and S. Folie, 183–192. Vienna: König.

Stevens, Q. 2007. *The Ludic City: Exploring the Potential of Public Spaces*. London: Routledge.

Stiefel, B. L. 2017. "Community Eruvin: Architecture for Semi-Public/Private Neighborhood Space." In *Community-Built: Art, Construction, Preservation and Place*, edited by K. Melcher, B. Stiefel, and K. Faurest, 85–101. London: Routledge.

Stone, P. R. 2006. "A Dark Tourism Spectrum: Towards a Typology of Death and Macabre-Related Tourist Sites, Attractions and Exhibitions." *Turizam: Međunarodni znanstveno-stručni časopis* 54 (2): 145–60.

Stoppani, T. 2007a. "Dust Projects: On Walter Benjamin's Passagen-Werk and Some Contemporary Dusty Makings in Architecture." *Journal of Architecture* 12 (5): 543–57.

———. 2007b. "Dust Revolutions: Dust, Informe, Architecture (Notes for a Reading of Dust in Bataille)." *Journal of Architecture* 12 (4): 437–47.

———. 2012. "The Architecture of Explosive Slowness." *Lo Squaderno* 26:9–14.

Storey, D. 2001. *Territory: The Claiming of Space*. Harlow: Pearson/Prentice Hall.

Strauven, F. 2002. "Wasted Pearls in the Fabric of the City." In Lefaivre and de Roode 2002, 66–83.

Strum, S., and B. Latour. 1991. "Redefining the Social Link from Baboons to Humans." In *Primate Politics*, edited by G. Schubert and R. D. Masters, 73–86. Carbondale: Southern Illinois University Press.

Tarde, G. 1890. *Les lois de l'imitation*. Paris: Alcan.

Taylor, R. B. 1988. *Human Territorial Functioning: An Empirical, Evolutionary Perspective on Individual and Small Group Territorial Cognitions, Behaviors, and Consequences*. Cambridge: Cambridge University Press.

Thom, R. 1983. *Paraboles et catastrophes*. Paris: Flammarion.

———. 1988. *Esquisse d'une sémiophysique*. Paris: InterÉditions.

———. 1991. *Prédire n'est pas expliquer*. Paris: Flammarion.

Thompson, D'A. W. (1917) 1945. *On Growth and Form*. Cambridge: Cambridge University Press.

Thrift, N. 2009. "Different Atmospheres: Of Sloterdijk, China, and Site." *Environment and Planning D: Society and Space* 27 (1): 119–38.

Tinbergen, N. 1951. *The Study of Instinct*. Oxford: Oxford University Press.

Tonboe, J., ed. 1994. *Territorialitet-Rumlige: Historiske og kulturelle perspektiver*. Odense, Denmark: Odense Universitetsforlag.

Torisson, F. 2017. *Utopology: A Re-interrogation of the Utopian in Architecture*. Lund: Lund University.

Trumbull, H. C. 1896. *The Threshold Covenant, or The Beginning of Religious Rites*. New York: Scribner.

Tsing, A. L. 2015. *The Mushroom at the End of the World*. Princeton NJ: Princeton University Press.

Tuan, Y.-F. 1977. *Space and Place: The Perspective of Experience*. Minneapolis: University of Minnesota Press.

Turley, L. W., and R. E. Milliman. 2000. "Atmospheric Effects on Shopping Behavior: A Review of the Experimental Evidence." *Journal of Business Research* 49 (2): 193–211.

Turner, V. 1969. *The Ritual Process: Structure and Anti-structure*. London: Routledge and Kegan Paul.

———. 1982. *From Ritual to Theatre: The Human Seriousness of Play*. New York: Performing Arts Journal.

Uexküll, J. v. (1934) 1957. "A Stroll through the Worlds of Animals and Men: A Picture Book of Invisible Worlds." In *Instinctive Behavior: The Development of a Modern Concept*, edited by C. H. Schiller, 5–80. New York: International Universities Press.

Valéry, P. 1957. "Je disais quelquefois a Stéphane Mallarmé." In *Œuvres*. Vol. 1, *1407–43*. Paris: La Pléiade-Gallimard.

Vandenberghe, F. 2007. "Régis Debray and Mediation Studies, or How Does an Idea Become a Material Force?" *Thesis Eleven* 89:23–42.

Vanderburgh, D. 1994. "Typification and the Building of Society: 'The Absent Patron.'" In *Ordering Space: Types in Architecture and Design*, edited by K. Franck and L. Schneekloth. New York: Van Nostrand Reihold.

Van Gennep, A. (1909) 2011. *The Rites of Passage*. Chicago: University of Chicago Press.

Vernant, J.-P. (1965) 2007. *Mythe et pensée chez les Grecs: Etudes de psychologie historique*. Paris: La Découverte.

Vernet, D., and L. de Wit, eds. 2007. *Boutiques and Other Retail Spaces: The Architecture of Seduction*. New York: Routledge.

Vidler, A. 1992. *The Architectural Uncanny: Essays in the Modern Unhomely*. Cambridge MA: MIT Press.

———. 2011. *The Scenes of the Street and Other Essays*. New York: Monacelli.

Virilio, P. 2004. *Ville panique: Ailleurs commence ici*. Paris: Galilée.

Warburg, A. (1929) 2010. "Menymosyne Einleitung." In *Werke*, edited by M. Treml, S. Weigel, and P. Ladwig, 629–39. Berlin: Suhrkamp.

Ward, C. 1961. "Adventure Playground: A Parable of Anarchy." *Anarchy* 7:193–201.

———. 1978. *The Child in the City*. New York: Pantheon Books.

Warnaby, G. 2018. "Taking a Territorological Perspective on Place Branding?" *Cities* 80:64–66.

Webster, G., and B. Goodwin. 1996. *Form and Transformation: Generative and Relational Principles in Biology*. Cambridge: Cambridge University Press.

Weil, S. (1942) 1991. "Expérience de la vie d'usine." In *Œuvres complètes*, edited by G. Leroy and A. Roche, 2:296. Paris: Gallimard.

Weizman, E. 2007. *Hollow Land: Israel's Architecture of Occupation*. London: Verso.

West, M. L. 1983. *The Orphic Poems*. Oxford: Oxford University Press.

Whitehead, A. N. (1929) 1978. *Process and Reality*. New York: Free Press.

———. (1933) 1967. *Adventures of Ideas*. New York: Free Press.

———. 1934. *Nature and Life*. Cambridge: Cambridge University Press.

Wikström, T. 1994. *Mellan hemmet och världen*. Stockholm: Symposion Graduale.

Willkens, D. S. 2016. "Reading Words and Images in the *Description*(s) of Sir John Soane's Museum." *Architectural Histories* 4 (1): 1–22.

Wolch, J. 2002. "Anima urbis." *Progress in Human Geography* 26 (6): 721–42.

Woodyer, T. 2012. "Ludic Geographies: Not Merely Child's Play." *Geography Compass* 6 (6): 313–26.

Wulz, F. 1979. *Wien 1848–1934*. Stockholm: Byggforskningsrådet.

Wunderlich, F. M. 2013. "Place-Temporality and Urban Place-Rhythms in Urban Analysis and Design: An Aesthetic Akin to Music." *Journal of Urban Design* 18 (3): 383–408.

Yeo, S.-J., and C. K. Heng. 2014. "An (Extra)ordinary Night Out: Urban Informality, Social Sustainability and the Night-Time Economy." *Urban Studies* 51 (4): 712–26.

Young, L. 2007. "Is There a Museum in the House? Historic Houses as a Species of Museum." *Museum Management and Curatorship* 22 (1): 59–77.

Index

Page numbers in italics refer to illustrations.

accumulation and collection, 65–66, 74
adventure playground. *See* playgrounds
affectio and *affectus*, 163
affects, 45, 49, 133, 155, 159, 163, 168, 192
affordance, 8, 14, 21, 37, 41, 153, 166, 167,
    168, 178–79, 181–83, 184–86, 202
Ainu people, 122
Aion, 5, 57–60, 62, 74, 75, 80, 81
Alice in Wonderland, 58, 75
alienworld. *See* homeworld and
    alienworld
allagmatics, 4, 95, 198
Alsthom factory, 151
Amin, Ash, 138
Amsterdam, 2, 8, 171–76, 178, 187
Anderson, Benedict, 23
animation, 4, 6, 9, 17, 31, 34, 104–18, 127,
    132–33, 138, 139, 185, 199; and domes-
    ticity, 114–15, 118–35; and formation,
    54, 83, 103–11, 113; inanimate, 85, 104,
    112; of rhythms, 159, 164; and thresh-
    olds, 17
anima urbis, 138
animism, 31–32, 103–4, 106, 108, 109, 112, 113
animistic moment, 6, 9, 17, 84, 86, 103–11,
    112–13, 133, 135, 138, 191, 199
archetype, 43, 67, 92–93
Arendt, Hannah, 133
Ariès, Philippe, 140

arrhythmia, 152, 158
Ascherson, Neal, 146
atmoculture, 46
atmosphere, 2, 4–5, 37, 38, 39, 45–49, 53,
    54, 69, 132, 136, 138, 175, 191
atmospherics, 47
atopon, 58

Bachelard, Gaston, 117–18, 132, 138, 148,
    152–53, 154, 156, 201, 202
Balata, 110
Barad, Karen, 32
Barthes, Roland, 154–55
Bede the Venerable, 10
behaviorism, 40
behavior settings, 184
Belarus, 123
Benjamin, Walter, 5, 17, 56, 61–62, 63–64,
    65, 68, 79, 98, 138, 148, 195, 197, 200
Bennett, Jane, 14, 32, 103, 138
Bergson, Henri, 17, 25, 152, 153, 154, 156,
    201, 202
Berlin, 146–47
Bettelheim, Bruno, 162
Biehler, Dawn Day, 119
Blom, Holger, 170
bodily activation, 178
"body without organs," 45
Bolton, Thaddeus L., 150, 201

boundaries, 44, 47, 99, 100, 104, 130, 181, 195, 201, 202; and form, 83, 94, 95; local, 185, 186; making of, 27–28; and organisms, 87, 92, 108; territorial, 6, 27–28, 99, 100, 105, 109, 112, 130, 135, 139, 147
Bowker, Geoffrey C., 28
Braudel, Fernand, 136
brick architecture, 2, 6, 105–6, 108, 109
brick making, 94–97, 105–6, 198, 199
Bridget of Sweden, 125
British Museum, 74
Britton, John, 78
Brown, Barbara, 16
building types, 5, 20, 46, 48, 57, 68, 70, 166–67, 177, 178, 184

Caillois, Roger, 149, 157, 166, 180, 183, 201, 202
Calais, 144
Canetti, Elias, 26, 97, 200, 202
Canguilhem, Georges, 17, 32–34, 39–41, 97
capital cities, 110
Central Asia, 120, 124
Christian eschatology, 197
Christianity, 125
Christian martyrs, 10
Christmas, 125
chronic, 60–66, 76, 77, 78, 80, 81, 98, 115, 150, 163, 198
chronological, 60, 66–68, 78, 115, 150, 163, 198; and antichronological, 76
Chronos, 5, 57, 66–68, 77, 80, 81
CIAM, 175
Coimbra, Leonardo, 152, 201
collection and accumulation, 65–66, 74
Constantine the Great, 110
Constantinople, 110
Copenhagen, 46, 169
corona muralis, 141

critical distances. See distances
Cronus, 61, 77
crowds, 21, 26, 38, 100, 119, 120, 121, 130, 138, 200, 202
Cyclopes, 125
Cyrus, 104

dance, 150, 159
Darwin, Charles, 41–42, 91
Darwinism, 34, 40, 41–42, 91; and anti-Darwinism, 196
Deakin, Richard, 11–13
Death Week, 123
deformation. See formation
de la Cadena, Marisol, 32, 132
Delambre, Jean-Baptiste Joseph, 28
Delaney, David, 16, 54
Delaplace, Grégory, 120, 128
Deleuze, Gilles, 17, 25, 32, 43, 45, 46, 58–59, 60, 61, 88, 192, 195, 196–97, 198, 199; and Félix Guattari, 43–44, 108, 137, 160–61, 196, 199; Logic of Sense, 5, 56
Delhi, 129
Deligny, Fernand, 161–62, 195
De Quincey, Thomas, 110
Der Golem (Meyrink), 104
Descartes, René, 39
Dickens, Charles, 60
Dimitry of Uglich, 104
display signs, 44
distances, 18, 21, 26, 101, 152, 164, 201
Dolidon, Annabelle, 155
domesticity, 6, 7, 73, 77, 80, 114–16, 119, 124, 128, 129, 130, 134–35, 169, 187; and domestication, 6, 115, 128, 134–35; and domestic spaces, 7, 69, 76, 111, 114–16, 118, 120, 132–34
domovoj, 22, 122–23, 124
Douglas, Mary, 116
Driesch, Hans, 34

Duisburg, 141
Dupuy, Gabriel, 50
Durkheim, Émile, 148–49, 153, 157, 198, 201, 202
dwelling, 48, 52, 114, 116, 117–18, 122, 128, 131–32, 140, 153, 197–98

Eesteren, Cornelis van, 171, 172
Egypt, 67, 77, 79, 170
Einstein, Albert, 40
élan vital, 17
Elden, Stuart, 15, 147
Emdrup, 170
Empson, Rebecca, 120, 128
entelechy, 31, 33
Entstehung, 17, 195
environment, 37, 38, 39–45, 46, 49, 53–54, 94, 99–100, 101, 102, 104, 113, 132, 136, 167, 178, 181–83, 184, 191, 197
environmentalization, 43
etengena, 200
Euclidean geometry, 51
eurhythmia, 150, 158, 201
Evans, Edward P., 104
Evans, Robin, 143, 145
Experimental Arch, 105–7
expression, 5, 22, 24, 55, 63, 81, 114, 133
Eyck, Aldo van, 171, 172, 174, 175

facialization, 108, 113
family resemblance, 52, 53, 197
Ficino, Marsilio, 85
fireplaces, 122–23, 125, 128, 132–33
flâneur, 65
fluidity, 14, 52–53, 69, 151, 153, 186, 197
formation, 2, 24, 43, 69, 82, 83, 86, 89, 90, 91, 97, 99–102, 103, 105, 106, 108–10, 111, 112–13, 120, 132, 134, 137, 139, 154, 160, 163, 165, 168, 169, 175, 177, 185, 188; and deformation, 51, 88–89, 91–92, 95,

98, 105, 110, 112, 200; psychic, 93–94; territorial, 1, 2, 7, 31, 55, 68, 110, 111, 113, 114, 138, 147, 148, 160, 165, 166; and "Will to Form," 88
formlessness, 50, 51, 99, 133
form-taking. See prise de forme
Franz Joseph I, 142
Freud, Sigmund, 7, 91, 93, 116–17, 131

Gagen, Elisabeth, 169
Gandhi, Ajay, 129–30
genius loci, 65, 114
Gerow, Aaron, 121–22, 200
Gesell, Arnold, 84, 179
Gestalt psychology, 181, 188
ghettos, 104, 143
Gibbon, Edward, 10
Gibraltar, 136
Gibson, James J., 41, 181–82, 183
gifts, 56, 68, 73, 79, 80–81, 122, 129, 135, 149–50, 184, 187, 201
Glissant, Edouard, 196
Goethe, Johann Wolfgang von, 8, 63, 89–90
Goffman, Erving, 157
Goldstein, Kurt, 40
Goodwin, Brian, 82, 103, 199
graffiti, 21
Grand Tour, 73–74, 78, 80
Greece, 79
Grosz, Elisabeth, 57
Guattari, Félix, 43–44, 108, 137, 160–61, 196, 199
Gyndes River, 104

haunted houses, 104
Haussmann, Georges-Eugène, 144
Hediger, Heini, 15, 195
Hegel, Georg Wilhelm Friedrich, 64
Heidegger, Martin, 117
Hippocrates, 40

Hokkaido, 122

home, 6–7, 30, 41, 44, 48, 52, 73, 111, 114–19, 120, 121, 122, 125, 127, 128, 130–35, 140, 144, 172, 173, 187, 192, 197; and homelessness, 118; and homemaking, 115; and home-museum, 77. *See also* house-museum

homeworld and alienworld, 115, 119, 130

house-museum, 2, 5, 57, 69–70, 73, 74, 75, 76, 78, 80, 81, 187, 198

Hugo, Victor, 60, 104

huldufólk, 132

Humboldt, Alexander von, 40

Husserl, Edmund, 136

hylomorphism, 84, 94, 95, 199

Iceland, 132

idiorrhythm, 154–55

ilinx, 180

imagined community, 23

in-between spaces, 131, 132, 162, 166, 168, 171, 174, 175, 201

in-between times, 60, 75, 149, 175

Indian Institute of Management (IIM), 105, *107*

individual collectives, 99

individual law, 34, 63, 196

individuation, 43, 84, 95, 98–100, 102, 103, 106, 108, 109

Ingold, Tim, 32, 103, 138

intensity, 12, 14, 45, 69, 137–38, 139, 156, 160, 162, 164, 165, 177, 179, 185, 188

interstices. *See* in-between spaces

interstitial moments. *See* in-between times

inwardness, 87, 108–9

irritation, spaces of, 185

Israel, 110, 144

Italy, 73, 90, 123

Jacobs, Jane, 167, 176

James, William, 58, 181

Janet, Pierre, 91, 93–94, 100, 201

Japan, 120, 121

Jaques-Dalcroze, Émile, 150

Jennison, George, 10

Jesi, Furio, 5, 56, 62

Jessop, Bob, 38

jijig hün, 120–21, 122, 130

Joseph II, 142

Jung, Carl Gustav, 67, 92–93, 98

Juppé, Alain, 144

Kahn, Louis, 2, 105–6, 108, 109, 110

kakorhythm, 150, 201

kamidana, 120

Kant, Immanuel, 196

karigurashi, 121–22, 129

Karoff, Helle Skovbjerg, 179

Klauser, Francisco, 140

Klein, Alexander, 153

koropokkuru, 122

Kracauer, Siegfried, 65, 79

Kronos, 5, 57, 60–65, 76, 80, 81, 197. *See also* Cronus

Laban, Rudolf, 138, 148, 150, 152, 201

Lacan, Jacques, 58

lararii, 120

Latour, Bruno, 159

Law, John, 52, 197

Le Corbusier, 104, 153, 171; *Le Modulor*, 104–5; *Ville Radieuse*, 104–5

Lefebvre, Henri, 7, 30, 137, 138–39, 147–48, 154, 155–58, 164, 200, 201, 202

Levi, Carlo, 123

Levinas, Emmanuel, 199

lignes d'erre. See wander lines

liminal encounters, 115

London, 2, 5, 57, 68, 70–81, 142, 143

ludus, 180, 183

Macdonald, Roderick A., 116
magic, 85–86, 103, 109, 112, 133
Malmberg, Torsten, 15
Manchester, playground of, 169
Mantua, 141
Marc, Franz, 87–88
Marx, Karl, 64
Marxism, 64, 154
Massey, Doreen, 30
Mauerspringer, 146
Mauss, Marcel, 138, 148, 149, 157, 198, 201
Mazzanti, Elisabetta Fiorini, 11
McLuhan, Marshall, 25
measure, 5, 21, 28, 34, 44, 55–56, 65–66,
   67, 78, 81, 137, 145, 150, 160, 163, 180,
   183, 192
Méchain, Pierre François André, 28
media, 21–22, 25, 40, 49, 102, 103
medial operations, 99
melodies, 4, 24, 29, 37, 42, 137, 138, 139,
   160–64, 165, 266, 183, 184, 188
Merleau-Ponty, Maurice, 41, 42–43, 84
metamorphosis, 6, 89–90, 98, 101, 198
metric expedition, 28
Meyrink, Gustav, 104
milieu, 39–45, 94, 98, 99, 101, 109, 132,
   148, 196
Mitchell, W. J. T., 103, 197
Mnemosyne Project, 151–52
Mol, Annemarie, 52, 197
monacicchi. See *munaciello*
monadology, 152, 201
Mongolia, 120, 128
monsters, 108, 111
Montessori, Maria, 179, 181
morphogenesis, 6, 54, 82–85, 89, 95, 97,
   99, 101–2, 108, 112–13, 198
Moryson, Fynes, 143
Mulder, Jacoba, 171
multitemporality, 5, 56–57, 80

munaciello, 2, 123–24, 128
mystery of appearances, 85, 86

Nablus, 110–11
Naples, 123–24
Napoleon I, 143–44
Napoleon III, 144
natural magic. *See* magic
Nazism, 34, 196
networks, 2, 4–5, 20, 37, 38–39, 49–54, 68,
   161, 168, 173, 174, 184, 191, 197
network urbanism, 50
Newton, Isaac, 39–40
Nietzsche, Friedrich, 32, 34, 88, 97, 150, 193
Norton, Mary, 121

Odense, 179
ongon. See *jijig hün*

paidia, 180
Palestine, 110, 144
Palissy, Bernard, 140–41
Papua New Guinea, 200
parasites, 119, 122, 129, 133, 134, 135
Paris, 142, 144, 201
parkour, 177
patriotism, 178
Payne, Lewis, 60
Penn, William, 141
Perec, Georges, 154
Peru, 32, 132
Philippopoulos-Mihalopoulos, Andreas,
   48, 196
Pinheiro dos Santos, Lúcio Alberto, 138,
   148, 152, 201
place(s), 9, 11, 14, 23, 24, 35, 38, 39, 49, 68,
   110–11, 115, 117, 120, 125, 131–32, 137, 146,
   166, 168–69, 173, 176, 183–84, 186; out
   of, 162, 173; public, 19, 185; and territory,
   14–15, 26, 35, 38–39, 49, 53, 186, 202

plant territorialization, 12

Plato, 83, 85

play, 8, 150, 161–63, 166–81, 184, 185, 186, 202; according to Roger Caillois, 180, 202; and the home, 131; practices of, 179; will to, 170

playgrounds, 8, 168–78, 184, 185, 186, 202; adventure, 170–71; in Amsterdam, 2, 8, 171–76, 187; critique against, 167, 170–71; and gender, 169; and nonplaygrounds, 183; in Scandinavia, 169–70; in Tokyo, 180–81; in the United States, 169, 170–71

policing, 141

Portmann, Adolf, 84, 86–87, 88, 92, 94, 100, 108, 109

potlatch, 201

power, 20, 22, 26, 38, 44–45, 54, 55, 60, 61, 62, 64, 94, 118, 148, 152; and form, 2, 6, 11, 44–45, 84, 87, 88, 94, 200; and territory, 2, 20, 22, 23, 26, 51, 54, 55, 143; will to, 88

Prague, 104

presence, 56–70, 73–81, 109, 120, 135, 139, 140, 146, 159–62, 185–86, 199; and absence, 64, 140, 146, 164, 165, 179; thick, 98

prise de forme, 94, 95, 101

Proteus, 90

psychasthenia, 93

Quechua people, 32, 132

Quran, 200

råde, 127

rågubbe, 127

refrains, 137, 161–62, 164

retailization, 19–20

retail spaces, 46–47, 159

rhythmanalysis, 7, 136–39, 147–48, 152, 154, 156–58, 163, 164, 190, 200, 201

rhythm machine, 166, 168, 171

rhythmontology, 152

rhythms, 2, 7–8, 14, 29, 37, 48, 55, 64, 67, 74, 78, 80, 105, 115, 128, 136–65, 166, 169, 171, 175–76, 177, 181, 183–88, 201, 202; and cadence, 151; and milieu, 44; and social bonding, 133, 159; urban, 20, 141–42

Rodia, Simon, 80

Rome, 9–12, 13, 14, 35, 38, 57, 110, 142

Russel, Edward S., 84

Russia, 104, 122, 124

Saint-Hilaire, Étienne Geoffroy, 90

Sandseter, Ellen Beate Hansen, 179

sarcophagus. See Seth I, sarcophagus of

Scandinavia, 124–25, 127, 131, 169–70, 200

Schmitt, Carl, 63, 64, 197

Schopenhauer, Arthur, 17

Schumann, Conrad, 146–47

Schütz, Alfred, 189

Sebastiani, Francesco Antonio, 11

The Secret World of Arrietty, 121–22

semiophysics, 87

Sennett, Richard, 140

Serao, Matilde, 123–24, 200

Serres, Michel, 119, 134

Seth I, sarcophagus of, 74–76, 77

shopping malls, 46, 48, 142, 190

Simmel, Georg, 5, 32, 34, 44, 45, 56, 63, 89, 114, 157, 192, 196, 198, 202

Simondon, Gilbert, 4, 43, 83–84, 86, 94–95, 98, 99–100, 108, 188, 196–97, 198, 199

singularities, 10, 88, 135, 160, 162, 198

singularization, 20, 115, 164, 165; and desingularization, 60, 163–64, 165

skateboarding, 177

skrammel-legeplads, 170

Sloterdijk, Peter, 45–46, 48

Soane, Elizabeth, 70, 73, 76
Soane, John, 2, 5, 57, 66, 68–81, 187; conflict of, with his sons, 73, 76–77; Grand Tour of, 73; purchase of sarcophagus by, 74–76, 77
Sørensen, Carl Theodor, 170
spacing and timing, 56, 80
Spinoza, Baruch, 163, 182, 192
spiritual crowds. See crowds
Srivastava, Amit, 105, 199
Star, Susan Leigh, 28
Steadman, Philip, 108
Stengers, Isabelle, 32
Stimmung, 114, 131
Stockholm, 169–70, 171
"stretched door," 145
structural stability, 89, 95
Strum, Shirley, 159
Studio Ghibli, 121
swarms and swarming, 6, 21, 110–11, 119, 120, 170
synchorization, 139, 143, 153, 155, 160, 163, 171, 200
synchronization, 20, 108, 137, 139, 155, 159–60, 163, 168, 169, 170, 171, 173, 174, 175, 177, 178, 181, 185, 200
synods, 148, 157

Tarde, Gabriel, 109, 152, 201
Team X, 175
temporality, 12, 29, 53, 55–56, 62, 65, 74, 80, 81, 129, 131, 132, 151, 158, 187, 198, 200; addictive, 65; chronic, 61, 63, 77; logistic, 68; multi, 5, 55–56, 57, 80; poly, 132
territorial appropriations, 19, 21, 44, 115, 118, 128, 173–74, 176, 177, 179, 201
territorial associations, 12, 16, 19, 49, 80, 109–10, 112, 115, 118, 127, 150, 162–63, 165, 168, 177, 178, 183, 184, 186, 200, 202

territorial bodies, 20, 160, 178, 185
territorial complexity, 14, 16, 19, 80, 183, 191
territorial conversion, 84, 168, 183, 184, 186
territorialized role, 182–83, 184, 186
territorial methods, 189–91
territorial motifs, 5, 38
territorial networks, 20, 49–53
territorial radiation, 178
territorial sorts, 5, 10, 20, 26, 52–53, 57, 68–69, 70, 74, 109, 163, 165, 166, 168, 177, 183, 184, 202
territorial strategies, 18, 19, 20, 54, 83, 109, 110, 118, 182, 173, 177, 184
territorial tactics, 19, 110, 118, 175, 177, 179
territoriographies, 190, 191
territoriology, 1–2, 3, 4, 6, 7, 8, 9, 15, 17, 27, 30, 31, 35, 36, 37, 43, 55, 80, 99, 114, 119, 120, 136, 165, 187, 188–91, 192, 195, 198
Tezuka Architects, 180–81
Thom, René, 8, 83, 85, 87–88, 89, 90, 94, 95, 98, 101, 102, 188, 198
Thompson, D'Arcy Wenworth, 91–92
time geography, 159
timing, 56, 80, 175, 200
tirakuna, 32, 132
Titus, 10
Tobolsk, 104
Tokyo, 180, 181
tomtar or tomtenissar, 2, 124–28, 130, 132, 200
topo-analysis, 118
Torah, 30
TPSN framework, 38
transdisciplinarity, 3–4
transindividuation, 108
Tsing, Anna, 32
typification, 115, 116

Uexküll, Jakob von, 33, 40, 41, 196
Umgebung, 40

Umwelt, 33, 40, 42–43, 136, 191, 196
undomesticated time, 61
unheimlich, 7, 116, 131, 134
urban walls. *See* walls
Urpflanze, 90
Urphänomen, 63, 196
Ursprung, 17, 63, 98, 195

Valéry, Paul, 102
valorization, 41
Venice, 68, 143
Vernant, Jean-Pierre, 61
Vespasianus, 10
Vienna, 142
Vischer, Friedrich Theodor, 104
visibility, 27, 28, 86, 87, 88, 97, 99, 111,
    113, 121, 132, 143, 169, 175, 187; and
    invisibility, 26, 28, 32, 40, 102, 117,
    121, 122, 128, 131, 200; and territory,
    20–23, 24
vitalism, 4, 30–34, 42, 103, 138, 192

Vitruvian man, 104

walls, 6, 77, 103, 105, 110–11, 113, 136, 137–
    47, 153, 175, 181, 188; and dewalling,
    142–43; and Kahn-walls, 109; urban, 2,
    7, 21, 48, 105, 139–42, 146, 191; and wall
    jumper, 146
wall technologies, 145
wander lines, 161–62
Warburg, Aby, 138, 148, 151–52, 192, 201
Ward, Colin, 167, 176
Webster, Gerald, 82, 103, 199
Weil, Simone, 138, 148, 151, 158
Weizman, Eyal, 110
Whitehead, Alfred North, 5, 32, 56, 57–58,
    98, 100, 182, 196, 197, 198, 199
Willkens, Danielle, 78

Yonebayashi, Hiromasa, 121

Zeus, 61

In the Cultural Geographies + Rewriting the Earth series

Topoi/Graphein: Mapping the Middle in Spatial Thought
Christian Abrahamsson
Foreword by Gunnar Olsson

Animated Lands: Studies in Territoriology
Andrea Mubi Brighenti and Mattias Kärrholm

Mapping Beyond Measure: Art, Cartography,
and the Space of Global Modernity
Simon Ferdinand

Psychoanalysis and the GlObal
Edited and with an introduction by Ilan Kapoor

A Place More Void
Edited by Paul Kingsbury and Anna J. Secor

Arkography: A Grand Tour through the Taken-for-Granted
Gunnar Olsson

To order or obtain more information on these or other
University of Nebraska Press titles, visit nebraskapress.unl.edu.

www.ingramcontent.com/pod-product-compliance
Lightning Source LLC
Chambersburg PA
CBHW020346270326
41926CB00007B/329

9 781496 221773